Islamic Law and Jurisprudence

Islamic Law and Jurisprudence

Edited by

NICHOLAS HEER

University of Washington Press

Seattle and London

Printed in the United States of America

Library of Congress Cataloging-in-Publication Data

Islamic law and jurisprudence / edited by Nicholas Heer.
p. cm.
Papers read at a conference in Islamic law held in honor of Farhat J. Ziadeh in May 1987.
ISBN 0-295-97006-5 (alk. paper)
1. Islamic law—Congresses. I. Heer, Nicholas. II. Ziadeh, Farhat Jacob.
LAW ISLAM 7 Isla 1990
340.5'9–dc20 90-12150
CIP

The paper used in this publication meets the minimum requirements of the American National Standard for Information Sciences—Permanence of Paper for Printed Library Materials, ANSI Z39.48-1984.

∞

Studies in Honor of Farhat J. Ziadeh

Contents

Preface

THIS VOLUME contains the papers originally read at a conference on Islamic law held in honor of Farhat J. Ziadeh on the occasion of his retirement from the University of Washington after a career of nearly forty years of teaching and research.

The conference began on Thursday evening, the 14th of May, 1987, with Professor Ziadeh's paper, "Integrity (*'Adālah*) in Classical Islamic Law." Ziadeh had been named one of three Solomon Katz Distinguished Lecturers in the Humanities for 1987 and his paper was presented as a public lecture in Kane Hall as part of the Solomon Katz lecture series.

The conference resumed on Friday morning with the papers of George Makdisi, John Makdisi, and Ann Mayer. William Ballantyne, Ian Edge, and David Pearl read their papers on Friday afternoon, and the conference came to a close after a final session on Saturday morning with the papers of David Forte, Wael Hallaq, Jeanette Wakin, and Bernard Weiss.

The order in which the papers were presented at the conference has not been preserved in the present volume. Instead the papers have been rearranged so that they fall under three main topics—Islamic jurisprudence, Islamic law and its relation to the West, and Islamic law in the modern period. Under the first topic, Islamic jurisprudence, are included the papers of Hallaq, Wakin, Weiss, and Ziadeh, all of which deal with certain principles of Islamic law. The second topic, Islamic law and the West, includes the papers of George Makdisi, John Makdisi, and David Forte. In each of these papers certain aspects of Islamic and Western law are compared, and in two of them it is argued that Islamic law has had an influence on Western institutions. The papers of Mayer, Ballantyne, Edge, and Pearl have been included under the third topic, Islamic law in the modern period. These papers deal with the place of Islamic law in the modern legal systems of some of the states in the Islamic world.

The editor wishes to acknowledge the contributions of all those who helped to make this volume possible. Thanks are due first of all to Professor Jere Bacharach, Director of the Middle East Center, whose idea the conference was and who arranged and organized it with the able assistance of Dr. Charlotte Albright, the Middle East outreach coordinator, and Ms. April Richardson, the secretary of the Center.

Thanks are also due to Dr. Theodora MacKay, Assistant Editor of the *Middle East Studies Association Bulletin*, who was responsible for all the computer operations necessary to prepare the volume for the press, and who made sure that usage and style were in conformity with current publishing standards.

The editor also wishes to acknowledge the help and support of the University of Washington Press, and in particular the contributions of Naomi B. Pascal, Editor-in-Chief, and Dr. Donald J. Cioeta, who together made sure that the volume appeared as scheduled.

Financial support for the conference was provided by the Graduate School Research Fund, the Henry M. Jackson School of International Studies, the Law School, the Middle East Center, the Department of Near Eastern Languages and Civilization, the Farhat J. Ziadeh Publications Fund, as well as the Exxon Corporation. Support for the publication of the papers was provided by the Ziadeh Publications Fund.

This book was set with Donald Knuth's TEX typesetting system, using Computer Modern fonts. The formatting commands were developed by Dr. Pierre A. MacKay. TEX is a trademark of the American Mathematical Society.

NICHOLAS HEER
University of Washington

Photo courtesy of *The Christian Science Monitor*

Introduction

BIOGRAPHY OF FARHAT J. ZIADEH

FARHAT JACOB ZIADEH, the son of Jacob Ziadeh and Nimeh Farah, was born on 8 April 1917 in Ramallah, Palestine. He attended the National Boys School and the American Friends Boys School, both in Ramallah. After graduating from the American University of Beirut in 1937, he studied law at the University of London, receiving the degree of LL.B. in 1940.

By that time the Second World War had begun, and Ziadeh found it impossible to return to Palestine. He went instead to the United States, where he found work as a legal clerk in the law office of Joseph W. Ferris in New York. From 1943 to 1945 he served under Professor Philip K. Hitti as an instructor in Arabic in the Army Specialized Training Program at Princeton University. It was during those two years at Princeton that he collaborated with Ībrahīm Furayjī on his first book, a history of the American people in Arabic, which was published by the Princeton University Press shortly after the end of the war in 1946. That same year, he returned to London where he became a Barrister-at-Law from Lincoln's Inn.

In 1946, he returned to Palestine to work in the law firm of 'Atalla and 'Atalla in Jerusalem. The following year he was appointed a magistrate in Safad by the Palestine Mandate Government. He remained in that post only until the end of the Palestine mandate in 1948, at which time he returned to Princeton as a lecturer in Arabic. His *Arabic Primer*, still remembered by some of his earlier students, was published the following year in 1949. On July 24th of that same year he married Suad Salem, who, like himself, was also from Ramallah. They have five daughters: Shireen, Susan, Rhonda, Deena, and Reema.

In 1950, Ziadeh began working with the Voice of America in New York as the editor of the Arabic desk. Since this was a full-time job, it meant that he could continue as a lecturer at Princeton only on a part-time basis. In 1954, however, when Princeton offered him an assistant professorship, he was forced to choose between a career at the Voice of America or one at Princeton. Fortunately for his students and the field of Islamic studies, he chose Princeton, even though it meant a substantial reduction in income.

Having returned to full-time work at Princeton, Ziadeh turned his attention to writing an Arabic grammar. He undertook this project in collaboration with his colleague the late R. Bayly Winder, and in 1957 *An Introduction to Modern Arabic* was published by the Princeton University Press. It was during this period also that Ziadeh began to work on his translation of Ṣubḥī Maḥmaṣānī's *Falsafat al-tashrī' fī al-Islām*. This project was sponsored by the American Council of Learned Societies, and Ziadeh's translation was published by E. J. Brill in 1961 under the title of *Mahmassani's Philosophy of Jurisprudence in Islam*.

In 1958, Ziadeh was granted tenure at Princeton and promoted to the rank of associate professor. He spent six months of that year in Cairo on a Ford Foundation grant doing research for a study on the development of the modern legal system in Egypt. This project, however, was temporarily put aside the following year so that he could begin work on *A Reader in Modern Literary Arabic*, for which he had received partial support from the U.S. Office of Education. This volume was subsequently published by the Princeton University Press in 1964, and was later reprinted by the University of Washington Press in 1981.

In 1962, Ziadeh had spent a sabbatical year in the Middle East, during which time he resumed the research begun in Cairo in 1958. The results of this research were published by the Hoover

Institution in 1968 in the volume entitled *Lawyers, The Rule of Law, and Liberalism in Modern Egypt*.

A turning point in Ziadeh's career came in 1966 when he was invited by the University of Washington to come to Seattle to develop and head a new program in Near Eastern studies. One of his first tasks after arriving in Seattle was to build up the Near Eastern faculty at the University. Prior to Ziadeh's coming, only two members of the faculty had been teaching Near Eastern subjects. One was an Ottoman and Balkan historian and the other an Arabist with an interest in Islamic theology and philosophy. Within the next few years, however, Ziadeh succeeded in getting authorization to fill four new positions, one each in Persian literature, Turkish literature, modern Hebrew, and ancient Near Eastern studies. Ziadeh himself taught courses in Arabic literature, as well as in Islamic law and institutions. Initially, the new program was housed in the Department of Classics. In 1970, however, the Board of Regents established a separate Department of Near Eastern Languages and Literature with Ziadeh as chairman. In addition to the new appointments in the Near Eastern Department, Ziadeh was also instrumental in securing appointments of Near Eastern specialists in the departments of History, Political Science, and International Studies.

In 1975, as a result of Ziadeh's success in developing the new Near Eastern program, the University was awarded a Federal grant for the establishment of a Near Eastern Center in what is now known as the Jackson School of International Studies. Ziadeh was appointed director of the Center and continued to serve in that capacity, and as chairman of the Department as well, until 1982, when he reached the age of sixty-five, the mandatory retirement age for chairmen and directors.

Although much of Ziadeh's time was taken up by administrative tasks, he was nevertheless able to find time to pursue his own research. While still at Princeton he had begun work on an edition of al-Khaṣṣāf's *Adab al-qāḍī* with the commentary of al-Jaṣṣāṣ. In 1972 he spent a six-months sabbatical in Egypt, where he was able to complete the editing of this text. It was subsequently published in 1979 by the American University in Cairo Press. In 1978, Ziadeh was again in Cairo, this time for research on property law in the Arab states. This research resulted in the volume *Law of Property in the Arab World: Real Rights in Egypt, Iraq, Jordan, Lebanon, and Syria*, published in 1979 by Graham and Trotman.

In 1983, having retired the previous year as Chairman of the Department and Director of the Center, Ziadeh took yet another administrative job, that of Director of the Center for Arabic Study Abroad, a consortium of eighteen American universities for training American students and faculty at the American University in Cairo, Egypt. His term of office in this position extended until 1989.

Throughout his academic career Ziadeh has served on numerous boards and committees and been elected to a number of offices. From 1975 to 1976, he served as president of the American Association of Teachers of Arabic. He was elected president of the Western Branch of the American Oriental Society for the year 1973–1974, and president of the Middle East Studies Association for the 1979–1980 academic year. He has been on the advisory board of the *Journal of the American Research Center in Egypt*, and on the editorial boards of the *Arab Law Quarterly* and the *Arab Studies Quarterly*. From 1969 to 1971 he was a member of the Board of Directors of the Middle East Studies Association.

In 1987, his last year at the University before his retirement at the age of seventy, Ziadeh was named Solomon Katz Distinguished Lecturer in the Humanities. His lecture entitled "Integrity (*'Adālah*) in Classical Islamic Law" was delivered on the evening of 14 May 1987 as the first of the papers read at the Islamic law conference of which this volume is the result.

BIBLIOGRAPHY OF FARHAT J. ZIADEH

Books

Arabic Speaking Americans (with H. I. Kātibah). New York: The Institute of Arab American Affairs, 1946.

Tārīkh al-sha'b al-amīrikī (with Ibrāhīm Furayjī). Princeton: Princeton University Press, 1946.

Arabic Primer. Princeton: Princeton University Press, 1949.

An Introduction to Modern Arabic (with R. B. Winder). Princeton: Princeton University Press; Oxford: Oxford University Press, 1957.

Mahmassani's Philosophy of Jurisprudence in Islam. Leiden: E. J. Brill, 1961.

A Reader In Modern Literary Arabic. Princeton: Princeton University Press; Oxford: Oxford University Press, 1964. Reprinted, Seattle: University of Washington Press, 1981.

Lawyers, The Rule of Law and Liberalism in Modern Egypt. Stanford: The Hoover Institution, Stanford University, 1968.

Al-Khaṣṣāf, *Kitāb adab al-qāḍī*. Cairo: American University in Cairo Press, 1979. (Editor, with introduction and notes.)

Law of Property in the Arab World: Real Rights in Egypt, Iraq, Jordan, Lebanon, and Syria. London: Graham and Trotman, 1979.

Articles

"Equality in the Muslim Law of Marriage." *The American Journal of Comparative Law* 5, no. 4 (October 1957): 503–517.

"'Urf (Custom) and Law in Islam." In *The World of Islam*, edited by J. Kritzeck and R.B. Winder, pp. 60–67. London, 1959.

"The Role of Lawyers in Egypt." *Law and Society Review* 3 (November 1968): 407–408.

"Report of the Image Committee." *Middle East Studies Association Bulletin* 8, no. 1 (February 15, 1974): 9–10.

"Haykaliyyāt" (Neologisms in Modern Arabic). *An-Nashra* 7, no. 2 (1974): 73–78.

"The Law of Property in Egypt: Real Rights." *American Journal of Comparative Law* 26 (1978): 239–271.

"Presidential Lecture" (Middle East Studies Association Meeting, 1980). *MESA Bulletin* 15, no. 1 (July 1981): 1–7.

"Al-Muwatta' as a Source for the Social and Economic History of the Hejaz." In *Studies in the History of Arabia*, vol. 1, part 1, pp. 25–33. Riyadh: Riyadh University Press, 1979. Reprinted in *Islamic Studies* 18, no. 4 (Winter 1979): 299–309.

"Land Law and Economic Development in Arab Countries." *The American Journal of Comparative Law* 33 (1985): 93–106.

"Prosody and the Initial Formation of Classical Arabic." *Journal of the American Oriental Society* 196 (1986): 333–338.

"Der Begriff des Eigentums im islamischen Recht." In *Beiträge zu islamischen Rechtsdenken* (co-author), pp. 93–115. Stuttgart, 1986.

"Shuf'ah: Origins and Modern Doctrine." *Cleveland State Law Review* 34 (1985–86): 35–46.

'Adab al-Qāḍī and the Protection of Rights at Court." In *Studies in Islamic and Judaic Traditions*, edited by W. M. Brinner and S. D. Ricks, pp. 143–150. Brown Judaic Studies, no. 110. Atlanta: Scholars Press, 1986.

"Permanence and Change in Arab Legal Systems," *Arab Studies Quarterly* 9 (1987): 20–34.

Book Reviews in the Following Journals

American Historical Review
American Journal of Comparative Law
Arab Studies Quarterly
International Journal of Middle East Studies
Journal of Near Eastern Studies
Journal of the American Oriental Society
Law Library Journal
Middle East Journal
Middle East Studies Association Bulletin
Modern Language Journal
Muslim World

I

ISLAMIC JURISPRUDENCE

1

On Inductive Corroboration, Probability and Certainty in Sunnī Legal Thought

WAEL B. HALLAQ

THE PROBLEM OF INDUCTION

RATIONALITY in drawing inferences means that the conclusion of an argument must follow from the premises and must not go beyond them; it must be true if the premises are true. The rational force of an argument may then be measured by the extent to which the evidence in it entails the conclusion. In valid deductive inferences this rational entailment must constantly hold true. But reasoning cannot be confined exclusively to deductive modes of argument, as the need often arises to draw a general conclusion from a limited body of evidence. Arguments proceeding from a certain number of particulars to a general conclusion do not follow the strict rules of logical entailment and rationality. In other words, they are not analyzable, after the fashion of deductive arguments, into premises and a conclusion; rather, they constitute a perception of relations that are not wholly subject to the rules of rational, deductive validity.

In these nonformal, inductive inferences the evidence does not entail the conclusion but lends it some sort of support or corroboration. Accordingly, the rationality and logical entailment in inductive arguments are a matter of degree and thus do not fit the neat paradigms of formal validity. The conclusion is not entailed by the available evidence but is more or less corroborated by it.[1] Here, there is no demonstrative confirmation unless it can be established beyond any doubt that the total body of evidence needed to prove a generalizing statement has indeed been provided. In such a case there is no problem, for when total evidence becomes available there is no question concerning the certainty of the conclusion if the particulars of the evidence which led to it are true. Instead, the real problem lies in the absence of total evidence, in drawing ampliative inferences by going from the observed to the unobserved with the inevitable result of reaching an uncertain conclusion. At best, therefore, inductive inferences—or inductive leaps, as they are sometimes characterized—establish their conclusions as probable.

This rudimentary conception of induction represents to a varying degree an essential assumption in the logic of Aristotle, of medieval Muslim logicians, as well as of modern Western philosophers.[2] Among the latter, David Hume restated the traditional problem of induction in terms of inferences from past experience to similar future events. If such events establish themselves in a law-like manner as being connected to current or past experiences, then what had applied to a particular case in the past must also apply to it in the future. Clearly, this argument presupposes a necessary causal connection between distinct events which neither Hume nor his posterity could establish.[3] In the absence of such

[1] The term "corroboration" is employed here in the non-demonstrative sense of gradational support. The use of "confirmation," though common among a number of prominent modern philosophers, will be avoided, for, as Salmon observed, this term implies a finalistic force in proving once and for all the validity of a hypothesis. See Wesley C. Salmon, "The Justification of Inductive Rules of Inference," in *The Problem of Inductive Logic*, ed. Imre Lakatos, (Amsterdam: North Holland Publ. Co., 1968), p. 28. Further on corroboration, see Georg Henrik Von Wright, *The Logical Problem of Induction* (Oxford: Blackwell, 1957), p. 117 ff.; A. J. Ayer *Probability and Evidence* (London: Macmillan, 1972), p. 63 f.

[2] William Kneale, *Probability and Induction* (Oxford: Clarendon, 1949), p. 24 ff., 53–56; H. W. B. Joseph, *An Introduction to Logic* (Oxford, 1906), p. 395; Ibn Rushd, *Talkhīṣ manṭiq Arisṭū*, ed. Gerard Jehamy, 3 vols. (Beirut: al-Maktabah al-Sharqīyah, 1982), 1:352, 353, 2:513–514; Salmon, "Justification," especially p. 25 ff.; L. S. Stebbing, *A Modern Introduction to Logic*, 7th ed. (London: Methuen, 1950), pp. 243–349, 402 ff.; Joseph Horovitz, *Law and Logic: A Critical Account of Legal Argument* (Vienna: Springer-Verlag, 1972), p. 4 ff.

[3] Von Wright, *The Logical Problem*, pp. 13–39; Nelson Goodman, *Fact, Fiction, and Forecast* (London: Athlone Press, 1954), pp. 63–65.

causal connection, Hume resorted to the next guiding principle in extending our present knowledge of things to yet unobserved instances, namely, the principle of the "uniformity of nature," which affirms that what held good in the past will hold good in the future.[4] But should this principle be grounded in an assumption that cannot be logically justified, then we have no good reason to trust any inference of this kind. Hume therefore concluded that inductive inferences cannot yield conclusive assurances but are at best highly probable.[5] To rephrase this argument and to eliminate the concern with future events—which is of no interest to us here—Hume's proposition comes down to the question of whether or not we are able to reach, on the basis of incomplete but highly corroborative evidence, a conclusion or a generalization which can be deemed conclusive. The answer, of course, is that we are not. Corroboration strengthens a generalization but does not render it certain; it enhances its credibility to the extent of the corroborative evidence.

While multiple pieces of corroborative evidence cannot establish the certainty of a proposition, it takes only a single negative instance to falsify that proposition. Like Greek and modern Western philosophers, medieval Muslim logicians acknowledged the validity of this principle. The oft-quoted and long-lived example of the crocodile was frequently introduced to illustrate this point. An investigation into the eating habits of animals, such as humans, horses, rabbits, birds, and so on, leads to the conclusion that "All animals move their lower jaw when they chew." This statement, however, is falsified when we examine crocodiles, which move their upper jaw, and which we failed to investigate before we formed our conclusion.[6] This example teaches that whatever the level of corroboration may be, there will always

[4] Frederick L. Will, "Will the Future be Like the Past?" in *Logic and Language*, ed. Anthony Flew (New York: Doubleday, 1965), p. 248 ff.

[5] For a lucid analysis of Hume's ideas on this issue see A. J. Ayer, *Probability and Evidence*, pp. 3–26; idem, *The Central Questions of Philosophy* (Middlesex: Penguin, 1976), p. 137 ff., 174 ff.; For a statement and critique of the same see Goodman, *Fact, Fiction*, chapter 3, especially p. 63 ff., 81 ff.

[6] Abū Ḥāmid al-Ghazālī, *Maqāṣid al-falāsifah*, ed. Sulaymān Dunyā (Cairo: Dār al-Ma'ārif, 1961), p. 89; Taqī al-Dīn Ibn Taymīyah, *Jahd al-qarīḥah fī tajrīd al-naṣīḥah* (being an abridgement by Suyūṭī of *Al-Radd 'alā al-manṭiqīyīn*), ed. 'Alī Sāmī al-Nashshār (Cairo: Maṭba'at al-Sa'ādah, 1947), p. 296 ff.

exist the possibility of falsifying the conclusion because of counter evidence. This problem of induction, whether in its basic Aristotelian and medieval Muslim form or in its highly articulated reformulation by Hume, Mill, Carnap, Keynes, and others, cannot be solved except in terms of probabilistic, nondemonstrative logic.[7]

MUSLIM USE OF INDUCTION IN LEGAL THOUGHT

In light of these fundamental problems of induction, I propose to investigate a number of central issues in Sunnī legal thought. My concern centers on the use which Muslim theoreticians of law made of the theory of induction, and the extent to which they diverged in their juridical formulations from the precepts of this theory. It must be immediately stated, however, that Muslim jurists were acutely conscious of the precarious logical status of induction, and had no illusions concerning its probabilistic nature. The oft-quoted ruling about *watr*, a type of prayer whose performance is recommended rather than obligatory, is particularly illustrative. On the basis of an inductive survey, it was found that, unlike *watr*, no obligatory prayers examined could be performed while on a journey. The ruling that the performance of *watr* is only recommended and not obligatory was deemed probable (*ẓannī*) rather than certain (*qaṭ'ī*) precisely because the inductive survey of prayers was admittedly incomplete, since *watr* was not included in the survey.[8] The judgment that the performance of obligatory prayers while on a journey was impermissible was reached on the basis of an examination of a number of individual types of prayer. In other words, there was a need for a reasonable number of prayers in order to establish this ruling as being highly probable. Reaching a ruling on the basis of examining a single prayer would have resulted in a ruling of a considerably

[7] Ayer, *Probability*, pp. 54–88; Max Black, "Induction," in *Encyclopedia of Philosophy*, 8 vols. (New York & London: Macmillan, 1972), 4:169–181.

[8] Fakhr al-Dīn al-Rāzī, *Al-Maḥṣūl fī 'ilm uṣūl al-fiqh*, ed. Ṭāhā J. 'Ulwānī, 2 vols., 6 parts (Riyadh: Lajnat al-Buḥūth wa-al-Ta'līf wa-al-Tarjamah wa-al-Nashr, 1979-1981), 2.3:217–218; Abū Ḥāmid al-Ghazālī, *Al-Mustaṣfā min 'ilm al-uṣūl*, 2 vols. (Cairo: al-Maṭba'ah al-Amīrīyah, 1324 A.H.), 1:51; Shihāb al-Dīn al-Qarāfī, *Sharḥ tanqīḥ al-fuṣūl*, ed. T. Sa'd (Cairo: Maktabat al-Kullīyah al-Azharīyah wa-Dār al-Nashr, 1973), p. 445.

lower degree of probability. Therefore, increasing the number of cases relevant to a certain issue constitutes added corroboration that raises the level of probability.

INDUCTIVE CORROBORATION AND THE NUMBER OF WITNESSES

The notion of inductive corroboration has indeed played a major role in the elaboration of a number of central concepts in Islamic legal theory. On the most basic level, this notion appears clearly in the discussions concerning the rationale behind the number of witnesses. Although the number of witnesses in a court of law was considered a divine prescription subject to no human stipulation, jurists argued for a rational explanation of the divine command.[9] As stated in the case of the *watr* prayer, reasoning on the basis of a single case would yield a conclusion with a rather low degree of probability. This principle was used to justify the unacceptability of one witness whose testimony without any corroboration is nearly as good as none (*testis unus, testis nullus*).[10] At least one other corroborating witness was thought to constitute a reasonably sufficient basis for deciding a case. While one witness's testimony would yield doubtful knowledge, the testimony of two trustworthy witnesses would enhance the credibility of testimonial evidence enough to render it highly probable. In the words of Sarakhsī, this highly probable knowledge assures our hearts and minds (*ṭuma'nīnat al-qalb*) that the probability of an error is quite slim.[11] To phrase it according to modern legal jargon, the testimonies of two genuine witnesses bring up the level of probability near enough to certainty for the verdict to be "beyond reasonable doubt."

In what may be termed an extraordinary legal case, where the Qur'ān stipulates punishments for committing adultery (*ḥudūd al-zinā*), four witnesses are required to satisfy the criteria

[9] Abū Ya'lā al-Farrā' al-Baghdādī, *Al-'Uddah fī uṣūl al-fiqh*, ed. A. Mubārakī, 3 vols. (Beirut: Mu'assasat al-Risālah, 1980), 3:856. For a contrary view see Shams al-Dīn Ibn Sahl al-Sarakhsī, *Uṣūl*, ed. Abū al-Wafā al-Afghānī, 2 vols. (Cairo: Dār al-Kitāb al-'Arabī, 1372 A.H.), 1:332.

[10] Muwaffaq al-Dīn Ibn Qudāmah, *Rawḍat al-nāẓir wa-junnat al-munāẓir*, ed. Sayf al-Dīn al-Kātib (Beirut: Dār al-Kitāb al-'Arabī, 1981), p. 91, ll. 7–8.

[11] Sarakhsī, *Uṣūl*, 1:290, 331, l. 10. For the definition of *qalb*, see Farrā', *'Uddah*, 1:89, ll. 3–6.

of evidence.[12] The importance attached to this particular case makes further corroboration necessary. The more serious the litigated issue is, the more witnesses the court requires. Although two trustworthy witnesses are normally sufficient in ordinary cases, and four in cases of adultery, the judge has the prerogative of requiring additional witnesses if he sees fit to do so. According to one prominent jurist, seeking testimonial corroboration beyond the required standard evidence is permitted by the Sharī'ah.[13]

Corroboration, however, does not depend merely on the number of witnesses required in a case. Rather, it must have as a prerequisite the condition of independence. What this means is that all testimonial statements relevant to a particular case must be given by independent witnesses. There must exist an intact means of transmission between the primal event and the subsequent utterance of the testimony. If one witness is told by another witness what to say, or is influenced by the testimony of another witness, or is involved in any kind of collusion with him, then the validity of his testimony becomes highly questionable, if not altogether worthless. For example, in a case where a man had a quarrel with the inhabitants of a village regarding a certain matter, the testimonial statements of the villagers in favor of each other were

[12] Insofar as procedural evidence and testimonial corroboration are concerned, a fully capacitated witness is a male witness. In "ordinary" cases the testimony of either two male witnesses or one male and two female witnesses is admissible. In adultery cases, on the other hand, only the testimony of four men may be accepted. The Ẓāhirī school seems to stand alone in recognizing the validity of women's testimony in adultery cases. Accordingly, Ibn Ḥazm accepts the testimony of eight women when four men are not available. See *Mu'jam Fiqh Ibn Ḥazm al-Ẓāhirī* (Damascus: Maṭba'at Jāmi'at Dimashq, 1966), 2:535, par. 17.

[13] Imām al-Ḥaramayn al-Juwaynī, *Al-Burhān fī uṣūl al-fiqh*, 2 vols., ed. 'Abd al-'Aẓīm al-Dīb (Cairo: Dār al-Anṣār, 1400 A.H.), 1:573. Cf. Joseph Schacht, *Introduction to Islamic Law* (Oxford: Clarendon, 1964), pp. 193, 195, who argues that a greater number of witnesses does not lend additional value to their testimony. Articles 1698 and 1699 of the essentially Ḥanafī text *Al-Majallah* (English trans. as the *Mejelle* by C. R. Tyser, et al., Lahore: All Pakistan Legal Decisions, 1967) not only deem a *tawātur* number of evidential testimonies valid, but also irrevocably conclusive. It must, however, be added that Article 1732 states that: "By reason of one of two parties having more witnesses than the other party, it is not necessary that it should be preferred, unless the number of witnesses amounts to the degree of tevatur," in which case (Articles 1698, 1733) any contrary evidence must be dismissed.

rejected on the grounds that they were made in collusion.[14] On the same grounds, the testimony of a father in favor of his son is deemed unacceptable in a court of law.[15] Thus, to yield a genuine corroboration, the testimonial statements must correspond with each other on points of fact and must be given independently of one another. They must not be adulterated by extrinsic factors. In fact, the quality of rectitude (*'adālah*) required of every Muslim witness may be said to have been intended as a safeguard against hampering the independent character of the testimonial evidence.[16] In due course, we shall observe the importance of the role which the principle of independence, as a validating condition of inductive corroboration, played in Islamic legal theory.

MUTAWĀTIR REPORTS

The *raison d'être* of witnesses in a court of law is obviously the creation of a connecting link between the judge and the facts or actual events of the case. Through true testimony our knowledge is extended to things beyond our individual experience, such as our knowledge of the existence of remote cities which we have never visited or, as in a criminal law suit, of events which took place sometime in the past. In a religion such as Islam, where the Prophetic past constitutes a fundamental source of religious belief and behavior, testimonial evidence of this sort is deemed indispensable. The theory of *akhbār* (Prophetic reports) and the various modes of their transmission draws heavily upon the very principles by which testimonial evidence is established. Not only cases of positive and substantive law, but also the methods and procedures through which these cases were established, found their

[14] The case, cited in Herbert J. Liebesny, *The Law of the Near and Middle East* (Albany: SUNY Press, 1975), p. 41, was decided by the renowned Ottoman Shaykh al-Islām Abū al-Su'ūd.

[15] Abū al-Barakāt al-Nasafī, *Kashf al-asrār sharḥ al-manār fī uṣūl al-fiqh*, 2 vols. (Cairo: Maṭba'at Būlāq, 1316 A.H.), 2:22, ll. 22-24. In the same vein, Article 1702 of the *Majallah* stipulates that "there must not be enmity as regards temporal things between the witnesses and the person against whom evidence is given." But Article 1701 accepts as valid the testimony of a person in favor of his friend, provided that the two cannot, by operation of the law, dispose of the property of each other.

[16] For the constitutive characteristics of *'adālah*, see Muḥammad Ḍiyā' al-Dīn Ibn al-Ukhūwah, *Ma'ālim al-qurbah fī aḥkām al-ḥisbah*, ed. and trans. R. Levy (London: Luzac, 1937-1938), p. 211 ff. (Arabic text).

source and rationale in these reports. The strength of a legal ruling or a method of interpretation (*ṭuruq al-ijtihād*) depended to a significant extent on the degree of authenticity of these Prophetic reports. The determination therefore of the status of reports was in matters of law of utmost importance for the purpose of assessing the epistemic value of legal premises. How then was the conclusiveness of the report determined with regard to the authenticity of the "testimony" it intends to convey? Let us begin with the *mutawātir* (recurrent) report.

The *mutawātir* report, whose authenticity is absolutely certain, reaches us through channels of transmission sufficiently numerous to preclude any possibility of collaboration on a forgery. Moreover, the persons witnessing the Prophet saying or doing a particular thing must be sure of what they saw or heard, and their knowledge of what they witnessed must be based on sensory perception (*maḥsūs*).[17] All of the above conditions must be met at each stage of the transmission if the status of *tawātur* is to be maintained.[18]

Epistemologically, this report yields necessary or immediate knowledge (*'ilm ḍarūrī*) in the mind of the hearer, a knowledge that is not inferred but directly imposed on the intellect.[19] In contradistinction to mediate knowledge (*'ilm muktasab* or *naẓarī*), where by definition inference is the means of its acquisition, necessary knowledge does not allow for any reflection; it simply occurs in the intellect without the awareness of the process—if any—through which knowledge is obtained. Now, when a person hears a report narrated by only one witness, he is presumed to have gained only probable knowledge concerning the authenticity of that report. To reach the stage of conclusive knowledge, the report must recur (*yajibu an yatawātara*) in the presence of the hearer a sufficient number of times, and each time it must be transmitted by a different witness. In the view of the great majority of scholars

[17] Qarāfī, *Sharḥ*, p. 349, ll. 9–10, 15–17.

[18] Muḥammad al-Izmīrī, *Mir'āt al-uṣūl fī sharḥ mirqāt al-wuṣūl*, 2 vols. (Istanbul, 1884), 2:199; Qarāfī, *Sharḥ*, pp. 349–350; al-Muḥaqqiq al-Ḥillī, *Ma'ārij al-uṣūl*, ed. M. Riḍwī (Qum: al-Maṭba'ah al-'Ilmīyah, 1403 A.H.), p. 139. On Ghazālī's theory of *tawātur*, see B. Weiss, "Knowledge of the Past: The Theory of *Tawātur* According to Ghazālī," *Studia Islamica* 61 (1985): 81–105, especially at 88–89.

[19] Farrā', *'Uddah*, 3:847, 848.

the report of two or four witnesses falls short of meeting the criteria of *tawatur*. Their argument for rejecting such reports takes its premises from the procedural law of testimony. Since, they assert, the *mutawātir* yields necessary knowledge, there must not be any intermediary stage of reflection between the actual reporting and the occurrence of knowledge in the intellect. Even when there exist as many as four witnesses, the judge must first establish their rectitude before accepting their testimony. The procedure of establishing rectitude is viewed by jurists as a prelude to the admission of their testimony, a prelude which *ipso facto* precludes the testimony of four witnesses from leading to immediate knowledge. As argued by the renowned theologian and jurist Bāqillānī, the testimony of four witnesses does not yield certain knowledge, much less immediate knowledge, because had it not been so, God would not have commanded us to investigate the character of as many as four witnesses before accepting their testimony as valid.[20]

While some scholars fixed the minimal number of witnesses in *tawātur* at five, other groups, basing themselves on some Qur'ānic verses or religious accounts, set the number variably at 12, 20, 40, 70, or 313.[21] It seems, however, that sometime during the fourth/tenth or early fifth/eleventh century there emerged a dominant view that the smallest number of transmissions constituting *tawātur* is known only to God.[22] In other words, to try to determine the number at which immediate knowledge obtains would be in vain. The impossibility of pointing to a particular number stems from the fundamental assumption that what leads to certainty in the case of one person may not lead to certainty in the case of another; the reason being that each instance of transmitting a report is surrounded by circumstantial evidence (*qarā'in al-aḥwāl*) which may be known to one hearer but unknown to the

[20] Abū Bakr al-Bāqillānī, *Tamhīd*, ed. R. J. McCarthy (Beirut: Librarie Orientale, 1957), pp. 384, 385. See also Qarāfī, *Sharḥ*, p. 352; Farrā', *'Uddah*, 3:856; Sayf al-Dīn al-Āmidī, *Al-Iḥkām fī uṣūl al-aḥkām*, 3 vols. (Cairo: Maṭba'at 'Alī Ṣubayḥ, 1968), 1:230.

[21] Āmidī, *Iḥkām*, 1:229; Juwaynī, *Burhān*, 1:569–570; Farrā', *'Uddah*, 3:856–857; Ḥillī, *Ma'ārij*, p. 139. The choice of 70, for instance, is based on the alleged number of the followers of Moses, and 313 on the number of Muslim fighters in the battle of Badr.

[22] Āmidī, *Iḥkām*, 1:229, ll. 7–19.

other. Knowledge of such evidence lends special corroboration to the number of reports so far heard, and consequently brings to one person a conclusive knowledge that has not yet been obtained by another person who has been exposed to the same number of reports but who has no special familiarity with the relevant *qarā'in al-aḥwāl*. A number of instances of transmission may yield equally conclusive knowledge in the minds of two persons at the same time only when the number of reporters are in excess of four and the circumstantial evidence relative to all instances of transmission are either absent or equally comprehended by the two persons.[23] This clearly implies that *mutawātir* knowledge is subjective in character; that is, that different people perceive it differently.

Another source of difficulty involving the determination of the minimal number of *tawātur* transmissions relates to the premise that the knowledge imparted by this type of report is immediate. A person simply does not know how and when he reaches such knowledge. Ibn Qudāmah gives as an illustration an example of the knowledge about the existence of Mecca gained by people who have never paid a visit to it. They can never determine the exact instance at which they became absolutely certain of its existence. Likewise, if a man were killed in the marketplace, and we were told by the first passing person that such a murder had taken place, we would think only that this event has probably happened. But when a second person informs us of the same news, and then we hear it from a third, fourth, fifth, and sixth person, the probability in our minds is increasingly strengthened until we become totally convinced that such an event has indeed taken place. We do not, however, know the precise moment or by which individual report we reached such a conclusive knowledge.[24] The precise degree of corroboration which draws the line between probable and certain knowledge is as impossible to determine as the exact day a person ceases to be a minor and becomes an adult, or the exact instant at which night ends and the light of day begins.[25]

[23] Ibid., 1:230, 232, ll. 6–18; Bāqillānī, *Tamhīd*, pp. 384, 385; Farrā', *'Uddah*, 3:856, ll. 2 ff.

[24] Ibn Qudāmah, *Rawḍah*, p. 88, ll. 18–22; Āmidī, *Iḥkām*, 1:229.

[25] Ibn Qudāmah, *Rawḍah*, p. 89, ll. 3–5.

The obvious impossibility of determining the minimal number of *mutawātir* reports leads us to resort ultimately to the intellect of the hearer as the point of reference for measuring qualitatively as well as quantitatively the reports leading to conclusive knowledge. It is the moment at which a person realizes that he is completely certain of a reported matter which determines the number of reports, not the other way around; the number may be decided only when conclusive knowledge is reached.[26]

The knowledge of the *qarā'in* surrounding an individual report and of its chains of transmission varies, as we have intimated, from one person to another. It is the number of instances of reporting plus the *qarā'in al-aḥwāl* that make up the body of knowledge in the mind. A report recurring a few times, say five, may lead, with the help of many *qarā'in*, to conclusive knowledge, while another report, recurring seven or eight times but without *qarā'in*, may fail to yield such knowledge. The corroboration through *qarā'in* may best be illustrated by the example of a suckling child. When we observe a mother nursing her child, we do not in fact see the milk reaching the stomach of the child. However, when we see the child sucking the breast of his mother, the movement of its throat, and its thorough satisfaction, and when we further know that it had not been fed for sometime and that its mother is in the nursing period, we come to the conclusive knowledge that the milk is indeed reaching the stomach of the child.[27] Although we have not seen the milk itself, the accompanying evidence conclusively proves that the child has taken it in.

Circumstantial evidence may be strong enough to take the place of what would have been additional instances of transmission. In throwing its weight behind the report, this evidence yields, together with the instances of transmission it accompanies, conclusive knowledge.[28] This means that when the number of instances

[26] Qarāfī, *Sharḥ*, p. 352, ll. 12–13; Farrā', *'Uddah*, 3:855, ll. 10–11; Ibn Qudāmah, *Rawḍah*, p. 89, ll. 10–11; Fakhr al-Dīn al-Rāzī, *Lubāb al-ishārāt* (Cairo: Maṭba'at al-Sa'āda, 1355 A.H.), p. 27.

[27] Ibn Qudāmah, *Rawḍah*, p. 87f.; Wael B. Hallaq, "Notes on the Term *Qarīna* in Islamic Legal Discourse," *JAOS* 108 (1989), 3:478f.

[28] Āmidī, *Iḥkām*, 1:232, 238; Ibn Qudāmah, *Rawḍah*, p. 87; "li-anna al-qarā'ina qad tūrithu al-'ilma wa-in lam yakun fīhi ikhbār, falā yab'udu an tanḍamma al-qarā'inu ilā al-akhbāri fayaqūmu ba'ḍu al-qarā'ini maqāma ba'ḍi al-'adadi min al-mukhbirīna."

of transmission is above four but still incapable of leading to conclusive knowledge, the quality of the circumstantial evidence may be such that it complements the instances of transmission with the result that conclusive knowledge is attained.[29] Conclusive knowledge is not attained when the number is less than five and the circumstantial evidence is not sufficiently persuasive.

DOES *TAWĀTUR* YIELD MEDIATE OR IMMEDIATE KNOWLEDGE?

The significance and weight of circumstantial evidence in this theory are given equal weight to the number of *tawātur* reports.[30] A few jurists went so far as to argue that when circumstantial evidence surrounds even a solitary report (*khabar wāḥid*), which necessarily falls short of fulfilling the conditions of *tawātur* and therefore leads by itself to probable knowledge only,[31] it sometimes renders the knowledge gained from that report conclusive.[32] Since circumstantial evidence is resorted to when the channels of transmission are less than the *tawātur* number, the knowledge

---

However, Ibn Taymīyah was among a smaller group of jurists who rejected the view that *qarā'in* in isolation of *ḥadīth* can yield certainty. See his *Raf' al-malām 'an al-a'immah al-a'lām*, in *Majmū' rasā'il* (Cairo: al-Maṭba'ah al-Ḥusaynīyah, 1323 A.H.), p. 67.

29 Ghazālī, *Mustaṣfā*, 1:135, ll. 4 ff., 138; Ibn Qudāmah, *Rawḍah*, p. 87–88. It should be noted that a number of jurists argued that immediate knowledge may obtain when the number is four provided that the instances of reporting are accompanied by strong *qarā'in al-aḥwāl*. See, e.g., Qarāfī, *Sharḥ*, p. 352, par. 2.

30 The great majority of jurists accepted this view of *qarā'in al-aḥwāl*. Abū Bakr al-Bāqillānī seems to have been in the minority in rejecting the role of *qarā'in* in the theory of *tawātur*. See Ghazālī, *Mustaṣfā*, 1:135.

31 Ibn Qudāmah, *Rawḍah*, p. 91. Āmidī, *Iḥkām*, 1:234, remarks that the majority of jurists (*al-jumhūr*) espoused the view that solitary reports can under no condition or circumstance yield certainty.

32 Kamāl al-Dīn Ibn al-Humām, *Al-Taḥrīr fī uṣūl al-fiqh* (Cairo: Muṣṭafā al-Bābī al-Ḥalabī, 1351 A.H.), p. 331; Juwaynī, *Burhān*, 1:576-577; Ḥillī, *Ma'ārij*, p. 141, 148; Ibn Qudāmah, *Rawḍah*, p. 91, 92; Ibn 'Abd al-Barr, *Jāmi' bayān al-'ilm*, 2 vols. (Cairo: al-Maktabah al-Salafīyah, 1968), 2:41–42. For the views of Ibrāhīm al-Naẓẓām, who is reputed to have been the first to propound this doctrine, and for their refutation see Sarakhsī, *Uṣūl*, 1:330 (also 2:321). Qarāfī, *Sharḥ*, p. 349, ll. 12–14, 357, considers this type of report as belonging to an independent technical category which is neither *āḥād* nor *tawātur*, because the report has not been transmitted through a sufficient number of channels and yet it yields certainty. According to Kamāl al-Dīn al-Anbārī (*Luma' al-adillah fī uṣūl al-naḥw*, ed. Attiya Amer [Stockholm: Almqvist & Wiksell, 1963], p. 34), the majority of jurists do not deem such a report conclusive.

that such a report imparts is necessarily mediate rather than immediate, for to ascertain the sufficient degree of persuasiveness of the circumstantial evidence involved, and to verify the uninterrupted chain of transmission of the solitary report—or reports—throughout generations of Muslims entails a good deal of contemplation and thought.

It may well be argued that even in cases of *tawātur* transmission the mind comes to a conscious realization of the instances of corroboration, whether they be instances of transmission or *qarā'in al-aḥwāl*.[33] In such cases, the knowledge obtaining in the intellect may be deemed inferential and thus mediate. The process by which this knowledge occurs is clearly cumulative and corroborative. The aggregation of statements made by trustworthy informants will increase the level of probability until certainty is achieved; and this is precisely the moment when we realize that what we heard is a *mutawātir* report.[34] But the problem that quickly unfolds here is the incompatibility of the assumed immediacy (*ḍarūrah*) of knowledge, on the one hand, and the intellect's awareness of the gradual process of corroboration that yields an increase in the level of probability, on the other, for any degree of such awareness naturally precludes knowledge from being immediate.

The solution to what seems to be an epistemological dilemma is claimed by jurists and theologians to be found in an inner psychological ability given to people by God, an ability to reach a level of certainty without consciously perceiving the gradation of evidential corroboration imposed on the mind.[35] In other words, the Almighty creates in us the power to attain conclusive knowledge through a *mutawātir* report without a conscious cognizance of the means and data through which that knowledge is attained. This argument may be explained only in terms of an unconscious method of inference in which the conscious intellect is totally oblivious to the hidden, ongoing cumulative process of constructing knowledge.

[33] Rāzī, *Lubāb*, p. 27; Ḥillī, *Ma'ārij*, p. 138.

[34] Ghazālī, *Mustaṣfā*, 1:44, ll. 3–8, 46, l. 12.

[35] In the exact words of Bāqillānī, *Tamhīd*, p. 10, this ability is "ḍarūratun tukhtara'u fī al-nafsi ibtidā'an"; Sarakhsī, *Uṣūl*, 1:331.

While the conscious intellect remains heedless of the inner process of acquiring *tawātur* knowledge, this process itself operates on the basis of a set of assumptions which are thought to justify the occurrence of immediate knowledge. Although God creates in us such knowledge,[36] there still exist outside the intellect certain conditions that must be fulfilled in order for that intellect to reach a state of immediate knowledge. As we have intimated earlier, in the fulfillment of these conditions the number of instances of transmission ranks supreme. A *mutawātir* number precludes any possibility of conspiring on a forgery or a lie. Lying within the framework of a *tawātur* number is impossible, the reasoning being that the *tawātur* transmitters cannot all have a single reason to lie, and therefore it is inconceivable that they should conspire to tell the same lie.[37] The differences between individuals, their multifarious ambitions and interests, make it impossible for them to agree on the same lie, since this cannot conceivably serve their divergent purposes and goals.[38] And even if they attempt to conspire on a lie, their great number will eventually bring their conspiracy into the open; it is simply impossible to preserve a secret among such a large group of people.[39] Thus, when they all transmit one and the same report, we know that the report is absolutely true.

Admittedly, the credibility of the thesis that a large number of people cannot succeed in conspiring on a lie cannot be justified on sheer objective grounds, for it is conceivable under given circumstances that such a thing might happen. But the nature of man and the world as created by God does not allow for a conspiracy under the conditions of *tawātur*. We know from God's habitual way (*'ādah*) of running things in this world that a *mutawātir* number of people simply cannot agree on a lie.[40] Abū Ya'lā al-Farrā' goes so far as to say that God directly creates in us such knowledge as soon as we hear a *mutawātir* number of people transmitting a Prophetic report, although He could also posit the same knowledge in us even without our actually hearing

[36] Farrā', *'Uddah*, 3:850, ll. 2-3.

[37] Rāzī, *Maḥṣūl*, 2.1:335-337; Farrā', *'Uddah*, 3:844.

[38] Nasafī, *Kashf*, 2:5.

[39] Bāqillānī, *Tamhid*, p. 382.

[40] Ibid., p. 382; Qarāfī, *Sharḥ*, pp. 349–350.

the report. This is precisely analogous, he asserts, to the birth of a child subsequent to sexual intercourse, although God has the power to create the same child without any such intercourse.[41]

Although it would seem that this theory of *tawātur* is on the verge of losing itself in a highly subjective justification devoid of any conception of causality, the attempt to argue for its credibility stems from the need to have a rational basis for believing the evidence of witnesses. Since individual instances of transmission (*āḥād*) cannot by themselves yield certainty, a large number of transmissions becomes indispensable as a guarantee for conclusiveness. As *tawātur* numbers cannot lead to anything but certainty, it is therefore assumed that the continued recurrence of transmissions will eventually yield immediate knowledge. The realization of having reached certainty with no reflection upon the means by which we attained that state of knowledge tells us that the number of transmissions involved is *mutawātir*, and therefore we *must* assume that the conditions which preclude the possibility of a conspiracy have been met. This theory then comes down to the fundamental requirement of number, since increasingly large numbers will preclude the possibility of a conspiracy and inevitably lead to immediate knowledge.

Here, indeed, lies the solution to the problem concerning the hearer's awareness of the very process by which immediate knowledge is attained. At a particular time, the hearer, after having reached a state of immediate knowledge, looks back and realizes that the report was transmitted a sufficient number of times. He does not, on the other hand, know for certain (nor is he expected to know) that the transmitters of the report did not lie. All he knows is that he heard the report a number of times sufficient to yield immediate knowledge in his mind. Presumably, he does not count the times of transmission, but realizes that they were sufficient to engender this knowledge in him. This is precisely analogous to the process of memorizing a lesson; you continue to repeat the lesson until you memorize it. You do not have to count the number of times you have read it, but you know that they were sufficient and that *now* you know the lesson by heart.[42] Furthermore, the

[41] Farrā', *'Uddah*, 3:850, ll. 3–6.

[42] Ibid., 3:843.

hearer does not attempt to establish the relationships among the transmitters of the report, but he assumes, *post eventum*, that those who relayed the report to him could not have met or conspired. This is certainly in consonance with the established theory. First, immediate knowledge occurs, and subsequently the hearer comes to the realization that the number of transmissions was a *tawātur* number, for if it were not, he would not have attained this knowledge. Second, once the number of transmissions involved is established as a *tawātur* number, we know that what the transmitters relayed is true, because God, in his *'ādah*, cannot allow for a falsehood to circulate among a *tawātur* group.

Each instance of transmission in a *mutawātir* report may be taken to constitute a member of a class of things—a class which is the *mutawātir* report in its entirety. According to the theories of inductive logic set forth in the first passages of this article, no conclusive knowledge can be attained with regard to a class until there is an exhaustive account of all the members of that class. The need for a full enumeration of members stems from the absence of any necessary relationship between the observed members of a class and its unobserved members. It is precisely here where the Muslim *juristic* conception of logic drastically differs from its Aristotelian and Western post-Aristotelian counterpart. A full account of all the instances of transmission, that is, all members of the class, is not deemed in the *tawātur* theory to be indispensable for conclusive knowledge. A relatively large number, but not necessarily the whole, suffices for attaining certainty. A person may therefore reach certain knowledge without having been exposed to all the instances of transmission in existence.[43]

[43] This is perhaps the most significant difference between logical induction and the *tawātur* theory. Nonetheless, it must be asserted that in principle *tawātur* operates within the framework of the general rules of induction. B. Weiss, "Knowledge of the Past," pp. 103–104, points out, and rightly so, two similarities between induction and *tawātur*, but a few lines later he says that there is, as implied by Ghazālī, an important difference between the two: that is, inductive knowledge is a generalization from particular experiences, whereas *tawātur* knowledge is not (p. 104). Weiss does not cite the place where Ghazālī implied this difference. Our sources, however, do not allow us to reach the same conclusion. Like inductive knowledge, *tawātur* knowledge is based on experience. This is why the validity of *tawātur* presupposes, among other things, that the knowledge of the report's contents must be grounded in sense-perception (*maḥsūsāt*) (see note 18 above, and pp. 88, 91 of Weiss's 1985

TAWĀTUR MA'NAWĪ

To stress the crucial importance of multiple transmission must not imply that individual instances of reporting are of no significance. Indeed, there is a fundamental epistemological value in solitary reports. Aside from the circumstantial evidence that may surround them and may thus lend them further support, the *āḥād*, merely by virtue of their having an uninterrupted chain of transmission from the time of the Prophet, boast a degree of probability in excess of 0.5.[44] And when two *āḥād* reports relayed by

article). The immediate knowledge which the *tawātur* engenders in the intellect eliminates, as we have already seen, any possibility of inference, thus connecting the original *maḥsūs* with the comprehension and sense-perception of the hearer. Therefore, when one hears a *mutawātir* number of identical reports transmitted, the knowledge that accumulates therefrom carries with it the actual original experience, almost as if it were the direct experience of the hearer himself. In *tawātur*, knowledge of past events stands on the same footing with particular sensory experiences, such as seeing a bird fly or experiencing pain when your finger touches fire. See Abū Isḥāq al-Shīrāzī, *Al-Tabṣirah fī uṣūl al-fiqh*, ed. M. H. Haytu (Damascus: Dār al-Fikr, 1980), pp. 291, ll. 4-6, 293, l. 6. The difference between empirical experiences and hearing a report may perhaps lie in the designation of certain senses as means of assimilating *tawātur* knowledge (e.g., hearing), while assigning to other senses the function of attaining *tajrībī* knowledge (e.g., smell). Fakhr al-Dīn al-Rāzī, *Maḥṣūl*, 1.1:100–101, observes that knowledge obtaining through rational faculties along with the sense of hearing is *tawātur*, but that which occurs through rational faculties along with other means of sense-perception is inductive (*tajrībī*). Ḥasan ibn Zayn al-Dīn al-Shahīd al-Thānī, *Ma'ālim al-uṣūl*, ed. Mahdī Muḥaqqiq (Tehran: Shirkat-i Intishārāt-i 'Ilmī va-Farhangī, 1985), p. 210, ll. 4-5. As we shall see later (pp. 24–29), Shāṭibī considers *tawātur* to be squarely based on inductive principles. It is also interesting to note that the Aristotelian theory of induction, which undoubtedly formed the main source of the Islamic theory of induction, insisted that knowledge of particulars, the backbone of any inductive inference, is possible only through sense-perception. See Von Wright, *Logical Problem*, p. 8. The connection between inductive and *tawātur* knowledge is discussed in clearer terms in works of logic. See, for instance, Ibn Taymīyah, *Jahd al-qarīḥah*, p. 316, who equates *tajrībīyāt* with *mutawātirāt*; also Quṭb al-Dīn al-Rāzī, *Taḥrīr al-qawā'id al-manṭiqīyah fī sharḥ al-risālah al-shamsīyah* [of Kātibī], (Cairo: Muṣṭafā al-Bābī al-Ḥalabī, 1948), pp. 207–208.

[44] Sunnī jurists are unanimous with regard to the *ẓannī* status of *āḥād* reports. The statistical probability of *ẓann* is certainly above half. According to Ghazālī, *ẓann* occurs when the soul is inclined to believe something but senses the existence of its opposite ("wa-yakūnu lil-nafsi sukūnun ilā al-shay'i wa-al-taṣdīqu bihi wa-hiya tash'uru binaqīḍihi ... wa-hādha yusammā ẓannan"). See his *Mustaṣfā*, 1:44, ll. 3-4. Therefore, the lowest degree of probability in *ẓann* is greater than 0.5. A degree of probability equal to 0.5 is termed *shakk*. Jurists also recognized degrees of probability higher than 0.5 but lower than 1.0, which they called according to an ascending order

different transmitters support a particular point or issue, their probability together increases to a significant degree. That is, if we assume that two solitary reports possess in common a given theme, and the probability that each report being true is, say, 0.51, the aggregate probability of their being true is increased to a degree significantly higher than 0.51 but lower than 1.0. When a greater number of *āḥād* reports, all having independent channels of transmission, possess in common one theme, the knowledge of this theme becomes conclusive as well as immediate. While the previous type of *tawātur* is known as *lafẓī* on the grounds that the wording of the report in all instances of transmission is identical, this type of *tawātur* is recognized as *ma'nawī*, that is, although the transmissions differ from one another in wording, they all share the same meaning (*ma'nā*).[45]

Although the justification of *al-tawātur al-ma'nawī* ultimately reverts to the same principles which underly *al-tawātur al-lafẓī*, those Muslim jurists who admitted the authoritative character of the former (and they were the great majority) seem to have stressed the element of inductive support as the cornerstone of its validity. The emphasis here is placed on the differences among the reports insofar as the chains of transmission and the verbal contents are concerned. Given the common theme that they convey, these reports cannot but enhance the argument that this common theme is unquestionably true. The degree of probability attached to them individually is immediately eliminated once they are grouped together as one aggregate.[46] In other words, the possibility that these reports are separately false is soon dismissed when, taken all together, they testify uniformly to a particular issue. An argument in favor of the certainty yielded by such corroborative evidence is the reputed generosity of Ḥātim, about whom there is no single *mutawātir* report. The multitude of the solitary reports which testify to his generosity,

---

of strength *ghalabat al-ẓann*, *al-ẓann al-qawī*, and *al-ẓann al-mutākhim lil-yaqīn*. See Abū al-Walīd Ibn Khalaf al-Bājī, *Al-Ḥudūd fī al-uṣūl*, ed. N. Ḥammād (Beirut, 1973), p. 30; idem, *Al-Minhāj fī tartīb al-ḥijāj*, ed. A. M. Turki (Paris: Maisonneuve et Larose, 1978), p. 11, ll. 4-5; Farrā', *'Uddah*, 1:83, ll. 3–4.

[45] Āmidī, *Iḥkām*, 1:232–233; Bājī, *Al-Minhāj*, p. 76; Ḥillī, *Ma'ārij*, p. 140; Ibn Taymīyah, *Raf' al-malām*, p. 67.

[46] Ghazālī, *Mustaṣfā*, 1:48.

however, collectively engender in us an immediate, conclusive knowledge.[47]

The process by which knowledge obtains in the mind through *al-tawātur al-ma'nawī* is similar to that which obtains through *al-tawātur al-lafẓī*. Without being aware of the actual process of reporting, the intellect accumulates knowledge until the point when it becomes entirely certain of the information reported. The process is purely corroborative and cumulative. It is likened by jurists to drops of water or small pieces of bread; individually they are insufficient, but when they are continuously consumed they will eventually quench the thirst and fill the stomach.[48] An outstanding example of the conclusive corroboration and complete confirmation that *al-tawātur al-ma'nawī* lends to what may first appear as a probable issue is the authoritative basis of Sunnī consensus. As there existed no clear Qur'ānic verse or *mutawātir lafẓī* report to the effect that the consensus of the community, represented by its scholars, is infallible, Sunnī jurists sought another means by which they could prove the infallible character of this central institution. What they found was a large number of *āḥād* reports all sharing the theme that God will not allow his community as a whole to fall into error. The individual reports, which were deemed to yield only probable knowledge, are now as a whole taken to yield certain as well as immediate knowledge. And to confirm even this conclusive knowledge, other corroborative pieces of evidence derived from the other "sources of Sharī'ah" were taken into consideration.[49]

TAWĀTUR AND CONSENSUS

The central role that the corroboration of multiple transmissions plays in bringing about certainty is obvious in the theory of

[47] Muwaffaq al-Dīn Ibn Qudāmah, *Taḥrīm al-naẓar fī kutub ahl al-kalām*, ed. and trans. George Makdisi (London: Luzac, 1962), p. 39, par. 68 (English trans. pp. 26–27); Āmidī, *Iḥkām*, 1:164, 232–233, 237–238. See another example given in my article "On the Authoritativeness of Sunni Consensus," *International Journal of Middle East Studies* 18 (1986): 445.

[48] Qarāfī, *Sharḥ*, p. 350; Sarakhsī, *Uṣūl*, 1:295.

[49] For a detailed analysis of this problem see my "On the Authoritativeness of Sunni Consensus," pp. 427–454, especially pp. 441–450. Also see Ibn Qudāmah, *Rawḍah*, pp. 118–119; Qarāfī, *Sharḥ*, pp. 338–339.

the *mashhūr* report, a report which originated as *āḥādī* but acquired the status of *tawātur* subsequent to the demise of the Companions and the Followers.[50] This report yields certain, though mediate knowledge. The assumption that the Companions and the Followers could not, by virtue of having lived in so early and pristine a phase of Islam, have lied or conspired on a forgery, precludes the possibility that this *āḥādī* report is probable. And once it becomes highly circulated after the Followers, the great number of instances of transmission will certainly secure its conclusiveness. The verification of the *mashhūr*'s early stages of transmission, however, presupposes an amount of conscious thinking, a fact which renders the knowledge obtained from it mediate rather than necessary.[51]

Despite their full awareness of the probabilistic nature of the early stages of the *mashhūr*'s transmission, the jurists who upheld this theory insisted on the impossibility of error or forgery when a sufficient—*mutawātir*—number of people were involved in its later stages. The mere fulfillment of the condition of *tawātur* number could, one is compelled to conclude, ensure infallibility and, consequently, certitude. *Tawātur* number as such can therefore be used interchangeably with consensus. Indeed, commenting on the *mashhūr* report, 'Alā' al-Dīn al-Samarqandī observes that "the *mashhūr* tradition is that which the scholars [of the age] have favorably received, so that there exists a consensus of the people

[50] For what seems to have been the beginnings of the notion of *mashhūr*, and for a highly interesting but unrepresentative view of *tawātur*, see the early treatise of Ḥasan ibn Sahl ibn Ghālib, *Al-Taṣdīq*, with a French translation by Marie Bernand-Baladi, "Des critères de la certitude: un opuscule de Ḥasan Ibn Sahl sur la crédibilité du dire transmis par un grand nombre," *Journal Asiatique* 257 (1969): 102–138. The translator's remarks in the introduction (pp. 98–100) to the text concerning the circularity of *ḥadīth* and consensus should be read with great caution.

[51] Sarakhsī, *Uṣūl*, 1:291–292; Nasafī, *Kashf al-asrār*, 2:6–7. While the majority of the jurists who recognized the category of *mashhūr* held that the knowledge resulting from this report is certain though mediate, a minority, such as 'Īsa ibn Abān, argued that such report can yield only a high degree of probable knowledge (*ṭuma'nīnah*). Against this last claim, Sarakhsī, *Uṣūl*, 2:292, cites *mashhūr* reports concerning the prohibition of usury and the prohibition of concluding a marriage with the maternal or paternal aunt of one's wife. Such reports, he asserts, are so certain that they may be used to abrogate verses from the Qur'ān. "Nothing can abrogate the verses of the Book unless it yields conclusive knowledge [*'ilm al-yaqīn*]."

of the age to accept it. Its status is thus that of consensus, and since the latter imposes certain knowledge, so does the former."[52]

In explaining the rationale behind the certitude of consensus, Sarakhsī insists on the significance of the number of people involved. Attaining certainty on the level of the community is tantamount to a combination of a great number of degrees of probability. Identical instances which are probable will conjoin to create certainty. In the section dealing with consensus he asserts that "what is established in sensory and legal matters by an aggregate of things (*ijtimāʿ*) cannot be established by individual things severally (*infirād*). Individuals cannot separately carry a heavy log; but if they group together they will be able to do so.... [This principle] we have already expounded when we dealt with the *mutawātir*."[53] The very principle of *tawātur* then constitutes the rationale for the certitude of consensus.[54] The association of consensus with *tawātur* comes out quite clearly in the debate about the number of qualified jurists (*mujtahid*s) who make up consensus. While such legists as ʿAbd al-Wahhāb al-Subkī refuse to accept as consensus any agreement from which even a less than *mutawātir* number of *mujtahid*s are absent, some Mālikīs and early Muʿtazilīs accept any consensus as valid as long as the number of *mujtahid*s who do not partake in it is less than *mutawātir*.[55] In either case, a

[52] Cited in A. Zysow, "The Economy of Certainty: An Introduction to the Typology of Islamic Legal Theory" (Ph.D. diss., Harvard University, 1984), p. 26. See also the discussion, pp. 24–29, concerning the Ḥanafī arguments against and for the *mashhūr*'s certitude.

[53] Sarakhsī, *Uṣūl*, 1:295–296. See also Saʿd al-Dīn al-Taftāzānī, *Sharḥ al-ʿaqāʾid al-nasafīyah*, ed. Claude Salāmah (Damascus: Wizārat al-Thaqāfah wa-al-Irshād al-Qawmī, 1974), p. 17, ll. 12-15.

[54] See Ibn ʿAbd al-Barr, *Jāmiʿ bayān al-ʿilm*, 2:41–42, who associates consensus with *tawātur* in the following words: "The Sunnah [of the Prophet] may be divided into two parts, one of which is a consensus transmitted through a sufficient number of people, generation after generation. This constitutes a conclusive proof if there existed no disagreement [concerning its transmission]. He who rejects this consensus would, in effect, be rejecting a divine text. The second part of the Sunnah is the solitary [*āḥād*] report...." It should be cautioned, however, that the association of consensus with *tawātur* should not imply that the argument for the authoritativeness of consensus involves a *petitio principii*, because whereas consensus rests on the notion of *tawātur*, *tawātur*, whatever its form, does not derive its authoritativeness from consensus.

[55] Qarāfī, *Sharḥ*, p. 336.

mutawātir number of *mujtahids* opposing consensus will certainly nullify that consensus.

If consensus grounded in *tawātur* acquires legitimacy, then a consensus in which all the scholars of the community partake will, *a fortiori*, lead to certitude. In such a consensus the enumeration of probable instances goes beyond the already conclusive *mutawātir* to encompass each and every instance, thereby reaching a conclusion squarely based upon summative induction. Each confirming instance, represented by a legal opinion of an independent *mujtahid*, is a member of a class. The *mujtahid* upholds an opinion which is admittedly probable. But in reaching this opinion, he, as an acknowledged authority on the Law, establishes himself as a self-contained agent; that is, he himself must reach the opinion through a direct analysis of the authoritative legal sources, and thus his opinion represents the ruling which was *probably* decreed by God. If all the other *mujtahids* who reached their opinions through similar, independent means agree on the same point of law, then they will be corroborating each other as well as conclusively demonstrating that the ruling of that particular case is certain. Here we attain a full enumeration of all the members of the class. The certitude resulting from this enumeration hardly needs any justification, especially in a system which is endowed with divine providence against error once *tawātur* obtains.

ABŪ ISḤĀQ AL-SHĀṬIBĪ

Partly grounded in what may be described as a subjective theological transcendentalism and partly in rational-cum-empirical justification, this theory of inductive corroboration stood as the underlying logical-methodological foundation for a number of material and theoretical legal principles, ranging from the various types of Prophetic reports to consensus. The theoretical elaboration and development of this inductive doctrine as part of legal theory came about after the introduction of Greek logic into *kalām* and *uṣūl al-fiqh*. Whether or not there existed a necessary connection between the introduction of Greek logic into the domain of law and the development of a theory of inductive corroboration, it remains true that it is only during the fifth/eleventh century and thereafter that this theory began to surface in the works of the jurists. In fact, it was not until the seventh/thirteenth century that logic, whether formal or inductive, made itself an integral part of an important segment of *uṣūl al-fiqh* works, and affected in one way or another the construction of theoretical legal precepts.[56] While the majority of *uṣūl*ists confined the use of the theory of inductive corroboration to problems such as those discussed above, we find that some others have utilized this theory even more extensively. In his *Al-Muwāfaqāt fī uṣūl al-aḥkām*,[57] for instance, Abū Isḥāq al-Shāṭibī (d. 790/1388) went so far as to anchor his entire theory of *uṣūl al-fiqh* in inductive principles.

Shāṭibī begins with the fundamental premise that general theoretical legal principles and the sources of law are firmly grounded in certitude and that they derive their authoritativeness from God, for should there be any degree of probability concerning these principles and sources, there might follow the ominous conclusion that such probability (*ẓann*) may well decline to a degree of doubt (*shakk*),[58] thereby rendering the Sharīʿah, the decree of God, mutable. The certitude surrounding the general principles and sources of the law must then be derived either from conclusive pieces of textual evidence (*adillah*) which, Shāṭibī admits, are rare if they exist at all, or through an inductive survey of the multitude of probable pieces of evidence supporting these principles.[59] Shāṭibī argues that the aggregation of such pieces of evidence is perhaps the main source of certainty in law. The *tawātur*, whether *lafẓī* or *maʿnawī*, derives its certainty from this principle. Each individual chain of transmission is undeniably probable, but when a sufficient number of transmitted reports are heard, certainty of the contents of the report obtains. He asserts that both the conclusive certainty concerning the Five Pillars of Islam and the indubitable authoritativeness of consensus and *qiyās* are established in this manner. Likewise, such fundamental juridical principles as the

[56] On the infiltration and assimilation of Greek logic in Sunnī legal theory, see part 1 of my article "Logic, Formal Arguments and Formalization of Arguments in Sunni Legal Theory," *Arabica*, forthcoming.

[57] Ed. M. M. ʿAbd al-Ḥamīd, 4 vols. (Cairo: Maṭbaʿat al-Madanī, 1969-1970).

[58] Shāṭibī, *Muwāfaqāt*, 1:10–12. For the distinction between *ẓann* and *shakk* see note 44 above.

[59] Shāṭibī, *Muwāfaqāt*, 1:13.

natural right to have a religion, to own property, to procreate, and so on, are advocated by the Sharī'ah in no uncertain terms, terms that are individually probable, but in their multitude they corroborate and affirm the validity of these principles beyond any doubt.[60]

The evidence that may be utilized in proving the certainty of legal principles may not be confined to the formal verbal expression contained in the Prophetic reports and the Qur'ān. Rather, these principles derive from the meaning which may be found, by means of induction, to permeate the entirety of *shar'ī* material sources. Induction in Shāṭibī's theory is not merely an exhaustive account of the reports that pertain in their totality to a particular issue, but rather a thematic induction (*istiqrā' ma'nawī*) of the spirit and the letter of the Sharī'ah. The evidence may not be especially decreed for a particular case, or may not even directly touch upon the issue in question, but its indirect relatedness to, and subsidiary support of, the issue yields certainty in the event of obtaining a sufficient number of corroborative instances.[61]

In other words, the certainty of the general legal principles results from the cumulative corroboration of statements and indications found in passages and contexts that are not as a whole necessarily relevant to these principles. Corroborative pieces of evidence may appear in passing, or as minor points in a larger body of evidence.[62] The conclusive knowledge of Ḥātim's generosity, for instance, obtains upon hearing countless anecdotes in all of which there exists, irrespective of the differing nature and contents of these anecdotes, a common theme to the effect of his generosity.[63] It is therefore the recurrence of a meaning or a theme in a Prophetic report, Qur'ānic verse, or any circumstantial evidence, which will inevitably lead to certainty in the mind of the hearer. Shāṭibī plainly states that widespread and constantly recurrent themes or statements ("mā ḥaṣala fīhi

[60] Ibid., 1:13–14, also pp. 15–16 (on the authoritativeness of *al-istidlāl al-mursal* and *istiḥsān*).

[61] Ibid., 2:35–36.

[62] Ibid., 1:15.

[63] Ibid., 3:189. See also Qarāfī, *Sharḥ*, p. 239.

al-takrār wa-al-ta'kīd wa-al-intishār") rank equally with decisive and conclusive texts.[64] In Shāṭibī's theory then, all *mutawātir* and *mashhūr* reports have a force equivalent to that of summative induction.[65] But what are the logical properties and logical justification of this induction?

In contradistinction to the particularistic nature of positive legal rulings (*furū'*), legal theory entails the construction of general principles and universal truths (*kullīyāt*). The great majority, if not the entirety, of these *kullīyāt* are based, as Shāṭibī has already intimated, on a multitude of probable instances or particular statements (*juz'īyāt*) which corroborate each other to the degree of certainty.

Shāṭibī is acutely conscious of the basic rule of induction which premises that to attain certainty with regard to a matter all the particulars or species subsumed under that matter must be enumerated and found to be mutually corroborative. If, on the other hand, one succeeds in reaching a *kullīyah* on the basis of enumerating the great majority of instances, then there should be no instance which will contradict the *kullīyah*. This curious assertion may be explained in light of his assumption that if a particular instance is proven to be in contradiction with the rest of the instances constituting a given *kullīyah* then one of the two, the instance or the *kullīyah* is invalid. But our author remains insistent upon the claim that once a *kullīyah* is reached on the basis of the great majority of relevant, corroborative instances, then such *kullīyah* cannot be invalidated by what appears to be a non-conforming or non-corroborative instance. Indeed, upon examining such an instance one would find that its essence (*dhāt*) differs from the essences of the other corroborative instances, a difference which justifies its unsubsumability under that *kullīyah*. The essences of the particulars under a *kullīyah* must be identical, and must not be subject to external influences (*umūr khārijah*). Take, for instance, the essence of humanity, namely, acting with intent and premeditation. You survey a great number of humans who will indeed corroborate and ultimately confirm this assumption. You may, however, come across

[64] *Muwāfaqāt*, 3:192, 194, ll. 17–18.

[65] Ibid., 1:13, ll. 1 ff.; 3:189, ll. 4-9.

an individual who does not act with premeditation because he is afflicted with a certain severe disease. This particular individual will not invalidate the *kullīyah* which premises that humans act with premeditation, for illness has effected a change in his essence. Likewise, the general principles of contractual law will not be rescinded just because the contract of *'arāyā* conforms to a different set of contractual legal assumptions.[66] Similarly, *tayammum* (ritual cleanliness with sand or soil) cannot abrogate the prescribed *kullīyah* of ritual purity (*ṭahārah*) which God intended as a means of cleanliness.[67] These non-conforming instances each have an essence, designed by divine wisdom (*ḥikmah*), which is not identical to the essences of the instances subsumed under that particular *kullīyah*.

That a particular species is proven to be unlike other species forming a genus and thus is rightly excluded from enumeration, creates no difficulty in Shāṭibī's theory. When a species is shown to have no common denominator with a number of other species, there would be, to begin with, no sense in utilizing it as a corroborative instance. But the logically problematic issue in Shāṭibī's theory is that he accepts as conclusive a *kullīyah* even though there has not been a complete survey of all the relevant instances. "In the Sharī'ah," he says, "the great majority of particulars [constituting a *kullīyah*] are considered as tantamount to a conclusive general, since the instances diverging from a *kullīyah* cannot constitute another *kullīyah* which can then compete with the first established *kullīyah*."[68] Put differently, a truly authoritative as well as conclusive *kullīyah* will not allow for a significant number of diverging instances to constitute another equally authoritative *kullīyah*. Therefore, Shāṭibī argues, an already established *kullīyah* will not be undermined because a single instance stands

[66] *'Arāyā* is a type of contract in which unripe dates on the palm tree are bartered against their value calculated in terms of edible dried dates. Although Islamic law does not allow the element of risk in contracts, the *'arāyā* contract was recognized despite the risk and uncertainty it involves. Taqī al-Dīn al-Subkī, *Takmilat al-Majmū'*, 12 vols. (Cairo: Maṭba'at al-Taḍāmun, 1344 A.H.), 11:2 ff.

[67] Shāṭibī, *Muwāfaqāt*, 2:36–37, 43–44, 3:7–8.

[68] Ibid., 2:37, ll. 6–7.

in opposition to it.[69] Only a significant number of competing particulars can weaken or undermine a *kullīyah*.[70]

In support of this thesis, Shāṭibī introduces the example of the solitary reports which are generally considered authoritative for practice (*'amal*) although some of them are dubious. In comparison with those sound reports, the few doubtful ones pale into insignificance. Similarly, in rational sciences a mistake remains isolated and unaccounted for, but once scholars continue to reiterate the same mistake, it becomes the rule rather than the exception. When exceptions are numerous in legal matters no general principle can be derived. It is only when the number of exceptions is insignificant that a *kullīyah* may be reached. Shāṭibī's awareness of his unconventional stance towards inductive logic seems to have compelled him to justify his thesis on the grounds that it is the only conceivable means by which general principles of law can be formulated.[71]

CONCLUSION

Although Shāṭibī's theory represents a novel approach to Sunnī legal theory, it can by no means be maintained that it was unique in its reliance on principles of inductive logic. The strictly logical presentation of the theory of induction in the context of legal studies appeared first in the works of Ghazālī, but it could not gain a foothold as an integral part of legal theory until the seventh/thirteenth or eighth/fourteenth century, with the emergence of such powerful writings as those of Taqī al-Dīn Ibn Taymīyah. But none of these scholars could, like Shāṭibī, build a full-fledged theory of law grounded solely in inductive logic. His is a consummate theory representing the most advanced stage in a prolonged

[69] Ibid., 1:119 ("waqad 'ulima anna al-kullīyata idhā 'āraḍahā al-juz'īyu falā athara lil-juz'īyi"); 2:36 ("al-kullīyatu ... la yarfa'uhā takhallufu āḥādi al-juz'īyāt"); 3:7 ("al-kullīyu la yankharimu bi-juz'īyin"). It is significant that Ibn Rushd, *Talkhīs manṭiq Arisṭū*, 1:352–353, distinguishes between demonstrative induction (*istiqrā' burhānī*) and dialectical induction (*istiqrā' jadalī*). The former must, in order to be valid, encompass all the particulars in existence, but the latter need only include those particulars which are deemed to have gained credence (*mashhūrāt*) on account of their acceptance by people in general.

[70] *Muwāfaqāt*, 3:5, l. 11 ("fa-al-i'rāḍu 'an al-juz'īyi jumlatan yu'addī ilā al-shakki fī al-kullī").

[71] Ibid., 1:84, 85.

process of theoretical development. The embryonic beginnings of this process first appeared in the fourth/tenth and fifth/eleventh centuries in connection with *al-tawātur al-ma'nawī* of *āḥād* reports. As one traces down the sources there emerges a clear pattern of attempts to lay down a general theory of *tawātur* in terms of the *tawātur ma'nawī*. In this theory, the traditional theory which came to be known as *al-tawātur al-lafẓī* played an important, but partial role. The central concept in this general theory was inductive corroboration, not necessarily of reports transmitted in a verbally identical fashion but of reports having in common the same meaning. Shāṭibī's concept of thematic induction (*al-istiqrā' al-ma'nawī*) represents an extension of *al-tawātur al-ma'nawī*; instead of restricting the application of the principle to Prophetic reports, Shāṭibī utilized it in extracting from the entirety of the *shar'ī* sources a set of principles of universal validity.

While Shāṭibī went beyond his predecessors in developing a legal theory of induction, he remained faithful to the logical assumptions underlying the already established theory of *tawātur*, which, as we have indicated, formed the basis for his general theory. The adoption of these assumptions, along with their logical properties, resulted in an inductive theory of law constructed of these same properties. *Tawātur*, which in practical terms is a state of immediate knowledge obtaining in the mind, is subjectively determined by the hearer and does not need, once reached, to exhaust the entirety of the instances of transmission in existence. The same degree of conclusive certainty is claimed to be reached in Shāṭibī's inductive theory, although the enumeration of all the members of a particular class may not be totally exhausted.

The intellectual world of Shāṭibī and his co-religionists was anchored in the premise that what makes things the way they are in this world is none other than the Almighty. The unshaken belief and faith in the words of the Prophet existed in the factual world of certainty, and that had to be explained in terms of divine intent and volition. Thus knowledge and the lack of it were the works of God; if we "know," it is because our knowledge has been granted and guaranteed by God. Had Hume been a Muslim jurist, he would certainly have found his otherwise aborted theory of necessary causal connection between events guaranteed to him by his Creator. And if this were not the case, he would have encountered no problem in constructing a world view based on the principle of the uniformity of nature; for, after all, Muslims were indeed the recipients of divine providence, expressed in the *ʿādah* of their Lord.

2

Interpretation of the Divine Command in the Jurisprudence of Muwaffaq al-Dīn Ibn Qudāmah

JEANETTE WAKIN

FROM THE PERSPECTIVE of the Muslim jurist, legal theory can be regarded as a "science of proofs," leading to standards that regulate human actions. These standards derive primarily from a discovery, through a defined set of sources and techniques, of the *aḥkām*, the qualification of actions or, more specifically, God's determination of the moral value of individual acts. Because anything that furnishes proof in discovering these *aḥkām* becomes part of the body of legal knowledge, the literature of *uṣūl al-fiqh* consists not only of legal reasoning and argument, but also contains extensive discussions on formal logic, dialectical theology, and linguistic theory. This represents a striking contrast to the more autonomous role of legal theory in Western society.

Furthermore, while Western legal theory studies questions of law and legitimacy in a social and institutional context, Islamic law sees these as an epistemological issue. That is, the approach of the Muslim scholar is primarily in terms of the nature of knowledge and, more precisely, the categories of certain knowledge as

This paper is based on a continuing study and translation of Ibn Qudāmah's *Rawḍat al-nāẓir wa-jannat al-munāẓir* made possible through the generous support of the National Endowment for the Humanities.

opposed to knowledge derived from a presumption of truth, or probability.[1]

Of great importance in explaining this is the Muslim view of the probative value of the two material sources and the role of the jurist in their interpretation. God's discourse, His address to men (*khiṭāb*), is conveyed to us through the Qur'ān and Sunnah. For the jurist, the most important difference between the two is in their mode of transmission, although this does not affect the status of either as revelation. The authenticity of the Qur'ān rests on its character as *mutawātir*, that is, it was so widely transmitted by so many individuals at the source that according to legal theory it is impossible to doubt the certain knowledge it conveys. This is also true of a small number of traditions. On the other hand, almost all the traditions are *akhbār al-āḥād*, falling short of this widespread transmission. The distinction is an epistemological one, because we cannot have certain knowledge when only one or a few individuals transmit the report. Therefore, the degree of acceptance of individual traditions—as regards both their authenticity and as a source for action—will vary according to the individual jurist or school of thought to which he belongs. However, nearly all jurists agree that the knowledge these traditions convey is not certain, but probable.

The jurists recognized other difficulties with their sources, such as conflicting norms (only partly overcome by the doctrine of abrogation), the obscure use of language, and the absence of a single uniform codex of traditions.

The work of the jurist is precarious. With this universe of God's discourse as his source, the jurist arrives at a rule through his powers of reasoning, a rule which is supposed to be a statement of God's transcendent will and intentions. His reasoning, which is itself fallible, will nearly always be based on knowledge gained from a presumption of truth and its results will be probability. Inevitably, there will be differences of opinion on what the

[1] This is not to claim that the jurists formulated a systematic critical theory of knowledge in the style of some theologians; rather, they took epistemological "positions" roughly related to the school of thought to which they adhered. These positions are best revealed in the chapters on traditions and logic in works of *uṣūl al-fiqh*.

law is. Consensus could, of course, confer the status of certainty on individual rules, but only a relatively small number of decisions can be the object of consensus (especially if those forming it are confined to the earliest generations of Muslims), and there is no higher authority to turn to beyond the jurists themselves. A divine law based on probability is surely a contradiction. Therefore, leaving out notable exceptions, the Sunnī jurists formulated a principle that became a persistent motif in *uṣūl al-fiqh* literature. This was the conviction that in matters of law certainty is an elusive goal; the jurist, through his utmost intellectual effort, hopes at best for high probability. Solutions arrived at through presumptive knowledge are binding.

I have attempted to look at this general theme in the context of the jurists' treatment of a heated and controversial issue—the legal status of an act performed in response to a command.[2] I will rely mainly on the arguments of the great representative of the Ḥanbalī school, the Syrian Muwaffaq al-Dīn Ibn Qudāmah al-Maqdisī.[3] The discussion, set forth in his *Rawḍat al-nāẓir wa-jannat al-munāẓir*,[4] also provides an important example of the preoccupation of the jurists with the linguistic premises of law.

We can easily understand the importance of the topic. The command is closely connected with the binding force of divine law. Since it has its source in the sacred texts, the jurist is more concerned than ever to exclude uncertainty as much as possible from the process of interpretation.

The problem can be dealt with in two steps. First, in the Qur'ān, we find that the imperative form is used for a number of

[2] The subject has not, to my knowledge, been treated in the secondary literature on *uṣūl al-fiqh*. However, see the dissertation of Aron Zysow, "The Economy of Certainty: An Introduction to the Typology of Islamic Legal Theory" (Harvard University, 1984), pp. 101–126, for the Ḥanafī treatment of some aspects of the topic.

[3] Born in Jerusalem in 541/1146 and died in Damascus in 620/1223. H. Laoust has provided a rich essay placing him in the context of Syrian Ḥanbalism in *Le précis de droit d'Ibn Qudāma* (Beirut, 1950), pp. ix–l. See also the *Encyclopædia of Islam*, new edition, s.v. "Ibn Ḳudāma al-Maḳdisī" (G. Makdisi).

[4] Published by the Salafīyah Press in Cairo, 1924, in two volumes, as part of a continuing effort by Rashīd Riḍā to produce a series of texts in the interests of the neo-Ḥanbalī movement. (Riḍā himself edited the *Kitāb al-mughnī*, Ibn Qudāmah's great compendium of *fiqh*, in 13 volumes in 1922.) The *Rawḍah* was edited with a brief commentary by the modern Ḥanbalī scholar al-Shaykh 'Abd al-Qādir Badrān.

significations. Are these uses of the imperative form commands?[5] Second, and more important, if there are no indications or additional information to specify how it is to be understood, what is the force of the imperative? Are God's commands always binding?

Many Qur'ānic verses convey the force of a command, or threaten punishment for disobedience to God's commands. On the other hand, the imperative is often used equivocally (*muḥtamalan*), so that it bears more than one meaning.[6] A command may indicate binding obligation (*ījāb*), as in the Qur'ānic verses that say "Perform the prayer!" It may also indicate recommendation (*nadb*). For instance, God says, "Take witnesses when you conclude contracts of sale!" (2:282). The verb "take witnesses!" (*ashhidū*) is in the imperative form, but this must represent only a recommendation, because even if there is nothing inherent in the text itself to indicate recommendation, we have the external evidence of the practice of the Prophet, who was known to have concluded contracts of sale without witnesses. This accompanying circumstance (*qarīnah*) influences the interpretation of the Qur'ānic verse, and allows the jurists to interpret the imperative form, in this case, as a recommendation.

Again, in such a command as, "Hunt for game! after you have completed the pilgrimage and have left the pilgrim sanctuary" (5:2/3), this imperative obviously indicates permission (*ibāḥah*), that is, the consent of the Lawgiver to go hunting again, it having been prohibited for pilgrims to hunt while they were in their ritually sanctified state in the precincts of Mecca.[7] Here the accompanying indication is not external, but is inherent in the wording of the text. Furthermore, in the Qur'ān, the imperative is used for threat (*tahdīd*): "Do whatever you will!" (41:40); to indicate powerlessness (*ta'jīz*), as "Be you stones or iron!" (17:50/53); to bestow honor (*ikrām*), as "Enter it in peace!" (50:34/33); to invoke God (*du'ā'*), "O Lord! Forgive me!" (14:41/42, etc.). The

[5] There is no disagreement about indirect expressions that convey the meaning of a command, such as *antum ma'mūrūna, faraḍtu, awjabtu 'alayka*—these clearly express obligation. Al-Ghazālī provides a fuller explanation, *Al-Mustaṣfā min 'ilm al-uṣūl* (Bulaq, 1322), 1:412–413, 417.

[6] *Rawḍah*, 2:65 ff.

[7] This example, among others, is also cited by I. Goldziher, *The Zahiris*, trans. W. Behn (Leiden, 1971), p. 67.

imperative is used for creation, even though an individual is unable to comply with it, as "O Fire, turn to coolness and become salvation for Abraham!" (21:69) or, to take a secular example, for wishing (*tamannī*), as when the poet said, "O long night, give way to dawn!" There are many more examples of different significations of the imperative form.[8]

These are all commands, even though they are qualified by indications specifying how we are to understand them. The imperative voice, then, appears to be used equivocally for statements that are not commands. But when God issues a command using the imperative, can it be equivocal?

Ibn Qudāmah denies that the form can be equivocal, even when there are accompanying indications. His argument is rationalist, drawn from linguistic usage. The function of language is communication and it has distinctive significations expressed by distinctive linguistic forms (sing., *ṣīghah*). This is like the clear-cut dichotomy between past and future time where each has its own exclusive signification. The imperative form is *if'al*, "Do this!" in the second person, and *li-yaf'al*, "Let him do this!" in indirect address. The notion of obligation, says Ibn Qudāmah, is so important that it is given a unique linguistic form. The imperative, in fact, is the only means we have for issuing a command, and is a natural verbal form in any language. To claim, as some do, that the form of a command in itself is equivocal or has no specific meaning, predicates incompetence on the part of God, who has established language, and deprives of their significance (*fā'idah*) all linguistic expressions that have no accompanying indications (*qarā'in*, sing. *qarīnah*). In other words, the imperative has a meaning which, by virtue of the form alone, is common to all imperatives. Thus all uses of the imperative are commands. Where there are circumstantial indications pointing to threat, permission, and the like, Ibn Qudāmah will allow only that the imperative term is used in an extended sense (*majāz*) rather than in its original strict meaning (*ḥaqīqah*).[9] Equivocal evidence merely adds

[8] To demonstrate their variety, al-Ghazālī gives a list of fifteen. *Al-Mustaṣfā*, 1:417–418.

[9] *Rawḍah*, 2:66.

to an incomplete expression, but does not affect the command as such.[10]

The definition of a command further reduces the possibilities. Ibn Qudāmah says it is "a summoning to an act, through speech, from a position of superiority."[11] The definition separates a command from a mere request to act (*iltimās, shafā'ah*), as it would be from an equal or from an inferior. If an inferior were to give a command to a superior, he might do so out of ignorance, but it would hardly be a command.[12] By insisting on oral speech, Ibn Qudāmah refutes the doctrine of "inner speech" held by the Ash'arīs, that meaning can subsist in itself,[13] that is, we can have meaning without speech. Ibn Qudāmah cites passages from the Qur'ān, the traditions, and especially usage. To take, for instance, a formulaic expression—because formulas are succinct examples of usage, linguistic convention in a nutshell—if a man swears an oath that he will not speak all day, and then talks to himself without articulating his words, he does not break his oath, whereas he necessarily breaks it if he pronounces his words aloud.

These remarks bring us to the next step in Ibn Qudāmah's discussion. A command calls for action. The crucial question is, how is that action to be qualified? What is its *ḥukm* or legal status if the command is detached from any circumstantial indications? Does a command impose obligation every time it is used?

With this question we come to what most jurists consider to be at the very heart of their discipline, the principle that any human act can be qualified according to the status of that action in the eyes of God. The jurists finally formulated five general categories of acts, the inclusion of an act within a category being determined by the criterion of whether its performance or non-performance is grounds for reward or punishment in the next world. In all schools

[10] Ibid., pp. 80–81.

[11] "Al-amr istid'ā' al-fi'l bi-al-qawl 'alā wajh al-isti'lā'." *Rawḍah*, 2:62.

[12] Thus most grammarians distinguished the imperative *li-* from the *li-* of request (*lām al-du'ā'*), while conceding that "it is really the imperative *li-*." Al-Shirbīnī in M. Carter, *Arabic Linguistics* (Amsterdam, 1981), pp. 128–129. As Carter points out, the distinction is purely out of theological scruples. Al-Ghazālī regards the superior/inferior distinction as irrelevant. *Al-Mustaṣfā*, 1:411–412.

[13] "Al-kalām ma'nan qā'im bi-al-nafs." For the arguments in support of this position, *Al-Mustaṣfā*, 1:412–413.

of law there may be differences of opinion concerning particular acts, depending on the interpretation of a quoted scriptural text or, if the texts are silent on a given question, on the results of an analogy.

If the command does not impose obligation every time it is issued, what *is* the legal status of the act? Which signification—certain obligation, recommendation, or permissibility—is the primary signification? Which conveys the most certitude? These questions are fundamental, because they involve the relationship between the command, divine authority, and *taklīf*, religious obligation.

The Ḥanbalī Ibn Qudāmah unhesitatingly adopts the view that a command signifies obligation. But before attempting to prove his own position, he reviews those of his adversaries. The most important among these is the view of the Muʿtazilah that an unqualified command (*iṭlāq al-amr*) entails not obligation, but recommendation. This is not argued on the basis of the imperative by itself, but negatively, because there is no accompanying indication that disobedience will be punished. In other words, we have not been supplied with the requisite information. The act, therefore, cannot be obligatory. Both recommended and obligatory acts are commanded, they claim, and although we know that performance of a recommended act is better than omitting it, we do not know whether punishment necessarily follows omission of the act, so we must reserve judgment on the question of responsibility. Therefore, the Muʿtazilah reason, the qualification has to be reduced to the least common denominator shared by obligation and recommendation. Second, a command is a request (*ṭalab*) for action, and a request indicates nothing more than the meritorious nature of the object sought. Now, a recommended act is meritorious, but anything above and beyond that belongs to a category that is not indicated—and not required—by an unqualified imperative. So, if there is a possibility of both qualifications, it follows that we must refer to the one that conveys certitude—namely, recommendation.

Ibn Qudāmah's reply to this is that the Muʿtazilī argument would be admissible only if an obligation were construed as a recommendation with augmentation. This cannot be the case, he argues, because the definition of a recommended act allows for its omission, whereas that never occurs when the act is obligatory. In other words, the two categories are mutually exclusive.

Others maintained that a command entails permission to perform an act, following more or less the same logic as the Mu'tazilah. Since permission is the lowest in the scale of positive categories, it is thus the one that most easily lends itself to certainty. It is certain to include all three qualifications. This position, argues Ibn Qudāmah, is logically absurd. A command is a request and a summoning to act, whereas permission gives someone unrestricted freedom to perform the act or not. Anyone can spontaneously recognize the difference between "Do this!" and "Do this if you wish!" A command is decidedly not laid down to admit choice.

Going even farther in the direction of uncertainty, still others held that the unqualified command had no primary signification at all, and maintained that judgment had to be held in abeyance until an indication emerged to clarify the qualification. These are the *wāqifīyah*, those scholars who suspend judgment.[14] We know, they say, when a binding command is laid down, either through the scriptural sources or through rational proof. When neither is discovered we must withhold judgment on the unqualified command. Ibn Qudāmah rejects this on several grounds. Since these scholars concede that a command enjoins performance rather than non-performance, they end up advocating the recommended act and disregarding everything above and beyond that—exactly like the Mu'tazilī proponents of recommendation. Furthermore, in a significant passage, he says, "If they suspend judgment because every possibility is open to them, then they are forced to suspend judgment in all established doctrines (*ẓawāhir*), relinquish every activity whose meaning is not absolutely certain, and reject most of the rules of the divine law, since the majority of them are established only by proofs based on presumptive evidence."[15]

In establishing the deontological value of the divine command, Ibn Qudāmah vigorously rejects all these expressions of uncertainty. The force of the imperative, by itself, is that of obligation, not only on the rational linguistic grounds just considered, but also because of the obvious evidence of the sources. The Qur'ānic

[14] For al-Ghazālī's defense of the position of *waqf*, *Al-Mustaṣfā*, 1:423 ff.

[15] *Rawḍah*, 2:75.

verses he cites all illustrate the force of a command or threaten those who disobey it. For instance, God says, "Let those who go against [God's] command beware, lest a trial befall them, or there befall them a painful chastisement!" (24:63). If the command did not entail an obligation, there would be no punishment associated with it. Several traditions show that the Prophet reacted to his Companions' failure to obey his command, or that his recommendation would have entailed obligation if he *had* commanded the act, such as cleansing the teeth as part of the ritual purification before prayer. In other words, the very existence of recommended and other acts shows that a command entails obligation. In a tradition concerning Barīrah, a slave woman whom 'Ā'ishah had set free, and who had chosen to leave her slave husband, the Prophet, out of compassion for the husband, asked Barīrah, "What if you were to take Mughīth back?" Barīrah replied, "Are you commanding me to do so, O Prophet of God?" The Prophet said, "I am merely interceding on his behalf." And Barīrah answered, "I have no need of him." Barīrah's response to the Prophet's intercession shows that he made a recommendation to her. Had it been a command, it would have given rise to an obligation to take her husband back.

There is, in fact, a whole body of evidence in the consensus of the Prophet's Companions, who by their actions unanimously asserted the binding character of any number of commands on the part of God and the Prophet. They enforced the Prophet's injunctions unquestioningly.

Finally, good Arabic usage, as endorsed by the grammarians, proves that an unqualified command gives rise to an obligation. If the master of a slave were to give him an order to perform a task, and the slave opposed him, the master would be justified in punishing the slave. If he were to give the slave permission to do something, or declare it unlawful for him, the slave would not be bound by an obligation. Let us not insult the Arabs, Ibn Qudāmah says elsewhere, by attributing to them a usage they did not intend.

Can a command ever convey a qualification other than certain obligation in Ibn Qudāmah's scheme of thought? Yes, in one case only—and here he agrees with the preferred opinion (*ẓāhir*) of the Ash'arīs. When a command follows a prohibition it requires the qualification of permissibility. Although he establishes several proofs, his main argument rests on empirical evidence. Most of the commands of the divine law occurring after a prohibition give rise to permission to perform an act. He cites, for instance, God's words in the Qur'ān, "When the prayer is finished, then disperse in the land [and seek benefit from God's grace]!" (62:10), indicating permission because of the preceding prohibition of doing business during communal prayer. The Prophet said, "I forbade you to visit graves, but [now] visit them! I forbade you *nabīdh* except in a water-skin; [now] drink it from all kinds of vessels but do not drink anything intoxicating!" In customary usage, a man may say to another who is not a member of his family, "Enter my house and eat at my table!" The prior prohibition is understood in that such a man, outside the degrees of kinship where he could freely circulate among the women of the house, would be forbidden from eating with them. This, says, Ibn Qudāmah, removes the prohibition without creating the binding obligation of a command with the words, "Eat at my table!" For this reason, it would not be appropriate to blame or reproach someone for failing to perform these acts.

A related question, and one that raised the argument to the level of theological rather than strictly legal discourse, was introduced by the Mu'tazilah. This was the question of intentionality, or God's volition (*irādah*). Are the divine command and the divine will identical? Is law the objective manifestation of the divine will?

The doctrine of the Mu'tazilah *mutakallimūn*, that God willed the acts He commanded, was a natural consequence of their doctrine that God's speech is one of His acts, rather than—as others held—inseparable from His essence. Therefore, argued the Mu'tazilah, His command had to be an act of willing.

Furthermore, we can see that if the legal status of the act belongs in the category of recommendation, as the Mu'tazilah claimed, then volition has to be involved. Since the linguistic form of a command designated a range of different possibilities,[16] then

[16] That is, that it was *mutaraddidah* or multivalent among obligation, recommendation, threat, and so on.

the command could be separated from what is not a command *only* by God's act of willing. Moreover, the imperative by itself is obviously invalid as a command because it can be uttered by those who do not exercise volition, such as someone who is asleep or habitually absent-minded. Now we know perfectly well, say the Mu'tazilah, that the aim of the speaker using this form without being absent-minded is to bring about the thing commanded. This is the very essence of an act of willing.

For Ibn Qudāmah, as for the other traditionalist theologians, if God's speech is one of His essential attributes, then volition cannot be posited as a condition for a command. God's will is *always* efficacious. Since His commands are not always obeyed, we must infer that God may command something but not will it. For instance, the Qur'ān tells us that God commanded Abraham to sacrifice his son but that Abraham did not do so. He commanded Iblīs to bow before Adam, but Iblīs refused. God did not will these acts, for had He done so, they would have taken place. To illustrate his point, Ibn Qudāmah takes the formula for an oath. First he cites the Qur'ānic verse that enjoins the Muslims to deliver pledges, or property left in trust, back to their owners (4:58/61). Then he says that if a man were to swear, "By God! I will surely deliver your pledge to you tomorrow, God willing!" and he does not do so, he is not considered to have broken his oath. If it were what God willed, he necessarily breaks his oath because God would have willed delivering the pledge He commanded. Ibn Qudāmah appeals to practice. A man gives an order to his slave, "Saddle my horse!" but the slave does not obey the order because he knows that the horse is refractory and that his master would be in danger of his life if he were to mount the horse, and the master knows this. But the slave must be chastised for disobeying the command, otherwise the master would be reprimanded by the authorities who happen to be present when this takes place. Was this a command whose disobedience deserves punishment? How does the master justify not punishing the slave? How could it not be a command when everyone present understands it as such? As for the command being uttered by an absent-minded or sleeping person, says Ibn Qudāmah, they fall outside the definition of a command, because these people are never in a position of superiority. God's will, then, for Ibn Qudāmah is not the force that links His command to human acts.

This analysis of the deontological value of the imperative hardly covered everything the jurists had to say about it. They were also concerned with the scope of the commanded act, including questions on its performance, and the conditions residing in the person commanded. The aim is always to exclude uncertainty as much as possible in the process of interpretation. Moreover, these discussions are concerned with another aspect of certitude, involving religious precaution (*tawarruʿ*, *iḥtiyāṭ*) to insure the fulfillment of one's religious obligations.

How often is the act to be performed?[17] Is the unqualified command continually valid for all time,[18] or is it meant for one instance of performance only? The issue is important because it is bound up with the notion of the individual's responsibility (*taklīf*), the obligations or restraints that God imposes upon him, connected with reward and punishment in the next world.

Ibn Qudāmah and others adopted the view that a person's responsibility for performing the act is discharged by performing it once. We can be certain of the obligatory character of that one instance. In the case of the command, "Observe the fast!" for instance, our certitude about the obligation is removed with one instance of fasting. Once the act is performed, we revert to our original freedom from abstract responsibility—an important notion in the Ḥanbalī school. For Ibn Qudāmah, linguistic practice supports this. If a man were to swear, "By God! I will surely fast!" he keeps his vow by fasting for one day. If he were to say to another man entrusted with his affairs, "Divorce my wife on my behalf!" he has no more than one pronouncement of divorce out of three. If a man were to command his slave to purchase goods for him, and the slave absolves himself of his trust by performing the act once, it would not be appropriate for the master to reprimand him.

Ibn Qudāmah's adversaries argued that the command "Observe the fast!" must be generally applicable to all time, because it is analogous to using a collective expression to apply to all

[17] *Rawḍah*, 2:78-85.

[18] The operative term here is *takrār*, "repetition" or "reiteration," in the sense of unceasing recurrence.

individuals in a category. Ibn Qudāmah replies that a command makes no allusion to time, but time, like place, is one of the self-evident qualities of a command (*ḍarūratihi*). Just as a man cannot perform an act in all places, neither can he perform it at all times.

Moreover, his adversaries claimed, commanding an act is prohibiting its opposite. A prohibition entails abandoning the prohibited act everlastingly. Since this is the case, a command necessitates everlasting observance of the fast when it is prescribed. Ibn Qudāmah refutes this on the grounds that such an argument functions to ignore what he perceives as the very quality that separates the command and prohibition. The difference between a command and a prohibition, he says, is that a commanded act exists in an absolute sense, while a prohibited act must be non-existent in an absolute sense. Absolute non-existence is general, whereas absolute existence is not general. That is, if something exists for a single instance it is existent absolutely; if something does not exist for a single instance, it is not non-existent absolutely. This may be illustrated by the following: if a man says, "I will surely fast!" he keeps his vow by fasting once; if he says "I will surely not fast!" he breaks his vow by fasting once. The fast exists absolutely or it is not non-existent absolutely. Thus, a command cannot be the opposite of a prohibition in this construction.

There is another difference between a command and a prohibition. A command entails positive action (*ithbāt*), while a prohibition entails absence of action (*nafy*). Absence of action with regard to an indeterminate person or thing (that is, an unqualified command) is general, while unrestricted positive action is not general. If someone says, "Do not do something once!" a general prohibition applies. If he says, "Do something once!" the action is necessarily specified. To put it another way, existence, by definition, admits the possibilities of both universality and particularity, while non-existence admits only universality. No one, says Ibn Qudāmah, can possibly disagree with this. We must conclude, therefore, that a command cannot be construed as the opposite of a prohibition, and binding in the future; it binds us for one instance of performance only.

The jurists were also clearly divided in their views on when the commanded act had to be performed.[19] Is the believer permitted to delay it, or must he perform it immediately?

The Shāfi'īs maintained that since the unqualified command entailed performance of the act and nothing else, the time of performance can be postponed.[20] Time, they said, like place, instrument, and the individual concerned, are inseparable attributes of the act (*lāzim al-fi'l*), not attributes of the command. Time only comes into being as a necessary quality of the act, and that necessary character would be dispelled if an act could be performed at any time at all, and not at the discretion of the individual. If a man were to say, "I will do [something]!" then at whatever time he performs the act he will have kept his promise (*kāna ṣādiqan*).

On the other hand, the dominant opinion of the Ḥanbalī school (and the Ḥanafīs) was that the act had to be performed immediately (*'alā al-fawr*). The key argument was the certitude of religious precaution. A command demands a time, and the best time of all is immediately after a command is issued because the believer will be certain to obey it and be absolutely secure from the danger of punishment. The absence of a specific determination in the command as to time must be treated differently from the place of the act. Indeterminate time leads to the lapse of the act, contrary to place. Furthermore, two places are the same in relation to an act, whereas the earliest possible time is better for the worshiper's security from danger and for absolving himself of his responsibility with certainty.

In addition to citing the Qur'ānic proofs, Ibn Qudāmah maintains that all the experts in the language concur that a command requires immediate performance. If a master were to say to his slave, "Give me something to drink!" and the slave postponed his task, he would be justified in reproaching the slave on the grounds that the slave disobeyed him. We also have parallels in the realm of legal undertakings, such as a sale, divorce, and the like, where the believer is bound to make the act immediately follow the contract—conforming to God's perfect knowledge of what is suitable (*ḥikmatan*).

[19] *Rawḍah*, 2:85–91.

[20] *'Alā al-tarākhī*, "at intervals," "discontinuous."

Now some acts, such as prayer, have a specifically fixed time of performance. If the believer has a legitimate reason not to perform his duty within that fixed time, these acts can be made up. But what of an act that has no specifically fixed time?[21] According to Ibn Qudāmah, these cannot possibly be postponed, for this would be inconsistent with the idea of obligation. In an argument by disjunction (*taqsīm*), in which the possibilities are narrowed down to zero, Ibn Qudāmah shows that there is, in fact, *no* time to which one can possibly postpone the act without changing its character as an obligatory act, or without putting the believer into such a position that the act would be incapable of performance.

What happens if the period of time designated for an act such as prayer lapses and the act has gone unperformed?[22] Is the obligation extinguished? Does making up the act depend on a new command? The solution preferred by Ibn Qudāmah is that a command gives rise to an abstract obligation to be performed in the future (*al-wujūb fī al-dhimmah*). Just as in private legal rights and claims, a person is not released from his obligation until he either performs the act at the time designated, or else is acquitted of his responsibility. The fact that time runs out does not affect whether or not these two have taken place.

Ibn Qudāmah addresses a series of issues that concern the religious responsibility of the individual commanded to perform an act. To what extent does later performance of the commanded act (*qaḍā'*) constitute valid fulfillment of the duty (*ijzā'*)?[23] What action is called for on the part of the believer should he fail to discharge the duty? Does a command affect the person who is absent when the command is given?[24] What of the indirect command, one given through another individual?[25] Whom does it bind? If a command is directed toward a group of people, does it give rise to a collective duty (*farḍ al-kifāyah*), binding on all but excused by the performance of some?[26]

[21] *Rawḍah*, 2:88–91.
[22] Ibid., pp. 97–93.
[23] Ibid., pp. 93–96.
[24] Ibid., pp. 105–107.
[25] Ibid., pp. 96–97.
[26] Ibid., pp. 97–100.

The opposite issue, whether a command directed toward one person should apply to the group[27] took on particular urgency because many commands in the Qur'ān are addressed to the Prophet. A small proportion of these use terms that convey specification (*takhṣīṣ*). That is, the obvious meaning or the wording of the text was clearly intended for the Prophet alone and no one else. On the other hand, most of the commands directed toward the Prophet could be interpreted as having general application, in which case they would be binding on the whole community of Muslims. The question skirts the periphery of one of the most complex and important questions of hermeneutics: Which is the more certain basis for action? Is it the term of general application, that is, the reference of a general term to every member of its denotation? Or does the particularization of a term convey greater certainty? Once again, the question of epistemology is at the center of interpretation.

On the question of whether a command directed toward the Prophet could be taken in the general sense, the community was clearly split. Those who argued that the ruling is specific to the person to whom it is directed, argued on the grounds of language. If a man commands one of his slaves to perform a duty, it is specific to him exclusive of his other slaves. If God commands us to perform an act of worship, the command in its unrestricted sense does not extend to another act of worship. An expression conveying general application cannot possibly bear the meaning of a particular application when the command is unqualified.

On the other hand, Ibn Qudāmah and others sought proof in the texts. In the Qur'ānic passage concerning the well-known incident when God gave the Prophet permission to marry the divorced wife of his adopted son, Zayd, God says, "So when Zayd had accomplished what he would of her, then We gave her in marriage to thee [Muḥammad], so there should not be any fault in the believers, touching the wives of their adopted sons" (33:37). Ibn Qudāmah reasons that God meant to establish the *ratio legis* (*'illah*), the reason behind the ruling that removes fault from other members of the community if they find themselves in the same circumstances. If the ruling were particular to the Prophet,

[27] Ibid., pp. 100–104.

then establishing such a rationale would be pointless. But, several verses later, there comes an expression of particularization: "If the Prophet desire to take her in marriage for thee exclusively, apart from the believers ..." (33:50/49). If the first expression had been particular to the Prophet, it would have been unnecessary to refer to him specifically with the second expression of particularization.

Furthermore, the Prophet is like other men in his obligations and responsibilities. A tradition reports that a man asked the Prophet about his duty to fast during the daylight hours of Ramaḍān without having performed the ritual ablutions when he arose from sleep in the morning. The man said, "The time of prayer comes unexpectedly upon me (*tudrikunī*) when I rise in the morning in a state of major ritual impurity (*junub*). Should I then observe the fast?" The Prophet replied that the same thing happened to him, and he observed the fast. The man replied, "O Messenger of God, you are not like us! God has forgiven you the sins you committed [before your prophethood] and those you committed later." The Prophet said, "I hope that I fear God more than you and that I know better than you those things which I should be fearful of!" The tradition acts as an authoritative proof (*ḥujjah*) in showing that the Prophet did not regard the permissibility of observing the fast as particular to him alone. He conforms to the norms established for the community. God's address to the Prophet is not specific to him. The Prophet himself suggested this when he said, "I am made forgetful only that I may direct men on the right path [when they are forgetful]" (*innamā ashū li-asunna*). A number of traditions are cited to show that the Companions, who certainly held differing views among themselves, always referred to the Prophet's practice to determine the community norms.

Once it is proven that the community shares in a ruling directed toward the Prophet, says Ibn Qudāmah, it is also proven that he must share in commands directed toward the community. The two are inseparable corollaries (*talāzum*) and what is proven with respect to one is proven with respect to the other.

The final issue I wish to take up is that of religious responsibility and its connection with a person's ability to perform the act, a problem also important in theology. What of a command on the part of God when He knows the individual does not have the capacity to carry it out? Is such a command possible?[28]

The response of the Mu'tazilah to this question is well known, as a consequence of their view of God as a Being who can do only what is rational. It is logically inconceivable that God would command an act when He knows that the condition cannot be realized. If a man knows that another person is unable to stand up, he cannot request him to do so; if he cannot make a request, he cannot give a command. How can the All-Wise request what is impossible of fulfillment?

Ibn Qudāmah, on the other hand, would not limit God's power to what is merely rational. A request on the part of God is not impossible even if He knows that the believer does not have the capacity to obey. A request from God is not the same as a request from a human being. God summons the worshiper to obedience for his very welfare, to facilitate his resolution to do good and shun wickedness. This is a sign of divine generosity, which *is* conceivable. In the realm of everyday matters, there is no reason why a man cannot appoint an agent to undertake the manumission of his slave tomorrow, despite the man's intention to manumit the slave himself today. It is through his command that he can test the way the agent carries out his professional duties and whether he will prove an easy man to work with.

However, more important for Ibn Qudāmah are the implications of the Mu'tazilī position. Clearly, if we were to adopt their position, we would be led to neglect many commands on the assumption that they are impossible to carry out. Therefore, Ibn Qudāmah insists that the fact that God knows the outcome of the command does not extinguish our obligation to obey it. It follows, then, that we must be in no doubt that there *is* a command and that it has an obligatory character. This is not a self-evident proposition.

Take the minor, who does not have religious responsibility and therefore lacks capacity. He is required to know and have a firm conviction that while he is still a minor and when he reaches majority and has capacity, he is commanded to observe

[28] *Rawḍah*, 2:107–111.

the prescriptions of Islam and refrain from illegal acts. He merits a reward for this even if there is no opportunity to perform an act of worship or if he is not in a position to engage in theft, for instance, or unlawful intercourse. Now, if the minor were to suppose that he is not subject to God's commands, because God knows he is unable to carry out acts of obedience, then he would necessarily be in a state of doubt about his being commanded and about what constitutes pious behavior. It is not an act of piety to obey what is *not* commanded and to refrain from what is not prohibited.

Not only must there be certainty about the command, but a religiously responsible person must know he has the capacity to obey. The law requires him, for instance, to observe the fast during Ramaḍān. But if it is clear to a man that he is going to die after the fast begins, and if he is in a state of doubt about his ability to obey, there is no command. How, asks Ibn Qudāmah, can an act of worship be binding when he is in doubt?

His adversaries would reply that it is binding because the normal assumption (*ẓāhir*) is that he will survive; the immediate actuality (*ḥāṣil*) is that the present circumstances are presumed to continue (*yastaṣḥib*), a basic principle on which other matters are built. For instance, if a man is approached by a ferocious animal, it would not be reprehensible for him to flee, even if there is a good possibility that the animal will be killed before reaching him (*dūnahu*). The present circumstance is his danger; he flees because he must presume present circumstances will continue. Ibn Qudāmah remarks that his opponents have forced themselves into this absurd position on account of their doctrines; for whatever leads to a logical absurdity is absurd. When a man flees a ferocious animal, he is in the worst possible predicament, whereas a remote possibility and doubt about his situation is sufficient. If a man has the slightest doubt about there being a ferocious animal on the road, it would be entirely right to take precautions! And here is the point: an obligatory duty is not established as binding in the presence of doubt and supposition! Otherwise we would be forced to say that a man who shirked the fast of Ramaḍān and then happened to die was not disobedient toward God because he adopted the other supposition—that he would die and therefore must be excused!

Thus the argument has been turned from God's knowledge about absence of capacity to perform a commanded act to man's certainty about his ability to do so. It is possible for God to command such an act, but it is not binding on an individual if his knowledge about his ability to obey is based on anything less than certainty.

This brief summary of some of the issues surrounding the interpretation of the divine command hardly does justice to the richness and comprehensiveness of the *uṣūlīs*' treatment.[29] Ibn Qudāmah, like other jurists, establishes authoritative proofs from the revealed texts, the consensus of the Companions, reasoned argument, the customary practice of Muslims, and what he regards as a sound knowledge of linguistic usage. The authority of "the people who know the language," the *ahl al-lisān*, meaning the early Arabs, is frequently invoked.[30] But the nature of the sources on which interpretation is based rarely allowed for certainty; in such cases the jurists—who took disagreement and individual expression for granted—were willing to settle for solutions based on probability.

[29] I have not touched on the question of the negative command, or prohibition, which is not simply the contrary of a command. For Ibn Qudāmah, at least, *tark al-fi'l* or *kaff 'an al-fi'l* is a charge to the believer to do something, to perform an act in its own right. It is discussed largely in terms of the legal categories of validity and invalidity, the concern being with the effectiveness of the act.

[30] These include, of course, the Companions, whose authority derives partly from the fact that they had a natural understanding of the Arabic language and could interpret the Prophet's speech.

3

Exotericism and Objectivity in Islamic Jurisprudence

Bernard Weiss

It is a fundamental principle of Islamic jurisprudence that the law properly so called—that is to say, the Sharī'ah—exists independently of all human deliberation, whether legislative or judicial. Islamic jurisprudence, in other words, carries the notion of law-as-object to its furthest conceivable limit. The law is, for the Muslim jurist, "out there" before human beings even exist.

"Out there" must of course be understood to be a metaphor, for the real "locus" of the law is within God, and God is beyond space and time. Islamic theology, which provides the philosophical underpinnings for Islamic jurisprudence, subsumes the law under the divine attribute of speech, and as the divine speech is eternal, without beginning and without end, so also is the law. The attempt of an early school of Muslim thought—the Mu'tazilī school—to place the divine speech entirely within the created order proved in the end to be of no avail; orthodoxy stood firmly behind the eternality of the divine speech.

But the concept of an eternal divine speech was not without its problems. The Mu'tazilīs had railed loudly against the notion of uncreated *ḥurūf*, the vocal sounds (or their written counterparts) out of which words, sentences, and extended discourse (*naẓm*) are constructed. The non-reflective rank and file of the orthodox movement had no problem with such a notion, but the reflective—those who delved into theological, as opposed to merely jurisprudential, disputation for the purpose of providing a coherent rationalistic basis for orthodoxy—saw that a problem clearly existed. The solution lay, for them, in the distinction between mental speech (*al-kalām al-nafsī*) and verbal speech (*al-kalām al-lafẓī*) This distinction was thought to correspond to a duality present in all languages: the duality of meaning (*ma'nā*) and emitted sound (*lafẓ*). When a speaker speaks, he is aware that before he actually utters sounds a kind of speaking is already taking place in his mind. It is that kind of speech which may be said to be, when God is its subject, eternal.

In itself, as pure object, this eternal divine speech is utterly simple, entailing no plurality whatsoever. That part of the divine speech which we identify as law is, therefore, at this rarified level which eludes conceptualization, indistinguishable from that part which we identify as something other than law. In itself the divine speech has no parts. We perceive it as divided into parts because we perceive it in its relatedness to the created world. The divine speech impinges upon our lives in different ways, and it is in respect to its impingement upon our lives as norm that we perceive it to be in part law.

That law, as is well known, consists of the divine *aḥkām*—judgments as to the ethico-legal status of particular human acts. Five possibilities lie before any given human act: it may be required, recommended, neutral, reprehensible, or forbidden. Which of these it in fact is depends wholly upon the divine judgment. Muslim orthodoxy, in rejecting the Mu'tazilī attempt to set up a rational foundation for the five categories, made a clean break with natural law thinking. There would be, in Sunnī Islam, no way whatsoever whereby the unaided intellect could acquire even the dimmest imaginable grasp of the status of any given act.

But the eternal law as object—along with the rest of the divine speech of which it is part—is of no value to human beings unless it becomes manifest to them. An object need not be manifest in order to be object; its becoming manifest in fact presupposes that it previously existed in a state of hiddenness. Orthodox Muslim thought maintains that the law exists as object before there are any human subjects to perceive it, and even when the human subjects are there, thanks to divine creation, it may still exist without their perceiving it. All human subjects initially stand awaiting the becoming manifest, the appearing, of the law.

The distinction between the manifest and the hidden, the exoteric and the esoteric, constitutes a great leitmotif within the religious culture of Islam, as also within that of Judaism and Christianity. For Muslim thinkers, all human experience begins with the raw data of immediate sensory perception and an intuitive grasp of the basic axioms which govern the process of discursive reasoning. All else is, in this primordial point of beginning, hidden. Included within this hidden is the very existence of God. That must become manifest to human beings as they process the raw sensory data in accordance with the laws of discursive reasoning. Muslim theology is embued with an unshakable conviction in the demonstrability of God's existence. Once this has become manifest, then the door is open for other things, such as the attributes of God and the truthfulness of His prophets, to become manifest through a similar exercise of discursive reasoning.

That God possesses the attribute of speech is thus a truth which becomes manifest through ratiocination. I shall not here take the time to recount the arguments which Muslim theologians put forward in support of this truth. I do wish to emphasize the point, however, that the becoming manifest of this truth is distinct from the becoming manifest of the divine speech itself. We may become aware that God possesses the attribute of speech without being cognizant of the actual speech.

Here we move from the domain of rational reflection to the domain of language. The instrument of manifestation—the *dalīl*—is now, not the rational argument, but the uttered word, the *lafẓ*. "Al-lafẓu yadullu 'alā ma'nan": the *lafẓ* signifies, makes manifest, a meaning. Without the *lafẓ* the meaning lies hidden within the mind of the speaker, unavailable to the hearer. Through the *lafẓ* it is transferred from the realm of the hidden to the realm of the manifest. To return to a distinction mentioned earlier: verbal speech is the means through which mental speech becomes manifest. Verbal speech is pure *dalīl*.

This is preeminently true of the divine speech. In itself hidden and beyond the reach of the creature, it becomes manifest and within reach through the instrumentality of the verbal speech—the ordered sequence of patterned sounds—heard by prophets and conveyed by them to mankind. In the case of all prophets except Moses, this verbal speech is heard upon the lips of an angel: only Moses is privileged to hear it directly from God. The Prophet Muhammad is instructed to transmit part of the speech heard upon the lips of the Angel Gabriel verbatim through recitation; that part becomes known as the Qur'ān. The rest he transmits by expressing its meaning in his own words or in his deeds; that part becomes known as the Sunnah. All that may rightly be called revelation—whether Qur'ān or Sunnah—is rooted in the verbal speech heard by the Prophet Muhammad upon the lips of the Angel Gabriel.[1]

This verbal speech heard upon the lips of the Angel belongs to the created order: it consists of *ḥurūf* and *naẓm*. The mental speech which it makes manifest transcends the created order: it lies within the eternal being of God. Here we have a distinctly Muslim understanding of a process wherein the eternal becomes manifest within time, within the creation. Harry Wolfson ingeniously coined for it the term "inlibration,"[2] modeled clearly on the Christian term "incarnation."

We thus have two instruments whereby the hidden may become manifest: the *dalīl 'aqlī*, or rational *dalīl*, and the *dalīl lafẓī* or verbal *dalīl* (also frequently identified with or subsumed under *dalīl naqlī*, or transmitted *dalīl*). Both are universally accepted

[1] The renowned jurist-theologian Sayf al-Dīn al-Āmidī (d. A.D. 1233) makes it clear that the eternal divine speech is "sent down" (*munazzal*) upon the Prophet in two forms: a recited (*matlūw*) form and a non-recited form (*ma laysa bi-matlūw*). The former is the Qur'ān, the latter the Sunnah. Sayf al-Dīn al-Āmidī, *Al-Iḥkām fī usūl al-aḥkām* (Cairo: Maṭba'at al-Ma'ārif, 1914), 1:228. Āmidī describes the Sunnah as "a source of information" (*mukhbirah*) concerning the divine speech rather than as an actual recitation (*tilāwah*) of that speech. Ibid., p. 227. As my own research over the last decade has concentrated heavily upon the writings of Āmidī, this paper is to a large extent an outgrowth of that research. My more limited reading of other medieval Muslim authors has, however, led me to the conclusion that Āmidī's statements on fundamental theological matters are representative of a widely held orthodoxy.

[2] Harry Austryn Wolfson, *The Philosophy of the Kalam* (Cambridge: Harvard University Press, 1976), pp. 244–248.

in some degree by Muslim thinkers. Through the latter—which consists of audible words heard upon the lips of angels, prophets, and all subsequent transmitters—the divine law, and all else that is contained within the divine speech, becomes manifest. Through the former, the groundwork for accepting the claims of prophets to have heard words upon the lips of angels is laid, not to mention the theistic framework required in order for the notion of a divine revelation to make sense. True, many Muslims in the period when theological disputation began to flower refused to apply methods of rational argumentation to the task of understanding the divine attributes. But even the most recalcitrant had to acknowledge the Qur'ānic summons to reflect upon the signs of the divine presence visible in the created order and upon the signs of prophethood. Never in Islam was such a crucial matter as God's existence and the veracity of His prophets left to be substantiated through an irrational leap of faith. That was to require, even for Christians, the services of modern existentialists.

That which becomes manifest through the *dalīl 'aqlī* and the *dalīl lafẓī* enters the public domain and thus stands in contrast to that which becomes manifest exclusively within the closed private world of individual experience. Accordingly, the word *ẓāhir* takes on in Muslim usage the sense of "exoteric," for the exoteric is precisely that which is manifest within the public domain. Since objectivity entails availability beyond the confines of an intrinsically private experience, "objective" becomes virtually synonymous with "exoteric." Objectivity can be assured only as the object becomes manifest within the public domain. Muslim thinkers never doubt that the law is an object, but at the same time they recognize that its objectivity is secured within human awareness by its being manifest to the human commonality.

The *dalīl 'aqlī* brings an object into the public domain by anchoring the object within a rational understanding of the world which all mature persons of sound mind possess. It is possible for persons to give inadequate attention to the *dalīl 'aqlī*—such that it will not bring the object into view, but in this case they close themselves off to the object; the object is not closed off to them. It is of great significance, I think, that in the later centuries of medieval Islam various theologians took up the task of mediating a certain portion of the disputational apparatus developed in the Kalām to the masses as though attempting to extend the function of the *dalīl 'aqlī* to the largest possible public domain. The very title of Muḥammad ibn Shāfi' al-Faḍālī's (d. A.D. 1820) so-called creed bears witness to this enterprise: "Kifāyat al-'awāmm fīmā yajib 'alayhim min 'ilm al-kalām" (the sufficing of the commonality in respect to that part of the science of the *kalām* which is incumbent upon them).

Since the law becomes manifest through the *lafẓ*, it is with the role of the *dalīl lafẓī* as an instrument of the exoteric that we are here primarily concerned. In relation to the *lafẓ* the exoteric emerges as a category or level of meaning. Exoteric meaning is meaning which the *lafẓ* itself engenders by virtue of a nexus between *lafẓ* and meaning which exists independently of the deliberations of any individual speaker and which, by virtue of its dissemination throughout society, belongs to the public domain. Exoteric meaning is, in other words, philologically determinable meaning, meaning which can be discovered with the aid of lexicography, grammar, and other sciences concerned with the exploration of the inner workings of the *lafẓ*. It stands in contrast to esoteric meaning, meaning which the *lafẓ* acquires from a source entirely outside itself and which no amount of philological investigation will reveal. Such meaning is not available within the public domain; those who seek it must draw upon wholly private resources or consult individuals privileged to be in possession of it.

Systems of esoteric meaning were built up by two major groups within medieval Islam, the Ismā'īlīs and the Ṣūfīs. Ismā'īlism, which looked to the living Imām as an infallible teacher of esoteric meaning, was never able to gain a hold over the minds of the great majority of Muslims and remained to the end a peripheral movement. Ghazālī called attention to the Achilles' heel of Ismā'īlī esotericism in his famous critique of the movement: if it was to find acceptance among the rank and file of Muslims it must offer a compelling justification, and if the Qur'ān and the Sunnah did not provide such a justification at the level of exoteric, publicly available meaning then human reason would have to come to the rescue. But a *dalīl 'aqlī* supporting the magisterium of the living Imām was hard to come by, as Ghazālī took pains to show.[3]

Ṣūfism, on the other hand, posited an esoteric meaning which became manifest through mystical experience. Mysticism required no justification outside itself; its claim to truth did not suffer from the vulnerability to counter-argument which beset the Ismā'īlīs. Accordingly, Ṣūfism eventually struck deep roots within large segments of Muslim society. In the earlier stages of its development—and to the occasional reformer in later Islam—Ṣūfism seemed at times to undermine the edifice of theology and law built upon the foundation of the *dalīl 'aqlī* and the *dalīl lafẓī*. The esoteric meaning which it affirmed was grounded in the subjective world of private experience, and the exoteric meaning which painstaking scholarship had erected over many generations could become, in comparison to that esoteric meaning, unimportant or even irrelevant. When a Ṣūfī caught up in ecstatic realization of oneness with the Sole Reality could exclaim that the central shrine of Islam, the Ka'bah, was circumambulating him in a world beyond space and time such that there was no need for him in this world to circumambulate it, Ṣūfism could readily seem to be a negation of exoteric Islam and especially of the divine law.

In order to protect the religion of Islam against such subjectivism and potential antinomianism, the guardians of orthodoxy understandably sought to bolster the objectivity of the law in every way possible. This objectivity could be guaranteed only by an uncompromising commitment to exotericism, to meaning which became manifest, not privately within the essentially noncommunicable experience of the mystic, but publicly through the normal functioning of the *lafẓ*. The words "al-lafẓu yadullu 'alā ma'nan" (the *lafẓ* points to, makes manifest, a meaning), which were cited earlier, give expression to a fundamental principle upon which the coveted objectivity was made to rest.[4]

[3] This critique, which is entitled *Faḍā'iḥ al-bāṭinīyah*, is available in English translation in Richard McCarthy, *Freedom and Fulfillment* (Boston: Twayne Publishers, 1980), pp. 218–261.

[4] This principle is not unknown in Western law. For example, the American Chief Justice John Marshall, in presenting his case for the Supreme Court decision on the historically crucial case of *McCulloch* v. *Maryland*, argued on the basis of what a key phrase in the U.S. Constitution, namely, "necessary and proper," means for speakers

The yearning for objectivity was, however, present among Muslims even before the advent of theosophic Ṣūfism. The vigilant had always sought to protect the law against the purely personal predilections or conjectures of the human creature. The whole movement to collect and codify *ḥadīth* arose largely for this purpose. Particularly as the sects began to proliferate, it became necessary for the faithful ever to be on guard against *bid'ah*, human innovation. *Bid'ah* amounted to an encroachment of human subjectivity upon the otherwise objectively determinable law.

It is the *lafẓ*, I have said, which makes manifest the law, and therein lies the objectivity of the law; for exoteric meaning—the meaning which words carry by virtue of their ordinary functioning as vehicles of communication—is an object, something "out there" waiting to be discovered. When someone says something to me in a language common to us both, he employs words which carry meanings independent of any deliberation on his part; and thanks to the objectivity of this word-meaning nexus I am able to apprehend the meanings of the words he has employed. Neither I nor the speaker created the word-meaning nexus, and that is why we are able to communicate freely one with another. We could presumably, if we so chose, invent word-meaning nexuses (I shall here prefer the English plural to the Latin *nexūs*), thus in effect creating our own language, but the communication which would result from this would be so unsatisfactory as to make the effort pointless. We could never invent and master a language of our own that would enable us to communicate as freely on a virtually unlimited range of topics as we are able to do in our inherited language.

The objectivity of the word-meaning nexus is the result of a primordial inventive process of which we have no record and about which we can only idly speculate. Muslim thinkers called this process *waḍ'*, and they debated the question of how this *waḍ'* came about—whether through divine or human agency—but were never able to come to an agreement.[5] They only knew it had taken

of English. This appeal to linguistic usage as a publicly attestable phenomenon may certainly be regarded as an attempt to safeguard the objectivity of the law. See Gerald Gunther, *Cases and Materials on Constitutional Law*, 10th ed. (Mineola: The Foundation Press, 1980), p. 84.

[5] Muslim scholars from the fifteenth century A.D. onward devoted an entire science

place, being convinced that the word-meaning nexus did not arise out of a natural affinity between word and meaning.

The word-meaning nexuses resulting from the primordial *waḍʿ* constitute what may be called the basic language of the particular linguistic community; but they do not represent the entire stock of word-meaning nexuses which are available to a given speaker. For language is subject to accretion. The basic language remains more or less constant through time, but as the needs of the community change new usages must be developed. Generally, this does not mean an invention of entirely new words in the sense of novel groupings of radicals (*ḥurūf*); rather, it entails the application of existing words to new meanings, which they will bear along with the old meanings. This process of developing new word-meaning nexuses is called in Arabic *ʿurf* and is distinguished carefully from the primordial *waḍʿ*.[6]

The law belongs entirely within the sphere of the meaning which the authoritative *lafẓ* has by virtue of the primordial *waḍʿ* which gave rise to the Arabic language or by virtue of subsequent *ʿurf*, and it is for this reason that the law may be said to be an object, something which exists "out there," something to be discovered, not created or developed, by human agents. Within the category of *ʿurf* must be included the *ʿurf* peculiar to the divine Legislator Himself, *ʿurf* which gives rise to the special "legal" meanings of words such as *ṣalāh* (the prescribed ritual prayer), *ḥajj* (the prescribed pilgrimage), and *zakāh* (the alms-tax). This legal *ʿurf* is very often placed under the heading of *sharʿ* and thereby distinguished from ordinary human *ʿurf*.

Through the *lafẓ* the law, which is *ab initio* hidden, becomes manifest. But this is not to say that through it the law becomes immediately or readily manifest or even that it eventually becomes in its entirety manifest. The process whereby the law becomes

---

to the subject of *waḍʿ*. On the nature of this science, see my doctoral dissertation, "Language in Orthodox Muslim Thought: A Study of "Waḍʿ al-Lugha" and Its Development" (Princeton University, 1966). This dissertation was completed under the supervision of Professor Farhat J. Ziadeh, who also gave me my first instruction in the field of Islamic law and jurisprudence. The interest in this field which he awakened in me has become the primary focus of my scholarly career.

[6] On the distinction between *waḍʿ* and *ʿurf*, see Āmidī, *Al-Iḥkām*, 1:36–39.

manifest through the *lafẓ* is a gradual one, one which in principle never ends and which is in fact still going on. In other words, at any particular point in time the law is only partly manifest to the community of scholars, which amounts to saying that it remains partly hidden. Furthermore, Islamic jurisprudence sets up degrees of manifestness, implying an ascending scale which begins with total hiddenness at the bottom and culminates in absolute manifestness at the top. The terminology employed in the description of this scale does not, however, entail an opposition between *ẓāhir* and *bāṭin*, the usual Arabic terms for "exoteric" and "esoteric," but rather an opposition between *ẓāhir* and *khafī*. *Khafī* means "hidden" and is thus a natural antonym to *ẓāhir*, "manifest." *Bāṭin* means "inner," and *ẓāhir*, when used as an opposite to it, takes on the sense of "outer." "Inner" and "outer" are of course related to, though not identical with, "manifest" and "hidden." When I look at an object, I call that part which is visible or manifest to me the outer part and the part which is hidden from me the inner part. There is, however, a distinction between *bāṭin* and *khafī* and between the two corresponding senses of *ẓāhir* which goes beyond the lexical senses of these words, a distinction which is of the utmost importance. *Bāṭin* refers to that meaning of the *lafẓ* which is hidden and may never become manifest through philological investigation; whatever is deemed to be *bāṭin* is in principle forever excluded from the realm of the *ẓāhir*. *Khafī*, on the other hand, refers to that meaning of the *lafẓ* which happens at the moment to be hidden but which may become manifest through philological investigation, thus entering the realm of the *ẓāhir*. *Ẓāhir* as an opposite to *bāṭin* includes, we must infer, all meaning which has actually become or is capable of becoming manifest through philological investigation, whereas *ẓāhir* as an opposite to *khafī* includes only that meaning which has actually become manifest in some degree. Both *ẓāhir* and *khafī* admit of degrees. A meaning which is *ẓāhir* can become more *ẓāhir*, that is to say *aẓhar*, while a meaning which is *khafī* may previously have been even more *khafī*, that is to say *akhfā*.[7]

[7] My discussion of the interrelationship between *ẓāhir* and *khafī* and the various degrees of each relies heavily upon Muḥammad Adīb Ṣāliḥ, *Tafsīr al-nuṣūṣ fī al-fiqh al-islāmī* (Damascus: Maṭba'at Jāmi'at Dimashq, 1964), pp. 87–127, 149–227.

The becoming manifest of the law through the *lafẓ* requires active involvement on the part of the human subject. If I wish to discover the law but do not know any Arabic at all, I must begin by learning Arabic grammar and the meanings of Arabic words. But proficiency in Arabic will not result in the law's becoming all at once fully manifest to me. There is yet much effort to be expended upon the task at hand. It is for good reason that the process of discovering the law is called in Arabic *ijtihād*, for it is indeed a long and arduous struggle.

I shall not here go into the problems involved in the determination of what constitutes an authentic *lafẓ*. Needless to say, the *lafẓ* which is before us will bear no authority unless it can be proven to be identical with the *lafẓ* which was heard upon the lips of the Prophet and of those who gave an account of his deeds. This requires consideration of the transmission process, which must be evaluated within the framework of the well-known distinction between widespread transmission (*tawātur*) and transmission through limited chains of transmitters, the so-called *asānīd*. I shall here confine my attention to the process of eliciting the law from the *lafẓ*.

The reason why the becoming manifest of the law through the *lafẓ* is a long and demanding process is that the *lafẓ* must always be treated as a totality embracing the whole of the Qur'ān and the Sunnah. If one considers the vastness of the Sunnah, not to mention problems relating to authenticity, one soon appreciates the difficulties that are involved in this holistic approach to the *lafẓ*. In speaking of a holistic approach to the study of the *lafẓ*, I mean that the Muslim scholar may never treat a discrete part of the *lafẓ* as a self-contained entity capable of making manifest a particular provision of the law, a particular *ḥukm*, entirely on its own. Every part of the *lafẓ* must be understood within its context, and this context can be nothing other, in the final analysis, than the *lafẓ* in its entirety. The part must, in other words, always be placed within the setting of the whole.

Very often the part itself *demands* placement within the larger setting. This is true, for example, of the ambiguous expression, called in Arabic *al-mujmal*, under which category is subsumed the homonym (*mushtarak*). A homonym may be said to make manifest two or more different meanings. But since only one of these meanings will in most cases be the meaning intended by the speaker, the homonym by virtue of its ambiguity both makes manifest and hides the intended meaning: it makes manifest the intended meaning in the sense that that meaning is among the meanings which it signifies by virtue of the primordial *waḍʿ* or subsequent *ʿurf* and it hides the intended meaning in the sense that it buries the intended meaning within a plurality of possible meanings. If the hiding effect of ambiguity is to be overcome, the revealing role of the ambiguous expression must be undergirded by the context. It is the combination of ambiguous expression *and context*, of *mujmal* and *qarīnah*, that will truly make manifest the law.

A prime example of the ambiguity which must be overcome in the making manifest of the law is the imperative form of the verb. Does an expression such as *inkaḥū*, "marry!" which appears in the Qur'ānic statement, "Marry such among the women as seem good to you," indicate that marriage is required, recommended, or merely permitted? Considering that the imperative form of the verb can be used for any one of these three meanings, it proves to be a rather imperfect vehicle for the making manifest of the divine *aḥkām*. Clearly imperatives demanded placement within a larger setting.

But even where a particular expression is not ambiguous, the larger context must still intervene if the law is to become fully manifest. A non-ambiguous expression makes manifest a single meaning in the sense that it signifies that meaning as its only proper meaning. The non-ambiguous expression enjoys a certain preeminence over the ambiguous expression since it allows a presumption to be made in favor of a particular meaning as the intended meaning. One cannot, on the strength of an ambiguous expression alone, make such a presumption in favor of any one meaning. One is thrown immediately upon the context as a basis for making any presumption at all. But with a non-ambiguous expression one may begin, on the strength of the expression itself, with a presumption as to the intended meaning. In this respect, a non-ambiguous expression provides a higher degree of manifestness of the law than an ambiguous expression. The non-ambiguous expression is, in fact, labeled *ẓāhir* in Ḥanafī jurisprudence, but in a specialized sense of that term distinct from the senses we have thus far considered. *Ẓāhir* here does not refer to an expression which has attained the highest possible degree of manifestness of meaning. Rather, it refers to an expression which, in allowing for a presumption as to its intended meaning, represents a crucial stage in the making manifest of the law, a stage not reached by the ambiguous expression. Accordingly, the ambiguous expression is, in Ḥanafī jurisprudence at least, placed under the category of *khafī*, "the hidden." It must be strongly emphasized that the application of the term *ẓāhir* to the non-ambiguous expression in the manner just described must be distinguished from its wider application to the whole body of philologically determined meaning.

But the non-ambiguous expression only prepares us to go on to further stages. For while it allows us to make a presumption as to the intended meaning, it does not afford us the certainty that our presumption is a correct one. For while the intended meaning of a non-ambiguous expression will generally be the proper meaning which it has by virtue of *waḍʿ* or *ʿurf*, this will not always be the case. Occasionally the speaker will have in mind a metaphorical meaning. Since metaphorical meanings are less commonly intended than proper meanings, one must initially rule them out in favor of the proper meanings. One must, as I have said, begin with a presumption in favor of a proper meaning. But this is only at the beginning, and one must move beyond the beginning. One must, in other words, test one's presumption in the light of the context. If a metaphorical meaning is intended, this will come to light from the context; if not from the immediate context, then from a remote context. A relevant contextual clue could arise from anywhere within the vast corpus of the authoritative *lafẓ*.

There is also the matter of general expressions. On encountering the Qur'ānic passage which says, "As for the thief, male or female, cut off their hands," one may, according to the opinion of the majority of jurisprudents, make a presumption in favor of an inclusive reference to all thieves. But then one must thereupon test this presumption in the light of the context, for general terms are very often subject to exclusions (*istithnā'*). Here again, the total context must be taken into account, not just the immediate context. There is nothing in the immediate context of the Qur'ānic passage just mentioned to suggest that certain thieves might be excluded from the penalty of amputation; but one may find indications elsewhere, either in the Qur'ān or in the Sunnah, that certain thieves are in fact excluded.

So long as a non-ambiguous expression is subject to the possibility that it carries a metaphorical meaning or that it carries a non-inclusive (that is to say, restricted) reference, it remains in the category of *ẓāhir*, in the specialized sense noted above. Once it has been established conclusively, on the basis of the larger context, that it does or does not have a metaphorical meaning or that it carries or does not carry a non-inclusive reference, then it may be raised to a higher degree within the ascending scale of manifestness, *ẓuhūr*. It becomes at this point, to use the Ḥanafī jargon, either *naṣṣ* or *mufassar* depending on the strength of the contextual evidence. But even when these issues have been fully resolved, there remains another question that must be asked of every part of the *lafẓ*: has it, within the period of live prophecy, been abrogated by some other part of the *lafẓ*? When the possibility of abrogation has been conclusively ruled out, then an expression or passage rises to the highest level of manifestness represented by the category *muḥkam*.[8]

These categories apply, generally speaking, to what may be called the explicit meaning (*al-ṣarīḥ*) of the *lafẓ*, that is to say, the meaning which the *lafẓ* bears by virtue of the word-meaning nexuses which arise out of *waḍ'* and *'urf*. But the law is not limited to the realm of explicit meaning; it may be present also in the implicit meaning, in the connotations and nuances, of the *lafẓ*. Implicit meaning is not at all the same thing as esoteric meaning, for the way to implicit meaning is through explicit meaning. To take an example, of which there are many: According to some Muslim scholars, the Prophet's saying, "The alms-tax (*al-zakāh*) is due upon free-roaming sheep," implied that the alms-tax was not due upon sheep which were not free-roaming. This implication would not be available to anyone who was not conversant with

[8] For a full discussion of the four degrees of manifestness (*ẓāhir, naṣṣ, mufassar, muḥkam*) developed in Ḥanafī jurisprudence; see Muḥammad Adīb Ṣāliḥ, *Tafsīr al-nuṣūṣ*, pp. 87–94, 104–111.

the explicit meaning of the Prophet's words; the very term "implication" indicates that it follows from the explicit meaning and is dependent upon it. Just how far the scope of implicit meaning could be extended was a matter of considerable controversy among Muslim jurisprudents. The Ẓāhirī school, for example, resisted attempts to go beyond the strict explicit meaning. The point which is important for us is that to the extent that implicit meaning was accepted as a valid representation of the law it was included within the realm of the *ẓāhir* in the broader sense of that term, that is to say, within the realm of the exoteric.

But does not the well-known method of determining the law on the basis of analogy (*qiyās*), a method which was accepted by the majority of Muslim jurisprudents, take us beyond even the implicit meaning of the *lafẓ*? Those jurisprudents did, it is true, treat the results of analogical reasoning as distinct from implicit meaning, although very often they would dispute whether a particular law was to be regarded as the result of analogical reasoning or an implicit meaning; the line between the two categories could be quite hazy. For our purposes, the all-important point is that the method of analogy did not, for those who accepted it, represent an activity of the juristic mind which was independent of the *lafẓ*. My reason for saying this is as follows. A law (*ḥukm*) which is analogous to some other previously established law has validity by virtue of a ground, called in Arabic *'illah*, which it shares with that other law. This ground must be rooted ultimately in the *lafẓ*. Islamic jurisprudence was to develop highly refined and liberal procedures whereby the ground of a previously established law could be determined, procedures that entailed in some cases consideration of the grand purposes of the law as a whole, the *maqāṣid al-sharī'ah*.[9] But even these had to be derived, by a process of induction (*istiqrā'*), from the *lafẓ*. Never could human rationality or ingenuity be determinative of the ground of a particular law. Whatever previously hidden parts of the divine law became manifest through this process had their anchorage within the philological determinable meaning of the *lafẓ*; a *dalīl lafẓī* was clearly

[9] The concept of grand purposes of the law is perhaps most thoroughly and systematically developed by the famous Mālikī jurist al-Shāṭibī in his *Al-Muwāfaqāt fī uṣūl al-aḥkām*.

involved. And the newly discovered parts of the law were clearly contained within the eternal divine speech whose function it was for the *lafẓ* to make manifest.

But what of the famous principles of *istiḥsān* and *al-maṣāliḥ al-mursalah*? Do these not take us beyond the limits of what may be derived from the *lafẓ*? As for the first principle, which is associated with the Ḥanafī school, whatever it may have entailed in the earlier stages of its development, it eventually came to be understood to be a basis for preferring one *dalīl* over another, a procedure which itself had to be justified from within the meaning of the *lafẓ*. The results of *istiḥsān* therefore embraced nothing which was not in some sense made manifest through the *lafẓ*. The idea of *al-maṣāliḥ al-mursalah*, of basing a law upon a consideration of public welfare, which could be found nowhere within the meaning of the *lafẓ*, though there was nothing within that meaning which ruled it out, is more problematic, and I shall leave it to others to determine whether a break with the *lafẓ* was involved. In any case, this idea was recognized in only one of the schools of Muslim jurisprudence, the Mālikī school.

It cannot be too strongly emphasized that problems of interpretation are always, in the view of the majority of Muslim jurisprudents, to be resolved within the framework of the philologically determinable meaning of the *lafẓ*, and that it is precisely this which guarantees the objectivity of the law and its transcendence over the vagaries of human subjectivity. Never is a problem in interpretation to be turned over to an agency or instrument outside the *lafẓ* itself. The meaning of the *lafẓ* can never be determined through judicial proceeding, for example. It is not a meaning or significance which may unfold in directions that go beyond the original intended meaning, not to mention setting aside, with an attitude of indifference, that original meaning. The *lafẓ*, taken in its totality, is to be treated as a fully self-executing instrument. There is consequently no part of the law that can be identified as a constitution, or *grundnorm* (to use the Kelsenian term), for the law is in its entirety a constitution.

I have not yet made mention of a subject which may seem at first to require some qualification of what I have just said: the consensus of the Muslim community. Does not the consensus represent an agency outside the *lafẓ* of the Qur'ān and the Sunnah which may resolve problems of interpretation? As is well known, orthodox Muslim thought affirms that the unanimous judgments of the community—or, rather, of its scholars—on questions of law are infallible. But what precisely is entailed in such judgments? According to the majority view, such judgments are necessarily grounded in the Qur'ān or the Sunnah: the consensus, in other words, grants finality to the results of the explorations of the meaning of the *lafẓ* carried on by individual scholars or to the results of their analogical reasoning from the meaning of the *lafẓ*. The question is whether the consensus *qua* consensus makes manifest anything which is not made manifest through the efforts of each individual scholar laboring on his own. The answer must clearly be no. The consensus is simply a sign that tells us that each individual scholar has arrived at an accurate understanding of the law which may never be set aside by any future generation. The consensus *qua* consensus has not introduced anything of substance which can be construed as lying beyond the realm of philologically determinable meaning. Through consensus we know that the philological enterprise has infallibly reached its goal. Against this view of the majority, a minority of Muslim jurisprudents maintained that the role of the consensus could extend beyond the results of the philological enterprise: it could give finality to a judgment arrived at without reference to the *lafẓ*.[10] It is not surprising, I think, that this way of thinking was generally rejected. It seemed to be setting up the consensus as a channel of revelation independent of the Qur'ān and the Sunnah. Just what relationship was posited, on this view, between the gratuitous affirmations of the consensus and the eternal divine speech is not clear. Were those affirmations, notwithstanding their circumventing of the *lafẓ*, nonetheless an expression of the divine speech? Since this view was not widely accepted among Muslims, this question need not detain us.

One final point remains to be considered before our discussion may be considered complete. Although Islamic jurisprudence considers the law as having the potential of becoming fully manifest through the *lafẓ*, it recognizes, as I have suggested, that the

[10] Āmidī, *Al-Iḥkām*, 1:374–378.

actual becoming manifest of the law is impeded by the limitations of human scholarly endeavor and that human beings must for the most part settle for what is less than fully manifest. The task of testing presumptions as to the meaning of a particular word, phrase, or passage through scrutiny of the larger context is, as I have emphasized, exceedingly arduous, owing to the vastness of that context, and very seldom, if ever, will the individual scholar claim not to have missed anything whatsoever in that context which might shed light on the word, phrase or passage in question. It is because of this virtual impossibility of penetrating with absolute thoroughness the entire corpus of *lafẓ*, not missing a jot or tittle, that the doctrine of *ijtihād* assumes such a crucial importance. What that doctrine affirms is that, when a qualified scholar has reached the point where he can say in all honesty that he has explored the larger context to the best of his ability and can do no better, he may then adopt the meaning determined at that point as constituting the law of God for him and for any others who may elect to follow his guidance. The process of fathoming the meaning of the *lafẓ*, while in principle unending, must for practical reasons be made to end somewhere. The doctrine of *ijtihād* seeks to establish a reasonable end.

Needless to say, the *ijtihād* process will yield varying results, and the doctrinal variations between the Muslim legal schools, not to mention variations within each school, confirm that this is so. This variation may seem to undermine the radical objectivity of the law which Islamic jurisprudence seeks to affirm, its transcendence above the vagaries of human subjectivity. If the law is internally consistent—and it is a conviction of Islamic jurisprudence that it is—then its objectivity, if it is to have any impact on human life, would seem to require uniformity among those human scholars whose business it is to expound the law. As I stated at the beginning of this paper, if the law-as-object is to have value for human beings, it must become manifest. A hidden object has no value. If much of the law remains, after the *ijtihād* process has been completed, hidden, while fallible human judgments as to what constitutes the law gain the force of law in the absence of the hidden parts, then it would appear that objectivity has given way to subjectivity.

In fact, objectivity is assured even in the presence of doctrinal diversity in two ways. First of all, to the extent that the principle underlying the practice of *ijtihād*, which is that whatever emerges out of the best efforts of a qualified scholar has by divine decree the force of law for him and his followers, can be shown with full certainty to be grounded in the *lafẓ*—and it seems to be assumed by Muslim jurisprudents that it can be—the validity of the diverse legal doctrines would seem to have a solid objective basis. Secondly, we must remember that when a scholar engages in *ijtihād* he is to be guided at all times by what words mean by virtue of either *waḍ'* or *'urf*, and that the word-meaning nexuses which emerge out of *waḍ'* and *'urf* are not of his making but have an objective existence quite apart from his deliberations. In all phases of *ijtihād*—even in analogical reasoning—the scholar is guided by some sort of *dalīl lafẓī*, and every *dalīl lafẓī* makes some sort of meaning manifest to the scholar, even if that meaning happens not to be the divinely intended meaning which constitutes the law or even if it happens to constitute a part of the law which was abrogated. For this reason *ijtihād* may be regarded as constituting from beginning to end a process wherein something beyond the individual scholar is becoming manifest to him. This meaning becomes manifest to him and then that meaning, until finally, if ever, the eternal law considered as the ultimate object of the entire search arises within his mind.

4

Integrity (*'Adālah*) in Classical Islamic Law

FARHAT J. ZIADEH

IN 1986 the well-known liberal and legal scholar Ronald Dworkin published a book entitled *Law's Empire* in which he argued that "*integrity* is the key to understanding legal practice." He says, "law's empire is defined by attitude, not territory or power or process.... it is a protestant attitude that makes each citizen responsible for imagining what his society's public commitments to principle are, and what these commitments require in new circumstances." The principle he is talking about is the "moral principle [which] is the foundation of law." To him "integrity means coherence in principle, and law must have integrity to have moral authority."[1]

Now, it is entirely possible to apply this theory of law, which explains primarily the Anglo-American legal system, to the Islamic legal system, especially because this latter system is based on religious and moral principles ultimately derived from the Qur'ān and the sayings of the Prophet Muhammad entitled the *ḥadīth* (traditions). The whole system is built on an analogical, but casuistic, methodology that honors basic moral principles. Each

[1] Ronald Dworkin, *Law's Empire* (Cambridge, Mass.: Harvard University Press, 1986), p. 413.

rule of law must be consistent, or "coherent," in the language of Dworkin, with the main body of law and the moral principles that support it. Anybody familiar with the Islamic law of contracts, for example, is struck by the fact that the rules governing contracts are devised in a way which would honor the wishes of the parties and at the same time avoid any interest taking or any speculation that resembles gambling. Both interest taking and gambling are prohibited by the Qur'ān as interpreted by scholars.[2] This coherence in principle, therefore, can be used to describe Islamic law or, for that matter, any system of law based on universal principles.

But it is not our task now to proffer more examples from Islamic law to support Dworkin's thesis. Instead, we shall take up the doctrine of integrity (*'adālah*) as understood in Islamic law and discuss its centrality to the ascertainment of one of the bases of law, namely the Traditions, and to the functioning of the court system. Integrity, in these cases, is that of the individual who transmits a tradition of the Prophet to a later generation, or whose testimony in court is a deciding factor in according or denying rights to parties in an action. Such an individual, to be considered trustworthy or upright for his role, must be coherent or consistent with the moral principles of his law. To repeat Dworkin's words, "Integrity is ... an attitude that makes each citizen responsible for imagining what his society's public commitments to principle are." Thus Dworkin's thesis as to the nature of law helps us in elucidating the importance of integrity in individuals who transmit traditions that might form a basis for law or whose testimony is decisive in the application of law in the courts.

One factor that has to be kept in mind in evaluating the importance of integrity is the nature of a traditional Islamic society compared to a Western state. In a Western state, law defines itself in terms of fundamental rights which are pitted against the "compelling interests" of the state. Islamic law, on the other hand, does not separate the individual and the state. The state is in fact the community itself, and the relations between the individual and the community are defined in terms of duties, not in terms of rights. In a Western state there are all sorts of safeguards, whether in law, constitution, or convention, that protect the rights of individuals

[2] Qur'ān 2:275; 5:90.

and groups, like separation of powers and the consequent balancing of authority in a state, writs of court (*habeas corpus, certiorari, mandamus*), impeachment of officials or rights of recall, and so on. In an Islamic society everything depends upon the integrity of individuals and those who administer the law. If that integrity is lacking, there is no other safeguard, except, of course, the resort to arms.

Even the traditional division of duties in Islamic law into five categories: acts that are commanded, acts that are recommended, acts that are free (in the sense that the law attaches no moral value to them), acts that are disliked, and acts that are prohibited—such a division assumes integrity in a society. For whereas the commanded and the prohibited acts are capable of being enforced by the authorities, the recommended and the disliked (hence, reprehensible) acts depend for their enforcement on the integrity of an individual or ultimately, of course, on the desire to find favor in the eyes of God.

Thus there is an assumption of a moral and religious society which is rightly guided by God and possesses the Truth. In the language of an adage or a maxim attributed to al-Ghazālī,[3] "it is not possible to have [a society] better than what has existed" (*laysa bi-al-imkān khayrun mimmā kān*). Life is not nasty and brutish so that men would join together in a compact to protect themselves and their interests. Life, although short, is well-ordered, and the individual is protected by God's law and the integrity of those who apply it. Hence the emphasis on integrity (*'adālah*) as a necessary characteristic of a person to assume public office, from that of caliph to court witness. In fact, as we shall see later, the mark of a "gentleman" in an Islamic society is the acceptance of his testimony at court (*maqbūl al-shahādah*). On the other hand, if a person does something dishonorable, or morally reprehensible, let alone criminal, his testimony might not be accepted in court. It is related that a judge in Egypt by the name of Tawbah ibn Namir (115–120 A.H./A.D. 733–738) entertained an action for divorce and divorced a woman from her husband. The judge then suggested to the man that he provide her with a separation gift (*mut'ah*).

[3] See Ibn Ḥajar al-Haythamī, *Al-Fatāwā al-ḥadīthīyah* (Cairo: Muṣṭafā al-Bābī al-Ḥalabī, 1325 A.H.), p. 40.

The man refused, but the judge did not say anything because such a gift is not legally obligatory.[4] Later, the man appeared in the judge's court as a witness in another case. But the judge would not accept his testimony because in the previous case he had refused to be charitable and God-fearing.[5]

The assumption of a moral society characterized by integrity is indeed enshrined in the Qur'ān. "Ye are the best community that hath been raised up for mankind. Ye enjoin right conduct and forbid indecency."[6] Integrity is even considered by some jurists to be of a stronger force than a judgment of a court. In grappling with the difficult task of evaluating the stability of judgments in a society compared to the moral integrity of an individual, jurists, for the most part, come out on the side of integrity. To be sure, stability of judgments is as important to an Islamic society as *res judicata* or *chose jugée* is in the West. But the outward stability should be tempered with an inner conscience. Consequently, if a judge should rule in favor of a man concerning a sale of a female slave to him or concerning his being married to a woman, while the man knows that such judgment was based on false testimony, the judgment is outwardly executory, but the man is conscience bound not to have sexual relations with either of them, according to the better opinion of the Ḥanafī school. If the subject matter of the judgment is property, personal or real, the man, as between himself and God, should not assume control of it.[7] This seems to be based on the Qur'ānic verse, "And eat not up your property among yourselves in vanity"[8] and on the saying of the Prophet, "He who cuts off for himself with his right hand [a piece] from the property of a fellow Muslim will have to face the anger of God."[9]

This integrity assumed in the general society must, as was said earlier, be evidenced in full measure among court witnesses and

[4] Following Qur'ān 2:236, this gift, which amounts to half the dower, is payable to the woman in lieu of dower if the marriage has not been consummated.

[5] M. al-Kindi, *The Governors and Judges of Egypt*, ed. Rhuvon Guest (Leyden: E. J. Brill, 1912), p. 344.

[6] Qur'ān 3:110.

[7] A. al-Khaṣṣāf, *Adab al-qāḍī*, ed. Farhat J. Ziadeh (Cairo: American University Press, 1979), p. 368.

[8] Qur'ān 2:188.

[9] See al-Khaṣṣāf, *Adab*, p. 370.

transmitters of the sayings of the Prophet because the order of society and the order of God's religion and law depend on it. We shall deal with court witnesses first.

As is well known among the experts in Islamic law, a fact can be established at court in any one of the three means of proof, namely, (a) the testimony of witnesses (in most cases two trustworthy male witnesses, with the possible substitution of two women for one man), (b) the admission of the defendant or accused, and (c) in the absence of the first two, the refusal of the defendant to take an oath denying the claim. There is no provision that would constitute writing as evidence, let alone an insistence that certain types of transactions be reduced to writing or be evidenced in writing, as some other legal systems do. Indeed, the Qur'ān itself says, "O ye who believe! When ye contract a debt for a fixed term, record it in writing."[10] Why, then, was writing not accepted as evidence (except in later times and in one school of law, the Mālikī, when qualified witnesses had attested the contents, and in another school, the Ḥanafī, when the witnessed document was actually deposited in the archives of the court for safekeeping)?[11] Was it only because a document, or a writing, can be subject to falsification and forgery whereas an upright witness cannot so easily be corrupted? Or is there some other reason for this phenomenon?

To answer this question we must understand the function of *shahādah* (witnessing or testimony) in the Islamic system of belief and practice. The *shahādah*, for example, is one of the five pillars of Islam, the others being prayer, fasting during the month of Ramaḍān, pilgrimage to Mecca, and payment of *zakāt*, or almsgiving. The *shahādah*, here, is witnessing that there is no god but God and that Muhammad is the Prophet of God. Like the other four pillars it is an action (*al-'amal bi-al-arkān*), not merely an inward belief. The *shahādah*, then, is standing up and being counted as a supporter of the faith. The individual becomes involved in the community and the community in him; he supports the community and the community supports him. Consequently, any public or legally binding act between individuals needs the

[10] Qur'ān 2:282.

[11] See Jeannette A. Wakin, *The Function of Documents in Islamic Law* (Albany: State University of New York Press, 1972), pp. 8–9.

support or the *shahādah* of the community. The presence of two adult and trustworthy male witnesses is necessary for the valid conclusion of a contract of marriage in Islamic law, and this presence is a matter of substantive law in Sunnī doctrine, not merely an evidentiary precaution as in Shīʿī doctrine.[12] The presence of witnesses is even necessary for the proper convening of a court of law, and the signature of a judge to a judgment is without any evidentiary value unless attested to by witnesses.[13] This involvement of the community in public acts through *shahādah* gives stability to these acts. A contract, of course, can be concluded without witnesses, but the parties would do so at their peril, because there would not exist the public support of the community through the *shahādah* to establish definitely the terms of the contract in case of dispute. Hence the insistence of the law on the oral testimony of witnesses and the characterization of such testimony as the best method of proof.

The involvement of the community in establishing legal rights took place in Islamic society before and after the emergence of a legal dispute. As we shall see later, trustworthy witnesses who attested legal transactions later became professional witnesses attached to the court, and their testimony, in case of a dispute, was just as decisive as the verdict of a jury in the common-law system. It is to be noted, though, that in the jury system the community gets involved after the emergence of the dispute, and therefore an investigative procedure of examination and cross-examination is set in motion to determine the truth. In Islamic society, by contrast, the judge merely listens to the testimony of the witnesses who had attested the legal transaction between the parties, and gives judgment in accordance with that testimony. The judge's mechanical role highlights the importance of witnesses and puts a premium on their integrity (*ʿadālah*).

Now, who is an *ʿadl*, or a person of integrity, who can be a witness at court? According to Abū Ḥanīfah (d. 767), the eponym

[12] J. N. D. Anderson, *Islamic Law in the Modern World* (New York: New York University Press, 1959), p. 46.

[13] This is especially emphasized in Mālikī law. See Emil Tyan, *Histoire de l'organization judiciaire en pays d'Islam* (Paris: Librairie du Recueil Sirey, 1938), 1:350, 363.

of the Ḥanafī school of law, all Muslims are considered persons of integrity (*'udūl*) to be witnesses for, or against, each other, unless their transgression or profligacy (*fusq*) is apparent. As a precautionary measure, however, a judge should inquire into the character of witnesses to ascertain their integrity in cases of grave crimes known as *ḥudūd*. The two students of Abū Ḥanīfah, Abū Yūsuf (d. 798) and al-Shaybāni (d. 805), on the other hand, insist that the judge should ascertain their integrity in all cases involving rights.[14]

What caused this glaring discrepancy in views between the master and his two students? Al-Jaṣṣāṣ (d. 980) in his commentary on *Adab al-qāḍī* by al-Khaṣṣāf (d. 874) explains that Abū Ḥanīfah's views were based on the integrity of the Muslim community in the generation of the Companions of the Prophet and the succeeding two generations known as those of the Followers and the Followers of the Followers, that is, up to the generation of Abū Ḥanīfah. Beyond that time, integrity seems to have slipped. Al-Jaṣṣāṣ advances a saying of the Prophet in support of that thesis: "The best people are those of the generation in which I was sent [as a prophet]. Then come those after them, then those after them. Then lying will spread."[15] Al-Jaṣṣāṣ then says, "As you can observe today, most people are not characterized by integrity. Thus there is no way out of investigating the character of witnesses in all testimonies."[16] This theory of gradual degeneration, coupled with the importance of *shahādah* in Islamic legal practice, gave rise not only to the institution of "witness clearance" (*tazkiyah*), similar to "security clearance" nowadays, but to the institution of witnesses "cleared" beforehand, or notaries.

How does witness clearance take place? We cannot here go into the details of the process, and shall be content with giving a synopsis of what al-Khaṣṣāf, one of the earliest jurists and writers on the subject, had to say:

> The *qāḍī* is to select for the scrutiny of witnesses the most trustworthy person he can find and the most knowledgeable in distinguishing

[14] Al-Khaṣṣāf, *Adab*, p. 289.

[15] A similar tradition is in Ibn Ḥanbal, *Al-Musnad* (Cairo, 1313 A. H.), 5:357.

[16] Al-Khaṣṣāf, *Adab*, pp. 290–291.

between people. He then hands to him in secret the names of the witnesses together with their description, their clan names and their place of residence. Such a person (*muzakkī*) is to inquire about them from the trustworthy among their neighbors, they being sagacious, not dupes.... The *qāḍī* may also appoint some other person to ask about the same witnesses independently of the first, before he proceeds with the case. He should then order the plaintiff to produce persons who would testify in public as to the integrity of the witnesses in the presence of the plaintiff, the defendant, and the witnesses. The *qāḍī* is to ask these persons about each one of the witnesses individually—about his name and that of his father, and about his integrity. Once that is done, the *qāḍī* should enforce the testimony of the witnesses.... The public scrutiny of the witnesses is necessary lest a man carry the name of another person [and a mixup in identity ensue].[17]

This meticulousness in the procedure of the *qāḍī* court contrasts sharply with the wrong perception of laxity and informality of such procedure that became for a while prevalent in the West following such a characterization by Max Weber.[18] Mr. Justice Frankfurter, in his dissent in the case of *Terminiello* v. *Chicago* (337 U.S. I, 1949), attacked the inclination of the majority to find a federal claim where none had been pleaded in the lower state courts, and said: "This is a court of review, not a tribunal unbounded by rules. We do not sit like a kadi under a tree dispensing justice according to considerations of individual expediency." Had Mr. Frankfurter read al-Khaṣṣāf instead of Max Weber he would not have fallen into this error!

Al-Khaṣṣāf even deals with the possibility that the defendant might contest the integrity of the witnesses after their integrity had been accepted by the *qāḍī*. In such a case the *qāḍī* is to repeat the scrutiny of witnesses by asking some other trustworthy people about them. If these latter should mention any factor that would nullify the witnesses' integrity, the *qāḍī* would do so, and would not give force to their testimony.[19]

[17] Al-Khaṣṣāf, *Adab*, pp. 292–296. The first judge in Egypt to inquire into the character of witnesses was Ghawth ibn Sulaymān who held his office from 758 to 761. See al-Kindi, *Governors*, p. 361.

[18] See Max Weber, *Max Weber on Law and Economy and Society*, ed. M. Reinstein (Cambridge, Mass.: Harvard University Press, 1954), p. 213.

[19] Al-Khaṣṣāf, *Adab*, p. 301.

As is apparent from the foregoing, the *qāḍī* must start with a base of trustworthy people who would later on establish the integrity of witnesses. But how is that base of trustworthy people to be established? Apparently the very first function of the *qāḍī*, when he is appointed to his post, is to carry on an investigation to ascertain who in the city of his jurisdiction is to be trusted. And he is to perform that duty in person. Al-Khaṣṣāf says:

> The *qāḍī* must acquaint himself as to the men of integrity [*'udūl*], confidence, and trust in the city to which be is appointed. If he is able to do so [even] before arriving there, he should attempt it. If some people are named to him, then when he enters the city he should summon them one at a time and ask them about each other ... until there develops a consensus as to who are [the men of integrity].[20]

Obviously, people who are not coherent with the purposes and morality of their society and law cannot be accepted as witnesses. Included in this group, according to al-Khaṣṣāf are the following: "gangsters, highwaymen, robbers, fornicators, homosexuals, those who drink grape wine or get drunk on date wine, those who participate in sessions of buffoonery, drinking and debauchery (even though they do not get drunk), singers and songstresses, hired mourners, both males and females, those who train pigeons and other birds, and those who play chess for gambling, or who allow chess playing to detain them from their prayers, or who, while playing indulge in swearing falsely."[21] The commentator al-Jaṣṣāṣ in explaining the inclusion of some of these persons says that singing and keening are undertaken by dissolute persons, and that trainers of pigeons, although not necessarily dissolute, are foolish and, therefore, unacceptable as witnesses. He presses home his point by saying that every action that indicates the foolishness of its doer nullifies his integrity, even though it does not prove his dissoluteness. "Don't you see," he says, "that if an old man should rise and wrestle with young boys in the mosque in the presence of people, or should stand in the market place and utter stupid and

[20] Ibid., pp. 83–84.
[21] Ibid., pp. 303–305.

ridiculous words, we would not accept his testimony even though his dissoluteness is not proven?"[22]

Aside from these failings in personal character that render a person unacceptable as a witness, certain practices would have the same effect. Thus, should a person be known to practice usury, or should he think lightly of the five daily prayers and wantonly disregard them, his testimony would not be accepted.[23]

Also, the question of legal capacity might come into play. Aside from the criterion of legal majority, the criterion of the free status of the witness is relevant. So, should the defendant claim that the witnesses against him were slaves, and therefore not fit to be witnesses, while the witnesses assert their freedom, the *qāḍī* would charge them with the burden of proving their freedom, whether it be an original freedom or a supervening one. Now, those familiar with the broad principles of Islamic law might think that the burden of proof has been misplaced here, since freedom is an original condition, and anybody claiming something contrary to an original condition, that is, the defendant in this case, must prove it. But al-Jaṣṣāṣ, the commentator on al-Khaṣṣāf, says that an original condition, or what is apparent (*al-ẓāhir*), cannot be used to assert a right against a third party (*la yustaḥaqqu bihi ʻalā al-ghayr*). To be sure, it can be used by a person to repel a claim against himself, thus placing the burden of proof upon the party asserting something contrary to what is apparent, or to the original condition, in relation to that person himself.[24] An example would be a person claiming another to be his runaway slave. Such a claimant must prove his contention, since there is a presumption of an original freedom on the side of the other.

To come back to our subject of integrity for purposes of testimony, jurists, being realists, also do not seem to insist that a witness be of an absolutely immaculate character. Abū Yūsuf says that if a person's affairs were mostly good, then he is trustworthy, provided that any failing he has had be minor, not major. This prompted a later jurist to say—and this is as close to a definition as I can find—"If the person be adhering to the community,

[22] Ibid., p. 305.
[23] Ibid., pp. 305–306.
[24] Ibid., p. 307.

performs his religious duties, be known for his honest dealings in gold coins (*dīnārs*), silver coins (*dirhams*) and goods, discharges trusts, and is truthful, then he is trustworthy, even though he might have committed a minor sin. In such a case he should ask forgiveness from God and not go back to sinning." The commentator al-Jaṣṣāṣ gives "honest dealings" prime of place, for without them, he says, a person cannot be trustworthy, although he might "adhere to the community." He supports his position by a *ḥadīth* from the Prophet: "The value of a person is [measured] not by the frequency of prayer and fasting, but by the discharge of trusts."[25]

What if the witness is a woman? Who is to ask about her character? Here jurists insist that only an able and wise woman who mingles among the people and is experienced should inquire about the witness's character. A woman of this persuasion, they add, would be like men in eliciting information.[26]

As can be seen, the ultimate acceptance or nonacceptance of a witness by a *qāḍī* can be a highly subjective matter, if one were to follow the prescriptions of the jurists. In fact, the legal literature preserves for us actual instances where a person's testimony was refused for one reason or another. Aside from the instance mentioned above, where a judge refused the testimony of a man for being uncharitable toward his divorced wife, the same judge would not accept the testimony of a North Arab (*muḍarī*) against a South Arab (*yamanī*) or vice versa.[27] Another judge would not accept the testimony of a poet because he incessantly slandered women of good reputation in his poems.[28]

The discretionary power of the *qāḍī* in accepting or rejecting the testimony of a witness placed in jeopardy the rights of the parties to a contract or any other legal transaction should a dispute arise between the parties, and should a witness, upon whom the enforcement of the contract depended, be declared nonacceptable. The practice, therefore, gradually grew, as described by Emil Tyan in his works, of the parties to legal documents

[25] Ibid., pp. 311–312.

[26] Ibid., p. 314.

[27] Al-Kindi, *Governors*, pp. 344, 346.

[28] See Tyan, *Histoire*, p. 351, and authorities cited there.

choosing witnesses who had already been declared trustworthy by the judge.[29] Thus arose the institution of professional witnesses (*shuhūd ʻudūl*) attached to the court who would authenticate documents, act as witnesses, and generally be influential in many ways.[30] Since judgments in all sorts of actions depended upon witnesses' testimony, they assumed an inordinate amount of power that could only be curbed by dismissal from their office by the judge. But often they and the judge formed a corrupt alliance that made a mockery out of integrity, upon which the whole system rests.

But, because of the power they assumed, the *shuhūd* were either looked up to or thoroughly denounced as corrupt and ungodly. Biographers of earlier generations of Muslims might mention a prominent person and then add that he was one of the *shuhūd* to emphasize his prominence.[31] But when in the year A.D. 827 a highly placed person took to task the *muzakkī* (the person who clears witnesses) for admitting as witnesses persons like a weaver, a street vendor, or a drink seller (obviously considered lowly crafts), he invoked God not to elevate the *muzakkī* and his descendants to the honorable position of *shuhūd* in the future.[32] The importance of the *shuhūd* or *ʻudūl* is even reflected in Jewish documents of later centuries found in the Cairo Geniza and studied by S. D. Goitein. Goitein says:

> No one could make a claim in [the Jewish] court without producing a Muslim document properly issued by *ʻudūl* approved by the government. This legal situation is reflected in many Geniza sources. And just as a government surveyor would assist the Jewish courts in deciding matters connected with the architectural aspects of a building, thus a Muslim notary, "great in the art of the notariate," would confirm property rights

[29] Ibid., and in *Le Notariat et le régime de la preuve par écrit dans la pratique du droit musulman* (Beirut, 1959).

[30] The first judge, we are told, who appointed official witnesses in Egypt was al-Mufaḍḍal ibn Fuḍālah. He appointed ten witnesses between the years 790 and 793, and by doing so seemed to have raised a furor. See al-Kindi, *Governors*, p. 386.

[31] See for example ʻAbdallāh Kh. al-Barrī, *Al-Qabā'il al-ʻarabīyah fī Miṣr* (Cairo: Dār al-Fikr al-ʻArabī, 1967), p. 200.

[32] Al-Kindi, *Governors*, p. 436. I read the word *muslimānī* as *sulaymānī*, a dispenser of a drink made of *sulaymānī* sugar.

by authoritative interpretation of a conveyance document submitted to him.[33]

He later says, "The Geniza contains a considerable number of ... deeds written by Muslim notaries in Arabic script. In most cases they tell us about houses, or parts of houses, acquired by Jews from other Jews, or from Christians or Muslims."[34]

Social and political privileges also could be established or denied by the testimony of witnesses. It seems that in the latter part of the second century A.H. (A.D. 801–809) the people of a village in the eastern part of Egypt, by the name of al-Ḥaras, wanted to establish for themselves an Arabian pedigree going back to the Arabian tribe of Quḍā'ah. Such a pedigree would raise their status from that of the conquered Copts to that of the conquering Arabians. It was opportune for them that the clerk of the court at the capital, Fusṭāṭ, was from the same village, and that the *qāḍī*, 'Abd al-Raḥmān al-'Umarī, a descendant of the second caliph 'Umar and a lover of the art of songstresses, was not beyond corruption. Some people from the Sharqīyah province and from the Syrian desert testified that the Ḥaras people were Arabians, so the judge at least had some evidence on which to base his rescript (*sijill*) that they were indeed Arabians. This decision raised a storm among the Arabians resident in Egypt, and many poets, who were the journalists and commentators of the day, had some choice words for both the Ḥaras people and the judge. One poet attacked al-'Umarī by saying: "If you should consider them Arabians, then you should find no objection to giving them your daughters in marriage"—an insult to a true Arabian. The matter was resolved in the year 809 when a new 'Abbāsid caliph, al-Amīn, dismissed al-'Umarī and appointed Hāshim al-Bakrī in his place. This new judge declared all those who had testified in the Ḥaras case to be not trustworthy and that the Ḥaras people were not Arabians, but Copts. He did so after receiving the testimony of "people of trustworthiness and abstemiousness."[35]

[33] S. D. Goitein, *A Mediterranean Society* (Berkeley and Los Angeles: University of California Press, 1983), 4:39–40.

[34] Ibid., p. 49.

[35] Al-Kindi, *Governors*, pp. 397–401, 411–414. For the location of Ḥaras and its luminaries see A. M. al-Sam'āni, *Kitāb al-ansāb* (Leiden: E. J. Brill, 1912), folio 163.

The *shuhūd*, though, like judges, must adhere to the political and religious philosophy of the day; otherwise they would not be "coherent," in the language of Dworkin, with the principles of their society. When the free-thinking movement known as al-Mu'tazilah, with its belief in the createdness of the Qur'ān, gained the upper hand in the first half of the ninth century, the caliph al-Ma'mūn instituted in 833 an inquisition and directed, among other things, that only persons who were both trustworthy and believed in the createdness of the Qur'ān be accepted as witnesses.[36]

Finally, one further aspect of the integrity of *shuhūd* for the Islamic legal system needs to be mentioned. It is their role in the transfer of testimony from one jurisdiction to another. In such a case, a plaintiff with a claim against a defendant who resides in another jurisdiction presents two trustworthy witnesses to the court of his own jurisdiction who support his claim. The judge then writes to the judge of the other jurisdiction, where the defendant resides, informing him of the testimony and of the trustworthiness of the witnesses, seals the letter and delivers it to two other trustworthy witnesses who were present at the taking of the original testimony. These latter witnesses then travel to the second jurisdiction, present the letter to the judge and testify in the presence of the defendant as to what they heard in the original testimony and as to the genuineness of the letter and the seal of the judge. When the judge is satisfied of their trustworthiness he gives judgment in accordance with the original testimony.[37]

To repeat, it is evident that a legal system like this sets high store by the integrity of witnesses. Idealistic jurists, in order to emphasize the requirement of integrity, relate precedents where important personages were denied acceptance as witnesses. One such instance was when al-Ḥakam I (A.D. 796–822), the Umayyad prince of Spain, who was known for his mirth and levity, was not accepted as a witness in the court of a judge whom he himself had

[36] Al-Kindi, *Governors*, pp. 445–446.
[37] Al-Khaṣṣāf, *Adab*, pp. 409–410.

appointed.[38] But there were instances, as we saw above, where integrity failed and thus resulted in denial of justice.

The requirement of integrity is even more stringent in its application to persons who claimed the authority to transmit a saying (*ḥadīth*) of the Prophet. As is well known, the formal sources of Islamic law are the Qur'ān (the very word of God), the *ḥadīth* (the sayings, actions, and tacit approvals of the Prophet), the consensus of those learned in religious sciences, and the analogical reasoning that would extend the provisions found in the first three sources to new circumstances. Thus, *ḥadīth*, the precedents of the Prophet, is of great importance to the legal system, second only to the Qur'ān. But to ascertain the *ḥadīth* is no easy matter, as the Prophet's mission lasted twenty-two years and practically all his Companions transmitted sayings from him throughout that period. Several generations elapsed before what were considered authoritative sayings, transmitted for the most part orally, were enshrined in formal collections. During those generations a considerable number of spurious *ḥadīth* was put into circulation for political, doctrinal, personal, or other reasons. As to the extent of spuriousness in the *ḥadīth*, scholars continue to disagree. In any case, Muslim scholars developed a methodology which they thought would ascertain the genuineness of the *ḥadīth*. It consisted of examining the *isnād*, or the chain of transmitters of the individual saying from the Prophet, across several generations, down to the time of the scholar doing the examining. The object of the quest is the *'adālah* or trustworthiness of persons in the chain of *isnād*. Questions looked into include the names and circumstances of the transmitters to ascertain where and when they lived, whether they had direct contact to make the transmittal possible, and whether they were pious, reliable, accurate, truthful, and not forgetful in their transmission. The saying itself, known as the *matn*, unless obviously outlandish, did not receive a comparable criticism.

This great concern for the men in the chains of *isnād* produced extensive biographical dictionaries of transmitters of *ḥadīth* that

[38] See Abū al-Ḥasan al-Nubahī, *Tārīkh quḍāt al-Andalus* (Beirut: al-Maktab al-Tijārī, 1967), pp. 48–50. For other instances, see al-Khushanī, *Quḍāt Qurṭubah* (Cairo: al-Dār al-Miṣrīyah, 1966), pp. 31–32.

became the forerunners of "Who Was Who" in practically every field of knowledge. For *ḥadīth* there developed a special branch of this genre known as *al-ta'dīl wa-al-tajrīḥ* (declaring people to be trustworthy or "wounding" their reputation), and a book, that we shall quote from often, deals specifically with those whose reputation has been "wounded," or is "out of commission," so to speak.

The stringency of traditionists in accepting or rejecting transmitters produced a myriad of jokes that often arise as a human reaction to stringency or authoritarianism. My favorite is the one often quoted in Arabic readers. It seems that a traditionist met a Christian on a boat. The Christian took out some wine, poured a glass and drank. Then he poured another glass and offered it to the traditionist, who grabbed it without thinking. The Christian felt it was his "Christian duty" to warn the traditionist and said, "Beware, it is wine!" The traditionist said, "How do you know it is wine?" The Christian said, "My servant bought it from a Jew." The traditionist drank it quickly and said, "I have never seen a more foolish person! We the people of *ḥadīth* transmit on the authority of so-and-so and so-and-so (and he named stringent traditionists). Am I to believe a Christian on the authority of his servant on the authority of a Jew? By God, I would not have drunk it, had it not been for the weakness of the chain of *isnād*."

A second story makes fun of the pedantry of *ḥadīth* transmitters and the lofty moral intent of the *ḥadīth*. The legendary comical character Ash'ab was asked by a certain Ṭālibid (a descendent of the Prophet's uncle Abū Ṭālib) whether he transmitted traditions. Ash'ab said, "I was told by Nāfi' on the authority of Ibn 'Umar that the Messenger of God said, 'A man in whom there are found two qualities belongs to God's chosen friends.'" The Ṭālibid asked what the two qualities were. Ash'ab replied, "Nāfi' had forgotten one, and I have forgotten the other."[39]

The epistemological process of ascertaining the words of the Prophet through an examination of the character of transmitters apparently was criticized by some Muslims as a form of character assassination or backbiting (*ghībah*), but, certainly, this is not the stand of the traditionists, let alone those among them who wrote books on those whom they considered weak and untrustworthy

[39] Franz Rosenthal, *Humor in Early Islam* (Leiden: E. J. Brill, 1956), pp. 29, 117.

transmitters. One such author, Ibn Ḥibbān al-Bustī (d. 965) denies that the process is backbiting and even quotes the Prophet to prove his point. Then he compares the process of ascertaining the veracity of a witness at court with that of a transmitter of *ḥadīth* and says, "If that process be permissible and proper for the sake of some nonconsequential material thing of this vain world, how much more would it be proper for defending the Prophet against mendacious words attributed to him!"[40]

Traditionists differ as to whether al-Bustī was stringent or liberal in declaring transmitters trustworthy.[41] He, therefore, can be considered a middle-of-the-road guide in this most difficult and controversial subject. In the introduction to his book *Kitāb al-majrūḥīn*, he divides those whose reputation has been injured into twenty categories ranging from atheists and heretics to outright falsifiers of *ḥadīth* who would invent *ḥadīth* to embellish the religious stories they recounted in mosques to elicit donations from their audience. We cannot, in this context, go through all these categories, but shall give some examples of persons from various categories not measuring up to what Islamic society at the time considered *'adl*.

Atheists, heretics, and evil doers are sometimes named, and sometimes just alluded to in order to warn against their type. We are told that such people enter cities, assume the guise of traditionists, and relate a false *ḥadīth* on the authority of a well-known transmitter, so that they would sow doubt in the hearts of men as to what is a true *ḥadīth*.

The famous Egyptian traditionist al-Layth ibn Sa'd (d. A.D. 791) is reported to have said, "There came to us from Alexandria an old man who related *ḥadīth* on the authority of Nāfi' [the well-known transmitter from Ibn 'Umar from the Prophet], and Nāfi' was still living at the time. So we approached this man and wrote on his authority and that of Nāfi' two long sheets. When the old man departed, we sent the two sheets to Nāfi' who recognized not a single *ḥadīth*."[42]

[40] Muḥammad ibn Ḥibbān al-Bustī, *Kitāb al-majrūḥīn*, ed. M. I. Zāyid (Aleppo: Dār al-Wa'y, 1976), pp. 17–19.

[41] See ibid., introduction, p. *lām*.

[42] Ibid., pp. 63–64.

Some do-gooders are another category. These are people who would create a *ḥadīth* and attribute it to a trustworthy transmitter in order to enjoin the good and censure sin, thinking that, by doing so, they were performing a meritorious act.[43]

Another category are those traditionists who, although pious, when they get old they get words and chains of *isnād* all mixed up, due to memory failure. Such people are usually treated kindly when reference is made to them, but are not considered authorities. One typical comment is "So and so is truly pious, but *ḥadīth* has its men."[44]

What traditionists considered plagiarism disqualified other men. As is well known, for a traditionist to have the authority to transmit a *ḥadīth*, he must personally hear it from the man he claims to have heard it from. One Isḥāq ibn 'Īsā says, "One day I mentioned to Muḥammad ibn Jābir [a certain *ḥadīth*], and immediately after, I saw that same *ḥadīth* in his written collection of *ḥadīth*, inserted between two lines, with the ink still fresh."[45] Even Abū Ḥanīfah, the eponym of the great Ḥanafī school of jurisprudence, has not escaped from a similar charge leveled at him by that same Muḥammad ibn Jābir. He says, "Abū Ḥanīfah asked me to give him the written accounts of *ḥadīth* I had heard from Ḥammād ibn abī Sulaymān, but I refused. So he intrigued with his son to obtain them from me, which he did. Now he narrates them directly on the authority of Ḥammād."[46] But, in view of the previous report about the character of Muḥammad ibn Jābir, and the fact that Abū Ḥanīfah was the student of Ḥammād, one can ascribe this charge to professional jealousy.

Other categories include those who often made mistakes, those to whose collections of *ḥadīth* false accounts were added by people the transmitter trusted, like a son or a bookseller, while the transmitter, unaware of the addition, continued to insist that the false *ḥadīth* was genuine, and those who were known for their unrighteousness. Of the latter category was a student of a famous traditionist, who was nevertheless wont to release scorpions in the

[43] Ibid., p. 64.
[44] Ibid., p. 67.
[45] Ibid., p. 74.
[46] Ibid.

holy mosque at Mecca, so that they would sting people, and to pour ink at night in the ablution fountains, so that people's faces would be blackened.[47]

The final category of untrustworthy transmitters are those who deviate from the main stream of Islam and become propagandists for an innovative philosophy or cult. Examples given by al-Bustī include a Qadarite free-thinker, a Muʿtazilite free-thinker, and a Shīʿite. All three were propagandists for their causes, and the Shīʿite used to say that ʿAlī will come back to this world.[48] Apparently, the disqualification of these people is attributed to their being propagandists. The eponym of the Ḥanbalī school of jurisprudence, Aḥmad ibn Ḥanbal (d. 855), was asked whether it would be all right to transmit *ḥadīth* from a Murji'ite (those who suspend judgment about presumed sinners until the time of the Hereafter) or a Qadarite, and he answered, "Yes, if he does not propagate his belief. But if he is a propagandist, then the answer is No."[49]

It is obvious, I think, that what constitutes integrity for an individual depends upon the role that individual plays in society. Integrity for a witness at court should reflect primarily honesty, since the rights of parties depend upon the testimony of a witness. It should also reflect the confidence of the court and the public in the witness, since he does represent the community's involvement in, and testimony to, the affairs of individuals. Accordingly he must be a person of dignity and of a character above reproach, not frivolous or even belonging to a despised craft, like tanning and weaving, that do not suggest dignity.

Integrity for a transmitter of *ḥadīth*, which is the speech of the Prophet, should demand more exacting requirements. This is especially so because most of the transmitters, at the time of looking into their integrity, would be dead, and therefore a thorough investigation of their background would be in order to establish their honesty, reliability, piety, seriousness, and all other characteristics that would insure the authenticity of *ḥadīth*. Religious humility or piety would be more pronounced in a transmitter of

[47] Ibid., pp. 76–80.
[48] Ibid., pp. 81–82, 208.
[49] Ibid., p. 82.

ḥadīth than in a witness at court, where worldly dignity would be more relevant. All other virtues insuring honesty would be practically the same, although the method of proving them would be different—in one case through "clearance" by the *muzakkī*, while in the other through proof of contact between persons in the chain of *isnād* and their reliability measured through truthfulness, good memory, lack of doctrinal bias, and so on.

The intimate relationship between the role a person plays and the virtues he must possess might become clearer if we compare the virtues a pre-Islamic Arabian leader had to have with those of an Islamic dignitary whose testimony would be accepted at court. In the tribal society of pre-Islamic Arabia the virtues were exemplified in the martial courage of the half-Black poet ʿAntarah, the tribal pride of the poet ʿAmr ibn Kulthūm, the munificence glorified by the poet Zuhayr, keeping one's word at the risk of even losing one's son exemplified by the Jewish-Arab poet Samaw'al, and battling extreme physical hardships depicted by the poet Shanfarah.[50] These virtues were necessary in a hostile desert environment. But in a civilized and urban Islamic environment, where rights and duties of individuals are spelled out by law, the order of society necessitates a different set of virtues that would enable that law to function properly.

A parallel transformation of virtues can likewise be traced in the West, as was so ably done by Alasdair MacIntyre in his book *After Virtue*. For Homer the example of human excellence is the warrior; for Aristotle it is the Athenian gentleman whose exercise of virtue leads to the achievement of the human *telos*; and for the New Testament the supreme virtues are faith, hope, and love.[51] But I am trespassing on a territory not my own, and must accordingly retreat gracefully.

This paper commenced with a quotation from Dworkin, and it might be fitting to end it with another quotation from him. He says, "We take an interest in law not only because we use it for our own purposes, selfish or noble, but because law is our most

[50] For all these poets and their lives see Reynold A. Nicholson, *A Literary History of the Arabs* (Cambridge: University Press, 1962), pp. 71 ff.

[51] Alasdair MacIntyre, *After Virtue* (Notre Dame, Indiana: University of Notre Dame Press, 1984), pp. 181–182 and passim.

structured and revealing social institution. If we understand the nature of our legal argument better, we know better what kind of people we are."[52] Similarly, if we understand the law of Islam and the legal structure of its institutions, like the institution of *'adālah*, we appreciate better the classical structure of Islamic society and how that society understood itself.

[52] Dworkin, *Law's Empire*, p. 11.

II

ISLAMIC LAW AND THE WEST

5

Lost, Strayed, or Stolen: Chattel Recovery in Islamic Law

DAVID F. FORTE

GETTING RID of one's personal possessions is easy. Getting them back is another story. I can will my pair of gold cuff links to my nephew, give my used overcoat to the Salvation Army, sell my washing machine to my neighbor, lend my lawn mower to my brother, or lease out my home computer. I can pledge a ring as collateral to a pawn broker. I can throw away an old chest of drawers, or abandon it to the next person who buys my house. I can lose my wallet, or my dog can stray from my backyard.

My goods can also be taken from me, sometimes by *force majeure*: flood, fire, and storm; sometimes with finality through legal action: taxes in kind, repossession, seizure for sale, escheat; or, they can be lost to me through the wrongdoing of others: theft, fraud, burglary, robbery, conversion, pilfering, embezzlement, false pretenses, vandalism, negligence. The English legal vocabulary is particularly rich in its descriptions of wrongful takings.

As usual, I am indebted to my colleague, Professor John Makdisi, for his research assistance and substantive comments. I also profited from the assistance of Professor Charles Donohue of Harvard Law School. Mostly, however, I am grateful to Farhat Ziadeh, whose work in Islamic property law inspired this piece and who becomes an instant friend to whomever he meets. To know Farhat Ziadeh is to have one of the special blessings of this life.

The ease with which one can part with one's belongings is rarely matched by any facility in regaining them. If some other person has my good—and it is still my good—how do I get it back? A man finds my stray dog. Another steals my book. The borrower of my automobile is unwilling or unable to return it. What are my remedies? On the other hand, how does the finder, the borrower, the good faith purchaser, protect himself from my demand if it is unjustified?

In any society, one's personal possessions have something of one's very person attached to them. Yet, to those things of mine that are lost, strayed, or stolen, every legal system provides but imperfect remedies. It is in scrutinizing these imperfections in remedies that we may begin to assay what particular values have precedence and priority over others in any legal system.

I limit my inquiry here to property that has left one's hands involuntarily, primarily through loss. I do so because the manner in which a legal system treats notions of ownership, of possession, and of the legitimate use of another's property is most starkly highlighted in how it disposes of lost or stolen goods. What are the owner's rights? What options does the finder have? What can be done with the goods pending resolution of the dispute? At base, every system of property has the notion that goods are to be used and to be available for use. Somehow these goods cannot be left fallow, but must be put to good use. Somehow title has to be quieted.

Let us compare how the early common law and contemporaneous Islamic law approached the problem. If I lived in medieval England or medieval Islam, around the eleventh or twelfth century, and I discover, say, that my cow is missing, what do I need to do to get it back? What if my neighbor finds the animal? What should he do to protect himself against a charge of theft or usurpation?

In both the English and Islamic systems, jurist authors gave confident and detailed answers. The very clarity and assurance with which the formulations are presented raise suspicions in all of us raised in a more pragmatic and factual historical tradition. Were these neat formulas in fact followed? We are today much more skeptical in fact about how law was actually applied in medieval England[1] and much needs to be learned about how law was applied in earlier Islam, but my point here is not so much to describe what actually took place, but what conceptions of wrong and remedy, of ownership and possession, animated the juristic system. So, for our starting point, let us look at what the jurists said should be done. What was their conception of property, of the rights and duties of owners and possessors?

The answer each system's jurist author gives to the problem of finding a lost good or strayed animal is revealing. Both systems require a ritual of pursuit or of proclamation. That in itself is significant. A detailed formula of physical actions in ritualistic form communicates first, that the substance of what lies behind the ritual is of great moment, and second, that one's rights or privileges depend on following the ritual. To fail the ritualistic requirements is to forfeit some right or to incur some liability. Thus, the one upon whom the ritual is placed has the burden. There is implicitly a suspicion the system places upon that party who can establish his *bona fides* only by the exactitude of following the procedure. If he fails the ritual, his remedies are unavailable.

The ritual form described here as taken from English common law deserves a preliminary comment. There is much doubt whether the procedure so confidently outlined by Pollock and Maitland took place in precisely that form. Actual legal procedures, especially in a primitive society, tend to be sloppier than the contemporaneous writers describe. But there was likely some form of pursuit, a taking hold of the object in question, and adjudication. The formalized description of the procedure highlights in sharp relief the legal values the jurist authors believed underlay the system. And it is those legal values that we are seeking to elucidate. We are comparing the jurist authors' notions of ownership, possession, and recovery in the early common law with those in the then more developed Islamic law. And, happily for this purpose, the actual operation of the law is not so directly relevant to our endeavor as it might be in an essay on legal history.

In accordance with an ancient action under Anglo-Saxon law, later known as an appeal of larceny or, as Bracton reported it,

[1] See S. F. C. Milsom, "Law and Fact in Legal Development," *Univ. of Toronto Law Journal* 17 (Toronto, 1967): 1–19.

actio furti, someone who finds his cow is missing needed literally to pursue the lost animal or forego recovery.[2] First, assuming it is my cow, I must have preliminarily taken some action to identify the cow as mine while I was still in possession of the bovine. In the presence of my neighbors, I would have had to make some distinguishing ear marks on the beast. Otherwise, the animal wherever found would have been only another piece of fungible currency. Then, once discovering that the cow had gone, I must raise the "hue and cry" in the area and, with my neighbors, go to "the four quarters of the neighborhood" and proclaim the loss. Under the earlier Anglo-Saxon law, I must follow the fresh tracks of the cow to the person whose land it winds up on and, grasping an ear, proclaim rightful possession. The grasping of the ear demonstrates that it is my particular cow (I made the earmark). It also reflects the nearly universal means of asserting rightful possession of ownership in ancient systems of law, namely, physically taking hold of the object.[3] Even in Islamic law, to have bare title is called *raqabah* or "neck," derived from the possessory grasping of the animal.

In the later appeal of larceny in common law, I ask the sheriff of the county to engage in the pursuit and I bring my claim in county court against the man found in possession. I can bring the claim without necessarily having to charge him with theft. If by chance the cow was stolen and the thief apprehended red-handed, he can be executed without any right to answer the charge.

Many cases were quashed for failure to prosecute the claim diligently, but if I have met these requirements, then the burden shifts to the one with "my" cow. He has a number of ways of defending himself, none of them very good.

If the cow was found on his property, and he fails to answer the summons to appear in court, he can be declared an outlaw and, true to the term, be outside the law's protection against anyone doing him harm, even killing him. In Norman times, he

[2] This summary is derived from F. Pollock and F. Maitland, *The History of English Law before the Time of Edward I*, 2 vols. (1898; 2nd ed.,Cambridge, 1968), 2:157–169. See also, W. Holdsworth, *A History of English Law* (London, 1976), pp. 78–82.

[3] Physical possession lay behind the purported ancient ritual of livery of seisin in the common law. Pollock and Maitland, *English Law*, 2:83–89.

can respond to an appeal of larceny by doing battle. If he declines battle and "puts himself upon his country," that is, seeks a jury trial, he has three defenses. First, he can claim original possession of the animal, that is, he can bring witnesses to testify that the cow was born on his farm. If he does so, then he and the appellor bring their contesting circumstantial evidence to the jury for final determination. Implicit in this defense is the notion (to be developed only centuries later) that original occupation, that is, being the first to possess and control, is the hallmark of ownership. This is the only way the finder can maintain possession. His other defenses only preserve him from the charge of theft if one is brought, but at the cost of giving up the good.

The most common of the other two defenses, the voucher of a warrantor, has been described in this manner:

> The appellee asserts that he acquired the goods from a third person, whom he calls upon to defend the appeal. There is a writ enabling him to compel the appearance of the vouchee. The vouchee appears. If he denies that the goods passed from him to the appellee, there may be battle between him and the appellee, and should he succumb in this, he will be hanged as a thief. If he admits that the goods passed from him to the appellee, then the appellee retires from the action. We see the goods placed in the warrantor's hand, and, when he is seised of them, then the appellor counts against him as against the thief or one who can name the thief. The warrantor can vouch another warrantor. The process of voucher can be repeated until a third, or perhaps a fourth, warrantor is before the court.... The convicted warrantor is hanged; the appellor recovers his chattel; but meanwhile the first appellee has gone quit; he is no thief, but he has lost the chattel.[4]

Finally, the holder of the cow, while giving it up, can assert he came by it honestly by producing witnesses who were present when he bought it, or again by using witnesses to show that he only found it and let all know the fact, or once again, by using witnesses to describe the animal which he brought back from the London Market.

The procedure I have described is probably too neat to have been the consistent judicial reality. Much of it came from Bracton

[4] Ibid., pp. 163–164.

(or those who wrote under that *nom de plume*) and Bracton was a jurist scholar versed in the Roman law who used that source to impose some conceptual rationality over what was undoubtedly a chaotic situation. Soon after Bracton, judges would come from the practitioner ranks, not the universities, and the juristic tradition present in Roman and Islamic law would fall away from the common law. In any event, later reforms in the common law provided alternate methods to ritualized pursuit for one to recover his property.[5]

Nonetheless, Bracton's description is of great value to our inquiry. For one thing, it came from the hand of a scholar jurist who was not dissimilar to the scholar jurists of Islam. For another, Bracton sought, in codifying this ritual, to describe what he believed really mattered in the common law at that time.

Who had the greater claim to the property? We see first of all that the common law was most concerned with the rights of possessors. Apparently, the very word ownership did not enter the English legal vocabulary until the fourteenth century.[6] The original "owner" or, more accurately, the prior possessor of the strayed cow had no chance to regain the cow unless he had previously marked it clearly, pursued its loss immediately, and found it in a short period of time. In other words, he who held a good was presumed to be in rightful possession, and to contest that possession, one had to show one had just momentarily lost control of it. There were other remedies that were developing, but for a while they were mostly limited to getting back the value of the good the prior possessor had, not the good itself from the current possessor. Thus, the notion of ownership of the thing against all others is secondary to the rights of possessors. If one is divested of one's good, one is seen as wronged, and the right is to be made whole by the wrongdoer. It is an interpersonal rectification the law looks to, not perfecting a property right in a specific thing. In

[5] See C. Donohue, *Property*, 2nd ed. (St. Paul, Minn., 1983), pp. 62–66; N. Arterburn, "The Early Liability of a Bailee," *Michigan Law Review* 27 (1927): 479–486; J. Ames, "The History of Trover," *Harvard Law Review* 11 (1897–1898): 277–289, 375–386.

[6] Pollock and Maitland, *English Law*, 2:153 n. 1.

Professor Charles Donohue's formulation, the former possessor is seen as one who is owed something, but not as one having owned something.[7] The action is *in personam*, not *in rem*. The juristic notion seems to have been to get the issue of possession settled quickly, so that the good's utility can be maintained.

When we turn to Islamic law, we find that the person who loses his property has no prescribed ritual which he must follow to recover it. All he need do is describe the lost object with sufficient specificity—the law books often refer to the wrappings and the manner of tying—to show reasonable proof of ownership. The owner does not even need to go to the *qāḍī* with his declaration, even if there are multiple claimants, but only to the finder who has the discretion to decide to whom he should return it. (Of course, recourse to the *qāḍī* is available if the finder refuses to return the good.)

Unlike early English law (at least as described by Bracton), where possession carried so much weight, in Islamic law, the finder of lost property gains no presumptive interest because of possession (although ultimately he may be able to treat property as if it were his own). Fundamentally, the finder is a trustee, whose duty it is to maintain the property for the benefit of the owner. Possession may have been lost to the owner, but the connection between the owner and the specific thing owned cannot, in theory at least, be broken while the good is still in existence. In opposition to the strong tradition in English law, many Islamic law scholars assert that so long as something is owned by another, possession, howsoever long, is never sufficient to acquire ownership. Rahim and Schacht, for example, hold that prescription is contrary to the strict theory of Islamic law. Others like Milliot agree but ultimately find some equivalent to it.[8]

Thus, if there are any ritualized obligations in the law of property in Islam, they are placed upon the finder and not the

[7] Donohue, *Property*, p. 61.

[8] J. Schacht, *An Introduction to Islamic Law* (Oxford 1964), p. 137; A. Rahim, *The Principles of Muhammadan Jurisprudence According to the Hanafi, Maliki, Shafi'i, and Hanbali Schools* (London, 1911; reprint ed., Westport, Conn., 1979), p. 281; L. Milliot, *Introduction à l'étude du droit musulman* (Paris, 1953), pp. 629–630.

owner. The one who finds the good is obligated to a certain form of proclamation:

> The finder is bound, during one whole year dating from the day on which the lost property was discovered and taken possession of, to publish and make known, without, however, mentioning any specific characteristics of his find, that such and such an object has been discovered.[9]

The publication must be made every two or three days, usually outside of the mosque in the district in which it was discovered. The finder himself should make the proclamation, unless, because of "rank and condition" he is unable to.[10] In that case, he should hire a man of good character or make use of the town crier. If, by chance, the good were discovered between two localities, the poor finder must publicize the discovery in both places.

If it turns out that the value of the found property is less than the legal minimum (*niṣāb*) then publication need be made for only a few days[11] or a reasonable time for the owner to discover his loss[12] or even, for some writers, not at all.[13]

The required ritual may be even more exact. For example, Nawawī requires that "notification should be repeated twice a day, that is, morning and afternoon, then once a day, then once a week, and lastly once a month, without interruption for the whole year. . . ."[14] Consigning the found object to the care of the court, however, renders publication unnecessary.[15]

Islamic law solves the complex problems associated with found property by the notion of resemblance (*shubhah*). A highly developed mechanism of analogy, resemblance is normally used to protect one accused of wrongdoing by comparing the action with one it closely resembles that is lawful. The entire notion of legal doubt is based on the same word. In their exposition of the law of lost objects, the jurists had at hand a rich set of resemblances

[9] Sidi Khalīl, *Maliki Law*, trans. F. H. Ruxton (London, 1911; reprint ed., Westport, Conn., 1980), p. 269.

[10] Ibid.

[11] *The Hedaya*, trans. C. Hamilton (London, 1870), p. 209.

[12] Nawawī, *Minhaj et Talibin*, trans. E. C. Howard (London, 1914), p. 238.

[13] Khalīl, *Maliki Law*, p. 269.

[14] Nawawī, *Minhaj et Talibin*, p. 238.

[15] Ibid., p. 237.

articulating relationships between owner and possessor. Some of these concepts, such as agency, pledge, deposit, lien, gift, and loan, were sometimes not referred to in terms, but solutions to the problems arising between owner and finder were derived from these concepts by analogical application.

The jurists are also concerned with keeping an innocent action free from resemblance to one that may be unlawful. Thus, in the case of found property, the finder is urged to seek witnesses to his finding. Letting one's neighbors know of the found property protects one against an accusation of usurpation. In English law, it worked to defeat a charge of theft. In Islamic law it also relieves the finder of having to pay indemnification to the owner if the good is later destroyed (provided it perished without fault by the finder).[16] The Shāfiʿī school, however, does not require the calling of witnesses to attest to one's discovery when it has been made.[17] With or without the need to gain witnesses, it is clear that the ritual of proclamation goes more to the obligations of the finder as trustee with the duty of due notice to the owner. The bias is in favor of the owner. Proclamation and witnessing only assist the finder against suspicion that he took the good wrongfully.

If, in fact, there was theft involved, then the stolen object must be returned if still in existence at the time of conviction and punishment. If not, the thief, if solvent, must pay compensation for the loss in ownership. However, if the thief is insolvent, the imposition of the *ḥadd* "rectifies" the crime and the debt is extinguished.[18]

Theft of property should be distinguished from unlawful use (*taʿaddī*), which is basically of two kinds: usurpation (*ghasb*) and breach of trust (*khiyānah*). Usurpation is the taking of another's good without right and with intent to convert to one's use on either a permanent or temporary basis.[19] The usurper is responsible in damages for virtually any type of loss to the owner's property. There is no *ḥadd* penalty to extinguish the debt.

[16] *Hedaya*, pp. 208–209.
[17] Nawawī, *Minhaj et Talibin*, p. 236.
[18] Khalīl, *Maliki Law*, p. 341.
[19] Rahim, *Muhammadan Jurisprudence*, p. 278.

Where the usurper has transferred the good or its value, the third party, even if he was a bona fide purchaser, is responsible for the loss of the property unless it was destroyed by *force majeure*.[20] If the third party innocently took usurped property by gift or succession, the owner must first have recourse to the usurper.[21] In all cases, the usurper and the third party are liable for contribution and indemnification.[22] By way of contrast, one who is the lawful trustee of another's property is responsible for loss only if he was at fault, that is, if he breached his duty of due care. If a trustee uses property of another, he can be guilty of breach of trust (*khiyānah*).

It is in the area of lost (not stolen or usurped) property, however, that the Islamic legal system's values most reveal themselves. In all of the law schools, the primary question is whether the taking up of lost property will help preserve it or not. In other words, how will the owner's interest be best preserved? Virtually all analogies to other property relationships work to protect the interest of the owner. Generally, it is not only permitted, but approved, to care for lost property, and, in fact, incumbent to take it up if the property may perish or be destroyed where it lay.[23] If one doubts whether one can care for the good safely, it would be blameable to take it up,[24] and absolutely forbidden if one is or fears himself to be dishonest in the handling of the good.[25]

In other words, as soon as property (or foundlings, for that matter) is placed in the way of one who can exercise safekeeping (*ḥirz*), an immediate fiduciary duty is created.[26] The would-be rescuer who turns away from the property would seem to have violated a trust (*amānah*), and although the writers do not speak directly of his liability in such a case, it would seem that, if the good subsequently perished, the erstwhile rescuer would be liable

[20] Khalīl, *Maliki Law*, p. 219. Obviously, if the third party took the property knowing it was usurped, he is fully liable for the loss. J. Hunwick, *Shari'a in Songhay: The Replies of al-Maghili to the Questions of Askia al-Hajj Muhammad* (New York, 1985), p. 83.

[21] Khalīl, *Maliki Law*, p. 220.

[22] Ibid., p. 218.

[23] *Hedaya*, p. 208; Khalīl, *Maliki Law*, pp. 268–269; Nawawī, *Minhaj et Talibin*, p. 236.

[24] Nawawī, *Minhaj et Talibin*, p. 236.

[25] Khalīl, *Maliki Law*, p. 269; Nawawī, *Minhaj et Talibin*, p. 236.

[26] *Hedaya*, p. 206.

for damages. On the other hand, picking up property intending or knowing one is likely to turn the good to one's use would make one a usurper with the obligation to indemnify the owner and be subject to *ta'zīr* penalties. Islamic law demands that the relationship between the finder and the good belonging to another be governed by the norm of integrity (*'adālah*).

The nature of a finder's fiduciary relationship having been established, the next question centers on what kind of care the found good needs. If the lost object is a stray camel, for example, then there is likely no need to care for it. A camel can fend for itself. It can survive in the desert, and is not subject to predators. Thus, the *Muwaṭṭa'* recommends leaving the camel alone.[27] A stray head of cattle should likewise be left alone if it is not subject to predators.[28] If it needs to be fed, however—for example, if found in a town without a place to graze—it should be cared for.[29] It follows logically that taking in a stray camel would have more of the *indicia* of usurpation than trust, for the only reason to do so would be to make use of it for one's own purposes. But not all the schools agree. Nawawī, less concerned with defenses against a charge of usurpation, permits taking in of a camel found in the desert for purposes of safekeeping until the owner turns up to claim it.[30] The *Hedaya* likewise applauds the caring for stray animals found in the desert, the reason being that it is reasonable in all cases to fear for the safety of the animals.[31]

The notion of trust (*amānah*) carries through the whole law on finding. If someone shows up and merely makes an unvarnished claim to the property, the finder is obliged not to return it.[32] If the finder does give it over and the true owner later shows up, the finder is liable for *darak*, a violation of the reasonable care a fiduciary is obliged to exercise. If, on the other hand, someone makes a plausible claim, with an accurate but only partial description of

[27] Mālik, *Muwaṭṭa'*, trans. Muhammad Rahimuddin (New Delhi, 1981), p. 327. See also *Hedaya*, p. 210, where it is asserted that Shāfi'ī agreed with Mālik on this issue.

[28] Khalīl, *Maliki Law*, p. 270.

[29] Ibid., p. 267 n. 2.

[30] Nawawī, *Minhaj et Talibin*, p. 237.

[31] *Hedaya*, p. 210.

[32] Nawawī, *Minhaj et Talibin*, p. 239; *Hedaya*, p. 212.

the property, the finder is advised to wait a short while in case someone with a better claim presents himself.[33] If a claimant provides a clear description of the property (normally its manner of packaging), the finder must return it forthwith. In doing so, he has acquitted his trust, and, according to the Mālikī school, even if another claimant—the true owner—should appear, the finder is free of any liability.[34] In the Shāfi'ī school, the person to whom the finder in good faith gave the good becomes surety to the finder if the true owner should later make a claim.[35] In the *Hedaya*, the finder may, but is not compelled to, return the good to a claimant who merely describes the packaging. The *qāḍī* cannot compel a return merely on that circumstantial evidence.[36] Showing an even greater concern for the true owner, the *Hedaya* cautions the finder that he will be liable to the true owner if he returns the good to a claimant only on the basis of an external description. The finder can protect himself only by affirmatively demanding and receiving surety from the first claimant. The *Hedaya* compels return of the good only if the true owner can produce judicially sufficient evidence before a *qāḍī*.[37]

As we have seen, a perusal of the Islamic treatment of lost articles indicates that once the good is properly in the hands of the finder it is seen as a form of trust (*amānah*). But there are different kinds of trust relationships. In most cases, during the year of publication, the lost good is the equivalent of a deposit for safe keeping (*wadī'ah*), and the developed notions of this kind of bailment in Islamic law control.[38] If the *res* (i.e., the object itself) of this kind of trust is destroyed, the trustee is not liable unless he was negligent about the care of the object. In *wadī'ah*, the bailor or owner is liable for the maintenance of the object.[39] Thus, the costs of publication of the lost object are charged to

[33] Khalīl, *Maliki Law*, p. 268.

[34] Ibid.

[35] Nawawī, *Minhaj et Talibin*, p. 239.

[36] *Hedaya*, pp. 212–213.

[37] Ibid.

[38] In *wadī'ah*, the owner typically asks another to hold his good safely, while the owner is absent for a while.

[39] Rahim, *Muhammadan Jurisprudence*, p. 318; Khalīl, *Maliki Law*, p. 210; *Hedaya*, p. 208.

the owner.[40] The actual moneys can be obtained from the public treasury as a loan made on behalf of the owner. But some jurists have some problem with the owner being liable for all the expenses in maintaining the object, for he has not consented to the deposit or to being bound by the rules of *wadīʿah*. Nawawī notes the difference of opinion when he says that "some others" would require the owner to recompense the finder only if the finder acts solely as a trustee of a deposit.[41] The Mālikīs have no hesitation in fixing the maintenance costs upon the owner without qualification. They also permit the finder the ordinary production of milk from stray cattle or sheep (but not the offspring, or the wool).[42] The *Hedaya*, on the other hand, once again forces the finder to seek authority and protection from the *qāḍī*. Without the *qāḍī*'s order, maintenance costs are seen as gratuitous on the part of the finder. With the *qāḍī*'s order, the costs become a debt of the owner, unless the found animals can be hired out to pay for their upkeep.[43]

It is at this point that the *Hedaya*'s requirement that the finder produce witnesses to his find makes its point. It will be recalled that witnessing a find protects the finder against a charge of usurpation. The *Hedaya* will not permit a *qāḍī* to fasten a debt on an absent and unconsenting owner, unless in law the good has been shown to have been taken for safekeeping and has not been usurped.[44] Nothing would have been more illogical than to have required an owner to pay for the upkeep of his wrongfully taken property. Thus, *Hedaya* seeks by judicial process to establish beyond doubt the nature of the found good as an object of trust. Only then, and only with the permission of the *qāḍī*, may maintenance costs be assessed against the absent owner.

What happens, however, if the costs of maintenance threaten to exceed the value of the good? The *Hedaya* reasons perceptively that this would "be no kindness" and, in an insightful comment,

[40] Nawawī, *Minhaj et Talibin*, p. 238.

[41] Ibid.

[42] Khalīl, *Maliki Law*, p. 270.

[43] *Hedaya*, pp. 210–211.

[44] Ibid., p. 211. Compare Khalīl (*Maliki Law*, p. 270), who requires that the finder of a lost sheep announce his find when he returns to an inhabited area.

notes that such an event would "eradicate the property."[45] Notice that the bias in favor of the owner remains and the notion of a virtually unbreakable connection between the owner and the physical object. It would be unreasonable to destroy the owner's chance to regain the property by fastening a cost to him equal to its value. The owner would then be buying back his own property, paying its full value, and therefore his original property would in fact have been "eradicated." The *Hedaya* consequently suggests maintenance for but a few days in such case. This gives the owner some chance to reclaim the object. But the author of the *Hedaya* realizes that the only way to safeguard the interests of the owner is to effect a forced sale. Thus the *qāḍī* is instructed to order the found object to be sold and the proceeds kept for the owner "in such a manner that the troves may be virtually preserved, in their value, because the preservation of them in their substance is impractical."[46] Thus the finder is still under a fiduciary duty to pay over the proceeds, but now the *res* of the trust is the proceeds.

If the *qāḍī* has authorized maintenance, and the owner returns to claim the good, the owner is now legally indebted to the finder for the costs. The owner can pay the costs or abandon his claim to the good to the finder.[47] Abandonment extinguishes the debt (*dayn*) and any residue in value of good goes to the finder.[48] If there are no maintenance costs due and the owner, out of gratitude for example, abandons the good to the finder, the transaction is regarded as a gift (*hibah*) of a deposit to a trustee.[49]

If the owner refuses to pay, the finder may detain the good and it becomes a pledge (*rahn*) or collateral. Some categorize the situation as a lien (*ḥabs*) by the finder on the retained good in which case the holder may make beneficial use of it.[50] If characterized as a pledge, the holder still has the trust obligation not to use the good for his own purposes.[51] The finder, if seen as a pledgee, has priority of claim over other creditors and may petition the court

[45] Ibid.
[46] Ibid.
[47] Khalīl, *Maliki Law*, p. 270.
[48] *Hedaya*, p. 631.
[49] Ibid., p. 484.
[50] Schacht, *Introduction*, p. 140.
[51] *Hedaya*, p. 633.

to order its sale to satisfy the debt.[52] Technically, the proceeds themselves also constitute a pledge in this case.[53]

The change in character of the object from deposit to pledge is significant, and not a mere change in wording. Generally, Islamic law regards the pledge as mutually exclusive of any of the trust relationships.[54] The pledge is based on an adversarial situation: a debt is owed. A trust is based on a cooperative venture. A trustee of a deposit is not permitted to indemnify himself from the trust *res* for a debt owed to him by the owner.[55] A pledgee may. In addition, upon demand and refusal, the pledgee may petition the *qāḍī* to imprison the owner until payment is made.[56] Interesting applications of the rule result. If the object perishes as a pledge, a sheep, for example, the debt is extinguished. If, however, the sheep died before the owner came to claim it, he will remain indebted for the maintenance costs, for the sheep had not yet become pledged to the debt.[57]

What happens if the property cannot be maintained for a year? Suppose it is food and will deteriorate quickly. In that case, the finder may dispose of the food. Some jurists allow only giving it in alms.[58] Others permit the finder to consume it,[59] or to sell the food.[60] Eating or selling the food signifies appropriating it for one's own use. It is obviously not an act of safekeeping. Nawawī asserts that if the owner returns and makes a good claim, the finder must make good the loss in kind.[61] It thus becomes a particular form of loan (*qarḍ*) whereby the lender (owner) parts with consumables or fungibles for a later return of payment of same type, quality, and quantity of good.[62] It is not, strictly speaking, a loan, for the thing given is not the very thing returned. It is, rather, an exchange of like kind goods. Thus ownership in the fungible actually passes. It

52 Rahim, *Muhammadan Jurisprudence*, pp. 319–320.
53 See *Hedaya*, pp. 632, 640.
54 Schacht, *Introduction*, p. 140.
55 Khalīl, *Maliki Law*, pp. 211–212.
56 *Hedaya*, p. 631.
57 Ibid., pp. 211, 633.
58 Ibid., p. 209.
59 Khalīl, *Maliki Law*, p. 270.
60 Nawawī, *Minhaj et Talibin*, p. 237.
61 Ibid., p. 238.
62 See Khalīl, *Maliki Law*, p. 172.

is one of the few ways where the finder actually gains technical title to the good with the contractual obligation to give in return a similar amount or weight of the same kind of good.[63]

The *Hedaya* relies on a different legal analogy. It states that although the food or something of insignificant value has been consumed, "it still continues the property of the owner, as transfer to a person unknown is invalid."[64] But indemnification, not payment in kind, is required.[65] Thus, the *Hedaya* sees the event not as a transfer of title (*qarḍ*), but lawful destruction (not usurpation) incurring an obligation for damages. It becomes *darak*, a default in ownership.

Khalīl treats this problem in a third way.[66] He also permits the consumption, but does not require any payment. It is neither *qarḍ* nor *darak*. But even here we do not receive the impression of a loss of title to the finder. Rather, it seems that since the food will naturally deteriorate anyway, the ownership interest would expire of itself. Thus, nothing is being taken from the owner. The finder, consequently, is relieved even of the duty to advertise, for notice of the owner's property when the property is expiring would be notice of nothing.

Suppose the object found is not likely to deteriorate, a head of sheep or cattle, for example, and still the finder consumes it. In that case, the finder is liable, either for a breach of trust or for usurpation depending on the circumstances of the taking. Khalīl, for example, relates the example of a man who finds a lost head of cattle where it could be attacked "by lions or perish for lack of food or water."[67] The finder's obligation is to care for the animal. To kill and eat it makes him liable to the owner for the destruction of his property, a violation of his trust, as would leaving it alone to perish. On the other hand, Khalīl seems to hint that taking and eating an animal found in the wild but not in danger would be usurpation, for there, nature would not have destroyed the animal, but the finder did.[68]

[63] See Milliot, *Droit Musulman*, p. 68.

[64] *Hedaya*, p. 209.

[65] Ibid., p. 208.

[66] Khalīl, *Maliki Law*, p. 270.

[67] Ibid.

[68] Ibid.

Finally, what happens if the owner does not show up to claim his property? In the case of ordinary property, if the owner does not claim the good within the year of publication, the finder may (1) give it in alms, as the agent (*wakīl*) of the owner, subject to the owner repudiating the gift and requiring indemnification from the finder or donee,[69] (2) appropriate it to his own use (only if he is poor, according to the *Hedaya*),[70] or (3) continue to hold it in safekeeping for the owner. In the second case, one is responsible for the value of the good plus compensation for deterioration in value if the owner ever returns.

This brings us to the issue of prescription. In all cases, the title of the owner is never formally extinguished, except in the case of consumables or fungibles where a technical exchange is effectuated (*qarḍ*). In the ordinary case, the law regards a year a long enough time to leave the good in limbo. Property, again, has its ultimate value in its utility. Yet Islamic law balks at extinguishing the title of the owner or leaving him without the right of indemnification for the *darak*. The law resolves the dilemma by allowing the holder to appropriate (*tamallaka*) the good. The appropriation is a form of "taking hold" of the property that is not only permitted but carries with it all the practical rights of alienation, use, and disposition available to owners of freehold *milk* property. *Tamallaka* is the same verb used to signify legitimate occupation of unknown or abandoned property by which it becomes one's own *milk* property. It is a different kind of "taking hold" from that signified by reception by the trustee (*qabḍ amānah*) or the usurper (*qabḍ ḍamān*) where liability for use is incurred.[71] Consequently, the finder (after a year) has appropriated the property and can utilize it as if he were the owner. All actions he makes in regard to the property are legally valid, including transfer. The only thing the holder has not appropriated has been the bare title (*raqabah*). The owner may still return and claim at least the value of the property. Bare ownership remains intact, in theory, forever.

Nonetheless, even the distant possibility of an owner returning apparently proved too chilling on the free use of property. No legal

[69] *Hedaya*, pp. 209–210.
[70] Ibid., p. 213.
[71] C. Chehata, *Etudes de droit musulman*, 2 vols. (Paris, 1973), 2:108–115.

system can abide the title and ultimate control of property to be suspended forever, even if the claim is limited to compensation for the value of the good. Among the schools, the Mālikīs wrote in a three year limitation for claims.[72] In the other schools where the logic of the Sharī'ah ran up against practicality, the Islamic state stopped it. Viewing state acts as part of Islamic law in addition to the Sharī'ah, we find that the state limited the *qāḍī*'s jurisdiction to ordering return of property after a certain amount of time. By this jurisdictional device, an effective statute of limitations was instituted. By operation of law, therefore, the owner was divested of his effective right to regain the property or its value and the finder became owner as against the rest of the world.

We can now summarize our findings on chattel recovery. We have seen that the Islamic jurists dealt with the issue of the return of chattels through the procedural device of ritual and the substantive use of the doctrine of resemblance (*shubhah*). Depending on the manner of taking up another's property, it could be theft (*sariqah*), usurpation (*ghasb*), or trust (*amānah*). Usually the property was held by the finder as a deposit (*wadī'ah*) or, if the owner failed to pay maintenance costs, as a pledge (*rahn*) or a lien (*ḥabs*). If the found property was fungible, it is treated as a loan or exchange of like objects (*qarḍ*). Beneficial use of a deposit or pledge by the finder is treated as a breach of trust (*khiyānah*), although such use of property under lien is permitted. Destruction of found property because of lack of due care creates a *darak*, a default of the owner's rights requiring indemnification to him.

The owner may abandon pledged property to the finder and the legal debt (*dayn*) becomes extinguished. If he abandons property having the status of a deposit, it is a gift (*hibah*). If after a year, the finder gives the property in alms, he does so as the agent (*wakīl*) of the owner. If the finder appropriates (*tamallaka*) the property, he takes it as *milk* property with all rights pertaining thereto except for the bare title (*raqabah*) which, in theory at least, remains with the owner.

When we compare the early English and the Islamic systems, we find that both are interested in the rights of the owner and the need for the possessor to make practical use of the property.

[72] Khalīl, *Maliki Law*, p. 309.

But what is striking is the difference in emphasis. The Sharī'ah insists on the integrity of the relationship between the good and the owner, whereas English law wants to get on with the job once possession is established. In English law, the burden of the argument is on him who wishes to contest possession. More often in the Islamic system, the rules place the burden on the one who is in the way of the owner's rights.

After a few more centuries, the common law caught up with the Islamic law of lost property. On taking up the good, the finder becomes a gratuitous bailee. If he knew or could have discovered the owner, appropriating the goods to himself makes him liable to a charge of larceny and conversion. The owner is liable for the reasonable costs of caring for his property. The theory, however, is one of unjust enrichment. A lien on the found property is not permitted. Notice and publication may be required, depending on the jurisdiction.[73]

The two systems still differ on the primacy of the owner's or the possessor's rights, although in practical terms they come to the same result. In the common law, owners are precluded from seeking the return of their property, traditionally after six years. But commentators insist that common law statutes of limitation are not primarily based on the notion of laches: the failure to prosecute a claim in a timely manner. It is not just to quiet title so that the use of the property can proceed without encumbrance. Rather, the limitation on the owner's right to recover is due to the favored position in the law that *de facto* possession enjoys.[74] It is the title that the adverse possessor claims in common law. In this sense, the common law retains its favored view of possession, while classical Islamic law remained more solicitous of the owner and his rights.

[73] See R. Brown, *The Law of Personal Property*, 3rd ed. (Chicago, 1975), p. 31.

[74] Ibid., p. 35. Note the critique of possessory concepts in D. Reisman, Jr., "Possession and the Law of Finders," *Harvard Law Review* 52 (Cambridge, 1939): 1105–1134.

6

Magisterium and Academic Freedom in Classical Islam and Medieval Christianity

GEORGE MAKDISI

HISTORIANS of the Middle Ages have traced the doctorate of the modern university back to the medieval "licence to teach," called in Latin *licentia docendi*. It conferred upon its holder a teaching authority, the origins of which were deeply rooted in monotheistic religion. Thus it was not a product of the culture of ancient Greece or of ancient Rome. But neither was it a product of Christian Byzantium, which continued the classical education it had inherited from Greece. Nor was it a product of the Christian Latin West, where, as will presently be seen, it was bound to come into conflict with the already existing teaching authority of the ecclesiastical hierarchy.

What were the origins of the doctorate? Where, why, and how did this new phenomenon come into being? What was the extent of its impact on medieval and modern intellectual culture? There can be no real doctorate without academic freedom, for the doctorate, at its origins, consisted of two things: *competence* and the *authority* or *right* to teach. Academic freedom is one of our most prized possessions of academia. The German language coined two technical terms for it: *Lehrfreiheit* and *Lernfreiheit*—that is, the professor's "freedom to teach," and the student's "freedom to learn." Where, how, and why did this academic freedom, long taken for granted, come into being? As this freedom is a university freedom, the prerogative of "academics," and as it is linked to the doctorate in the case of the professor and, in that of the student, to his status as a bona fide member of the university community, our inquiry must go back to the birth of the university and to the forces that brought it into existence. The *licentia docendi* meant an authorization, a "permission to teach." Why should there have been any need for *permission* to teach? Permission from whom? to teach what?

Long before the *licentia docendi* appeared in the medieval Christian university, it had already developed in Islam, with the same designation, expressed in Arabic, word for word: *ijāzat al-tadrīs*, "permission to teach." Thus the doctorate may be said to have traveled through history under three main designations: (1) the classical Islamic-Arabic *ijāzat al-tadrīs*, (2) the medieval Christian-Latin *licentia docendi*, and (3) the modern doctorate. In its first and third periods, this licence shared the same essential attributes, whereas in the middle period, the Christian Latin Middle Ages, it was subjected to some modification required by the circumstances of its new environment.

The modern doctorate involves not only the ascertainment of the doctoral candidate's competence in a given field of knowledge; competence was always a requirement for teaching in any intellectual culture worthy of the name. It involves also the doctor's right to do research and to publish his findings in the classroom, as well as in public through his publications. It is this right that is referred to as "academic freedom" based on the authority to teach, called in Latin, *magisterium*.

Long before the *licentia docendi* appeared upon the scene with its teaching authority, its magisterium, Christianity had developed the councils in which the magisterium devolved upon the college of bishops in union with the pope. This magisterium is defined in the *New Catholic Encyclopedia* as:

> the perennial, authentic, and infallible teaching office committed to the Apostles by Christ and now possessed and exercised by their legitimate successors, the college of bishops in union with the pope.[1]

[1] See J. R. Lerch, "Teaching Authority of the Church (Magisterium)," in *The New Catholic Encyclopedia* (New York: McGraw-Hill, 1967), 13:959–965.

In view of such a definition, how could a professor of theology in a medieval Christian university claim an independent teaching authority? Herein lay the reason for the modification which the licence had to undergo in the Christian West.

Note that early in the universities of the Middle Ages, all of which were Christian, three terms were applied to the teacher. They were synonymous, but each term laid stress on a particular attribute or function. These terms were *master* (in Latin: *magister*), *doctor*, and *professor*. *Master* put the accent on competence; *doctor*, meaning teacher (from the Latin verb *docēre*, to teach), emphasized the teaching and guiding function; and the term *professor* emphasized the professing of one's own personal opinions.

Authority to teach in our day is conferred upon the doctoral candidate who has proven his competence in a field of scholarship to which he has contributed an original thesis. His academic freedom to profess his thesis, his "opinion," is recognized, and the thesis is accepted and applauded for its originality, because it is based on his own intellectual labor. Henceforth, the new doctor, the new professor of original personal opinions based on his personal research, is authorized to profess these opinions freely, unhindered by any outside force, be it religious or secular.

Such, in summary, is the doctorate's authority, the dignity of the doctoral degree, in its third main stage of development. Such also was the doctorate's dignity in its first period of development. For nowhere in the world of the Middle Ages did this phenomenon first come into being except in classical Islam, in the sole field of the religious law. The doctorate, as just described, was that of the Muslim doctor of the law, the jurisconsult, called *faqīh, mujtahid,* and *muftī*. He was a member of one of the Sunni *madhhab*s. These *madhhab*s, as mentioned elsewhere, were the professional guilds of the masters of the religious law. As a master-jurisconsult, in one of these professional guilds of law, the doctor had the authority to profess opinions regarding the law, based on his own personal research. There was no higher authority, religious or secular, which could force him to submit his opinions for approval before professing them.

The licence to teach, an institution of the religious law of Islam, was an *intrusive* element in medieval Christendom. Christianity had no need for it. Its own teaching authority was already in place, solidly established for well over a millennium. The new *licentia docendi* was a source of conflict to the established order of things. It had come to the Christian West along with all the learning that medieval Christendom was avidly importing from Islam by way of knowledge. It had come as part of the tools and methods that were part and parcel of that knowledge.

The remark was previously made that this licence of religious origin was not the product of ancient Greece or ancient Rome. Could then this licence, deeply rooted in religious law, have developed in Christianity or in Judaism? The religions of Judaism, Christianity, and Islam share the same attribute of monotheism, thanks to their concept of a personal, omniscient, and omnipotent God. However, in addition to being of religious origin, the licence to teach was the product of an individualistic system; as such, it could not have developed in an ecclesiastical hierarchy or in any other system of authority higher than that of the individual doctors. It was specifically the product of a guild, a group of individuals who were subjected to the same specialized training and whose authority, once granted, was independent of all outside forces, and above which there was no other authority. Consequently, it could not have developed in Christianity with its ecclesiastical hierarchy, or in Judaism where the higher authority of the Gaon was recognized, head of the Academy in Babylon (Iraq), "the major seat of learning and authority in the Jewish world."[2]

It is true that the functions of the Jewish rabbi and the Muslim *muftī* were parallel; but they were parallel only up to a certain point. Judaism did not encourage the layman to seek out more than one rabbi when in need of an answer to a question on the religious law. The layman went to the highest authority in his locality and ventured no further. In Islam, however, the layman was free to consult a number of *muftī*s, and he was free to make his own choice from among the opinions he received. This

[2] J. Mann, *Texts and Studies in Jewish History and Literature*, vol. 1 (Cincinnati, 1931), p. 87 f., *apud* T. Groner, *The Legal Methodology of Hai Gaon*, Brown Judaic Studies 66 (Chico, California: Scholars Press, 1985), p. 10.

distinction between the two systems is crucial, as will be seen presently.

Nor could the doctorate, as described, have originated in Shīʿite Islam, which may be described as a "church of authority" in contrast to Sunnī Islam, a "church of consensus." In Shīʿism, the teaching authority was vested in the *imāms*; they represented the highest authority. Any religious doctrine, to be regarded as authentic, had to be referred back to the authority of one of the *imāms*.[3]

The teaching authority inherent in the doctoral degree, as known in modern times, derives, in its origins, from a religious system fundamentally *consensual*; that is to say that the final criterion of a doctrine's orthodoxy was the unanimous consensus of the doctors of the law, considered as equals. Here is how the system worked in Sunnī Islam; it differed significantly from that of Shīʿite Islam, as well as from those of Judaism and Christianity.

The road leading to consensus began with the layman soliciting a legal opinion from the jurisconsult on a point of religious law. Each of the elements of this process was designated by a technical term. The layman, when soliciting an opinion, did so in his capacity as *mustaftī* (i.e., one who seeks an opinion from a *muftī* on a point of law). The legal opinion he solicited was called a *fatwā*. The jurisconsult, in his capacity as a professor of legal opinions, was known as the *muftī*. And the process itself, when viewed from the position of the soliciting layman, was called *istiftā'* (i.e., the solicitation of legal opinions) and, when viewed from that of the jurisconsult, *iftā'* (i.e, the issuing of legal opinions). The legal opinion, when received, did not obligate the layman to accept. It was only a legal *opinion*, handed down by a jurisconsult; it was not a legal *decision*, handed down by a magistrate. The layman was free to solicit yet a number of other opinions, from as many jurisconsults, on the same point of religious law. These opinions were generally presented in written form, in answer to written requests.

[3] See I. Goldziher, *Vorlesungen über den Islam* (Heidelberg: C. Winter 1910, reprint 1958), p. 215; French translation by F. Arin, *Le dogme et la loi de l'Islam* (Paris: P. Geuthner, 1920), p. 215; English translation by A. Hamori and R. Hamori, *Introduction to Islamic Theology and Law* (Princeton University Press, 1981), the chapter on "Sects," last paragraph of section 10, p. 191.

With all the opinions now laid out before him for consideration, the layman was free to choose the one to follow. This practice was much the same as the modern day practice of soliciting second and third opinions from medical practitioners; the only limitation being, in both cases, the size of one's purse.

When the layman made his eventual choice from among the opinions received, his choice was referred to as *taqlīd*. This technical term has usually been misunderstood in the case of the layman. In reality, the term has two quite opposed meanings. In the case of the *mustaftī*-layman, the term meant "investing with authority," "clothing with authority." The choice he made clothed with authority the opinion chosen. It was his right to practice *taqlīd*. Commendatory when applied to him, *taqlīd* was, on the other hand, a term of disapprobation when applied to the *muftī*-jurisconsult. A *muftī* had no right to "clothe with authority" the opinion of another *muftī*. Therefore, in his case, *taqlīd* was considered "servile imitation." A servile jurisconsult was one who had abdicated his authority, violating his sacred mission and the process leading to consensus. He eventually lost his reputation and was no longer considered an authoritative jurisconsult. An authoritative jurisconsult was one who, conscious of his sacred mission, based his opinion on his personal research, an activity called technically *ijtihād* (literally, to exert unsparingly one's effort, to do one's utmost). As a practitioner of that activity he was called *mujtahid*, an authoritative jurisconsult-theologian.

If two laymen were to choose, from among the opinions they received on the same point of doctrine or practice, diametrically opposed opinions, each would be free to follow the opinion chosen, though neither of the opposing opinions had the sanction of consensus. Pending that eventual sanction for one or the other opinion, each would have the sanction of the layman's *taqlīd*, investing it with authority, in the meantime. Orthodoxy thus functioned on two levels: (1) the initial level of the layman's *taqlīd*, and (2) the final level of the consensus of the jurisconsults, the doctors of the religious law.

The jurisconsult, in arriving at his opinion, did so on the basis of his own individual research (*ijtihād*), based on his own interpretation of the sources. He performed his task alone, not as part of a committee of jurisconsults, though the result of his research could well be in agreement with that of another, or others, on the same question. He was not bound by the opinions of any jurisconsults, past or present, not even by those of his own guild of law (*madhhab*). More than this, he could not follow even one of his own past opinions on the same, or a similar, problem; he had to arrive at a fresh opinion resulting from a fresh effort of research. He was free to form his own personal opinion independently of all outside forces. No power or authority could legitimately coerce him to arrive at a predetermined one. Not only was he free and independent to practice his research and proclaim his findings, he was encouraged to do so by a promise of reward in the Hereafter. A prophetic tradition (*ḥadīth*) rewarded the jurisconsult for his research, even if eventually he was proven to have been mistaken; he was doubly rewarded if he proved to be right. Another such tradition held every jurisconsult to be right, in the sense that he had discharged his obligation conscientiously to the best of his ability.

These two freedoms, the layman's and that of the doctor of the religious law, could not exist in a system that had an ecclesiastical hierarchy, with councils and synods to determine orthodoxy. Islam had neither councils nor synods; it therefore had to determine its orthodoxy through a process consistent with its own circumstances. As the individual answers of the doctors of the law to the questions of the laymen gave rise to conflicting opinions; as the doctors, in relation to one another, stood on an equal footing; and as there was no higher religious authority of last resort to appeal to for solutions to controversies, the method adopted was that of *consensus*, that is, the consensus of the doctors of the religious law. But Islam had no formal organization for the determination of consensus; indeed there could never be certainty that any organized effort to collect the opinions of the doctors could be complete. Yet the consensus had to be unanimous; even one authoritative dissent could vitiate it. In view of such considerations, the consensus had to be determined retroactively and negatively. Consensus was determined by whether authoritative doctors had raised their voices in the past against a certain doctrine. In the absence of a negative opinion, the doctrine was considered as having been accepted as orthodox. *Dissent was therefore the most important single element in the process of determining orthodoxy.*

In Islam, dissent was not merely allowed, or simply encouraged, it was virtually prescribed as an obligation incumbent upon each and every Muslim. It was *a fortiori* incumbent on each and every doctor of the law, when, in conscience, he considered an opinion to be at variance with the truth as he saw it. In dissenting, the jurisconsult was following the precept of "ordering the good and prohibiting evil." This precept not only enabled him to proclaim his dissent, even when his opinion was not solicited by a layman, it enjoined him to do so, discouraging his silence. If through timidity, apathy, or negligence he remained silent, his silence was taken as tacit approval (*taqrīr*); it had positive value. Between consent and dissent, the system made no room for abstentions.

The importance of dissent in Islam explains the existence of, and the role played by, one of the most prolific genres of Islamic legal literature, called "dissent" (*khilāf*). This literature appeared very copious to the eminent Islamist Ignaz Goldziher, at the end of the nineteenth century. Sensing its importance, he felt the need to draw attention to it, calling for the detailed study of its bibliography.[4] Over half a century later, Franz Rosenthal rightly reiterated the need, reminding Islamists that Goldziher's call had not yet been answered.[5]

At the outset, one may well be puzzled by this prolific legal literature that "codified," so to speak, *dissenting opinions* on matters of doctrine and practice. The uncertainty disappears, however, when one grasps the function of dissent in the determination of orthodoxy. *Khilāf*-works were in fact all that Islam needed to determine orthodoxy on the two levels previously mentioned.

[4] I. Goldziher, *Die Zahiriten, ihr Lehrsystem und ihre Geschichte* (Leipzig: O. Schulze, 1884), p. 37 n. 1; English translation by W. Behn, *The Zahiris: Their Doctrine and Their History* (Leiden: E.J. Brill, 1971), p. 36 n. 1. In the Arabic of Goldziher's note, read *jarrada* instead of *jawada*, a misprint repeated in the Arabic of Behn's English translation.

[5] F. Rosenthal, in Ibn Khaldun, *The Muqaddimah: An Introduction to History*, 3 vols., Bollingen Series 43 (New York: Pantheon Books, 1958), 3:30 n. 289. On *khilāf*, see G. Makdisi, *The Rise of Colleges: Institutions of Learning in Islam and the West* (Edinburgh University Press, 1981), esp. p. 107 ff., and s.v., index.

The initial level of orthodoxy consisted of the contrary opinions regarding a given doctrine or practice, and the second level of consensus was determined by the absence of dissenting opinions. This explains why Islam does not have a legal literature "codifying" orthodox doctrines. The *khilāf*-literature performs that function negatively. *Khilāf*-books, though negative in aspect, were positive in their effect. They served to define orthodoxy on the two levels previously mentioned: (1) if the question was cited with conflicting opinions, this meant that no consensus was reached, and that the opinions were therefore equally orthodox on the initial level, and (2) if the question was cited with only one opinion, the absence of conflict meant that the opinion was orthodox on the level of consensus. In the first case, the jurisconsult-author of the *khilāf*-work could give preponderance to one opinion over another or others; but the layman was left with his freedom of choice. In the second case, the absence of authoritative conflict indicated consensus.

With the development of the professional guilds of religious law, and the institutionalization of legal studies, no longer could any student of law claim mastery of his subject arbitrarily. He now had to be formally educated, pass qualifying examinations, and receive the licence proclaiming him doctor of the law. The examination consisted in his presenting a series of theses, that is, opinions, and defending them successfully. The examination simulated the very function for which he had been trained: namely, the function of the jurisconsult, a doctor of the law consulted by members of the Muslim community on matters of doctrine and practice. Besides issuing legal opinions as part of his teaching function, he had to prepare himself to defend them against possible opposing opinions of other jurisconsults. This function required training in the art of disputation.

Issuing legal opinions and defending them was in fact his primordial function, the one he was certain to perform. For then, as today among many of our new graduates with doctor's degrees, the new doctor did not always succeed in finding a teaching post. But unlike today's new doctor, he still had the authority to profess his opinions, and he was paid for them by the soliciting faithful. This authority inhered in his position as *muftī*. The full title of his authorization was "the licence to teach law and profess legal opinions" (*al-ijāzah bi-al-tadrīs wa-al-iftā'*) For this professorship of legal opinions he was granted a lifetime tenure, responsible to God alone. His competence to teach, to do research, and proclaim his findings in legal opinions and publications, were matters strictly within the control of the individual doctors of the law, acting in the context of the professional guilds of law, free and independent of all outside forces. He received his authorization from his teacher, a doctor of the law in one of the guilds. The governing power had no say in the matter whatsoever.

The give-and-take of disputation, of argumentation and debate, was vital to the Islamic process of determining orthodoxy. Islamic orthodoxy owed its determination to the free play of opinions of the doctors of juridical theology. In Islam, the method of disputation was thus not a mere school exercise. On the other hand, that is exactly what it was in the medieval universities of Christendom. Here, where Christianity had its councils and synods to determine orthodoxy, the method of disputation was merely a school exercise. It had come from Islam as part of the influx of Arabic learning, the translation and assimilation of which lay at the basis of the rise of universities in the Christian West. But the method of disputation was soon to perform in Christianity the function for which it was created in Islam. That is to say that Christianity was to witness the rise of another teaching authority in its midst, another magisterium, which was exercised, not by the college of bishops in union with the pope, but rather, as in Islam, by the doctors of theology.

From its beginnings in Christian antiquity down to the High Middle Ages, the magisterium consisted in the faithful transmission of the teachings received, and apostolic succession was the form and the guarantee of the tradition, with the bishops often performing the role of theologians. With the rise of universities in the Middle Ages, and the advent of the method of disputation, later to be called the "scholastic method," a magisterium came into existence which paralleled the pastoral magisterium and threatened to outclass the authority of the bishops. St. Thomas Aquinas distinguished between these two magisteria: a pastoral magisterium, which he called the *magisterium cathedrae pastoralis* or *pontificalis*, and the *magisterium cathedrae magistralis*. The first was a preeminence of authority, the second, a personal competence publicly recognized. According to Saint Thomas, the pastoral magisterium has jurisdictional authority behind it; it is concerned with preaching and public order in the church. This magisterium, which belongs exclusively to the bishops in union with the pope, is the only authoritative magisterium.[6] The professorial magisterium is concerned with academic questions; the professors teach by knowledge and argument rather than by their official status. Their conclusions are no more valid than the evidence they are able to adduce. Though they may be valid, they do not become authoritative unless and until they are adopted by the pastoral magisterium. By itself, the professorial magisterium is unauthoritative. The forms of the magisterium and its relation to the doctors have been studied by the French theologian Yves Congar, who also studied the semantic history of the term magisterium.[7]

Over a century before the excellent studies of Father Congar, back at the mid-point of the nineteenth century, Charles Thurot had drawn attention to this phenomenon, in his work on education at the University of Paris in the Middle Ages. Here is a translation of his text on this subject:

> The Faculty of Theology assumed the power of passing final judgment on whether a religious doctrine was true or false, orthodox or heretical. The bishop and in the last resort the Pope could only exercise judicial and coercive power; they simply applied the punishment. Indeed it was necessary to give a theological reason for the condemnation; and this was impossible without having recourse to the science of theology, that is to say, to its depositories, the doctors of theology. Accordingly, the pope himself could not pass final judgment in matters of dogma. Such was the system applied by Peter of Ailly, in 1387, before Pope Clement VII.

[6] See A. Dulles, "What is Magisterium?" in *Origins* 6 (1976): 85.

[7] See Y. Congar, "Pour une histoire sémantique du terme 'magisterium'," *Revue des Sciences Philosophiques et Théologiques* 60 (1976): 85–98; "Bref historique des formes du 'magistère' et de ses relations avec les docteurs," Ibid., pp. 99–112, esp. p. 103, and the summary on p. 98.

This situation being a curious development in the Christian world, Charles Thurot goes on to explain:

> These pretensions were not illusory. Composed of regulars of all the orders and of seculars from all the nations, the Faculty of Theology of the University of Paris was, so to speak, the only one. No other university was composed of more members and of more distinguished doctors. All the nations were admitted to the Sorbonne; all the religious orders were represented in Paris by the elite of their Brethren. It looked as though there could not be found anywhere else a more impartial and more enlightened tribunal.[8]

Thus we witness in Christianity an interesting phenomenon: a metamorphosis of a method that was, in the Christian West, strictly scholastic, transferred out of the realm of a school exercise and charged with the strictly ecclesiastical role of determining orthodoxy. This function of the scholastic method was in essence Islamic, necessary in a religion with no ecclesiastical hierarchy; it did not belong in a religion endowed with such a hierarchy and charged alone with the "teaching authority," the magisterium.

The substance of the theologian's magisterium consisted in his scholarly *competence*; the substance of the pastoral magisterium consisted in the *jurisdictional authority* of the bishops. In the period before the rise of universities, magisterium simply meant the post, function or activity of someone in the position of *magister*, that is, a scientific competence in a definite field. But with the rise of universities, in the latter part of the twelfth and early part of the thirteenth centuries, Islamic seeds were planted for what was soon to be become a second magisterium in Christianity, that of the professors of theology. Such was the situation described by Charles Thurot and Yves Congar.

This phenomenon was something new; it had never existed before. This role of the theologians reaches its climax at the Council of Basel, a climax which Congar calls *malsain* (pernicious). At

[8] See Ch. Thurot, *De l'organisation de l'enseignement dans l'Université de Paris au Moyen Age* (Paris, 1850), p. 160; G. Makdisi, *Rise of Colleges*, p. 279; idem, "Freedom in Islamic Jurisprudence: *Ijtihad, Taqlid*, and Academic Freedom," in *La Notion de liberté au Moyen Age: Islam, Byzance, Occident*, The Penn-Paris-Dumbarton Oaks colloquia, IV: Session des 12–15 Octobre 1982, ed. G. Makdisi et al. (Paris: Les Belles Lettres, 1985), pp. 79–88, esp. p. 85.

this council, the 34th session held on June 25, 1439, there were 300 doctors of theology, as compared with only 13 priests and 7 bishops! This, says Father Congar, explains the importance that Luther placed later on his title of doctor (i.e., his function and mission as doctor). Even the level-headed theologian Godefroid de Fontaines (d. 1306) upheld the right of the doctors of theology *not* to follow the episcopal decision, but rather to "determine" (a technical scholastic term meaning to resolve, to arrive at solutions) in those matters belonging to the jurisdiction of the pope, because, in his words, "ea quae condita sunt a papa possunt esse dubia" (those matters that are established by the Pope can be uncertain).[9]

In Christianity, conflict over the magisterium came about *after* the rise of universities with their doctors of theology. In Islam, that conflict took place *before* the rise of the colleges of religious law. In Islam, the magisterium flowed from the Prophet Muhammad to his disciples (*aṣḥāb, ṣaḥābah*), and to their followers in succession, in their capacities as teachers of the religious law. The conflict in Islam occurred after the introduction, translation, and assimilation of Greek learning from Byzantium. It came to a head with al-Ma'mūn. This caliph espoused the philosophical theologians' thesis on the Qur'ān as being the created word of God, against the juridical theologians who believed the Qur'ān to be coeternal with God. A fifteen-year inquisition (*miḥnah*) ended in mid-ninth century with the reversal of caliphal policy under al-Mutawakkil. Sensitive to popular sentiment, this caliph opted in favor of the traditionalist juridical theologians.

The failure of the rationalist-inspired inquisition had the effect of reestablishing the doctors of the religious law squarely in the seat of authority. Solidly settled in that position, they created their professional guilds of law, the *madhhab*s, established their program of legal studies in exclusive colleges of law, and systematically excluded philosophical theology from the curriculum. The colleges were charitable trust foundations which encompassed the endowed buildings and the farmlands and other properties whose revenues paid the beneficiaries, namely, the

[9] See Y. Congar, *Revue des Sciences Philosophiques et Théologiques* 60 (1976): 103–104.

teachers, the students, and the administrators. The doctors of the law were the authors of the law of the charitable trust, as well as its interpreters and its guardians. Nothing was to be the object of a charitable trust which could be construed as inimical to the tenets of Islam, and the doctors of the law were those who decided what was inimical to those tenets. The institutions which had served as learning centers for the philosophical theologians, called "House of Wisdom" (*dār al-ḥikmah*), "House of Learning" (*dār al-'ilm*), and so on, gradually disappeared in favor of traditionalist institutions called "House of the Koran" (*dār al-Qur'ān*) and "House of the Prophetic Traditions" (*dār al-ḥadīth*).

Thus Islam, and later Christianity, experienced conflict over the question of the legitimate teaching authority, the magisterium. In the one case, the authority to teach was transmitted from the prophet, in the other, from Christ. In Islam, there being no ecclesiastical hierarchy, the Prophet's successors were the scholars of the religious law; in Christianity, the successors of Christ were the bishops and the pope, that is, the ecclesiastical hierarchy. Conflict occurred in both cases when a foreign element was introduced. In Islam, this element was Greek philosophy, a pagan element in the midst of a monotheistic religion; in Christianity, it was the doctorate, Islamic in origin, a new teaching authority superimposed on the legitimate authority already in place. Islam, lacking councils and synods, had need for a "teaching authority," and the doctors supplied it; Christianity, already endowed with a teaching authority, had no such need.

In Christianity, conflict over the magisterium arose *after* the rise of the guilds, that is, the university and its doctors. In Islam, that conflict arose *before* the guilds of law came into existence. It was the conflict itself, between the philosophical theologians, on the one hand, and the juridical theologians, on the other, that led to the creation of the guilds of law. These guilds gave their members not only *autonomy*, but also made it possible for them to *exclude* all undesirable elements, among these the philosophical theologians. In Christianity, the cause of the conflict was the extraneous, intrusive element: the Islamic doctorate with its scholastic method. To understand the impact of this doctorate's intrusion upon the intellectual culture of Christianity in the Middle Ages, it would be well to sketch briefly the doctorate's development from its origins in Islam.

The doctorate was granted in Islam after an examination involving the method called the "method of disputation," in Arabic, *ṭarīqat al-naẓar* or *al-munāẓarah*, a term humanists of the Italian Renaissance were to dub derisively the "scholastic method." It was previously stated that three terms were used to designate the person licensed to teach, namely, *doctor*, *professor*, and *master*, each of these terms emphasizing a particular attribute or function. In Arabic the three terms were *mudarris*, *muftī* and *faqīh*. The parallel terms *mudarris* and *doctor* emphasized the teaching function; those of *muftī* and *professor*, the function of professing opinions; and those of *master* and *faqīh*, competence. The mastership was the highest rank the guild could give, and the term *faqīh* meant one possessed of a masterful understanding of the religious law.

The only teaching guilds in Islam were the guilds of law. The only field of knowledge for which an authorization to teach was necessary—in other words, the only field in which a doctorate was required—was the field of religious law. In the whole field of Islamic education, in the three major divisions of Islam's classification of knowledge, namely, the Islamic religious sciences, the foreign (Greek) sciences, and the whole array of the Arabic literary arts, *there was no other doctorate*. The reason for this is simple: the magisterium, the "teaching authority" was not involved in fields other than the religious law. A grammarian did not need a religious authority to teach grammar; hence, there were no doctors of grammar. The grammarian was free to teach grammar without a licence for his field. He did, however, have a licence for one or more specific books. But this was an entirely different kind of licence. Its function was to guarantee the authenticity of the book's contents, on the basis that it was studied under the author himself or under a professor belonging to a chain of authoritative transmission reaching back to the author. Such was also the case with all other fields of knowledge, especially the religious sciences and the ancillary literary arts.

Transplanted from Islamic soil, the doctorate had to become acclimated to its new environment, in which a teaching authority already long-established resided in the ecclesiastical hierarchy. As in Islam, teaching in Christendom was also a religious function; therefore the granting of the licence to teach became an ecclesiastical act. The licence had to be obtained from the chancellor of the cathedral church. Historians of the medieval university tell of the protracted conflict between the chancellor and the university professors. Even when the professors finally escaped from the control of the chancellor, they did so only to come under that of the pope. The professors did not achieve that complete autonomy enjoyed by their colleagues in Islam, the professors of the guilds of law, and the failure was, of course, predictable. They failed not only in Paris, but also in the University of Bologna, where Honorius III in 1219 enjoined that the doctorate could not be granted without the consent of the Archdeacon of Bologna. Authority belonged to the ecclesiastical hierarchy alone; the university professors of theology taught by virtue of the hierarchy's mandate. Thus, in the Christian West there was a distinction between the two concepts of pastoral authority and professorial competence. In Islam, however, where there was no ecclesiastical hierarchy, authority and competence were *both* invested in the professors of the religious law, an investiture which set them apart from all other professors.

Classical Islam produced an intellectual culture that influenced the Christian West in university scholarship. It furnished the factor which gave rise to the university, namely, the scholastic method, with its concomitants the doctorate and academic freedom. This freedom can only have existed in an intellectual culture in which all the "teachers" involved were considered equal in their authority or right to teach. It could not have existed where the teaching authority belonged exclusively to an ecclesiastical hierarchy. Academic freedom in classical Islam, in the jurisconsult and the layman, is coterminous with the modern concept for that freedom in the university professor and the student.[10]

[10] It should be said, parenthetically, that the student's freedom to learn ought to be understood in its original meaning as the freedom to exercise one's critical judgment regarding the opinions of the professors, an exercise which is a basically essential part of the university student's education in developing his critical sense, in anticipation of his eventual accession to the freedom to *profess*. Student freedom,

In modern university scholarship, as in the religious scholarship of classical Islam, "orthodoxy" is consensual; that is to say that the "orthodoxy" (so to speak) of the results of scholarly research is judged by the consensus of the community of scholars themselves. Dissent plays a vital role in these two intellectual cultures. But in a religion where the legitimate teaching authority is vested in an ecclesiastical hierarchy, dissent is bound to be considered, in the words of Yves Congar, as leading to heresy, and eventually to separation from the communion of the faithful.

Classical Islam, having no ecclesiastical hierarchy, had to develop a mechanism for the determination of orthodoxy. That mechanism was scholarship in the religious law, based on the method of disputation, with the arbiter being the unanimous consensus of the doctoral scholars of the law. Its learning and methods influenced the medieval university, and through that institution, university scholarship in modern times. The roots of the doctorate are firmly implanted in the legal scholarship of classical Islam, in its scholarly research, and in the freedom of its jurisconsults and laymen. That is to say that classical Islam's legacy in the realm of intellectual culture is to be found, among other things, in the doctorate and the academic freedom of professor and student. These have come to modern times from the medieval university, which owed them in turn to classical Islam.

in this context, is therefore not meant as a justification for the elective system. That system was strictly a local development, the credit for which may only be claimed by Harvard's President Elliot, and from the pernicious effects of which university faculties have for some time been at pains to find remedial relief.

7

An Inquiry into Islamic Influences during the Formative Period of the Common Law

JOHN MAKDISI

IN TWELFTH-CENTURY ENGLAND, land law was largely focused on the feudal relationship between lord and tenant. This was not the landlord-tenant relationship we know today. Feudal society was a pyramidal structure wherein a tenant enjoyed lifetime possession of a piece of property in return for services he performed for his lord, who in turn owed services to a higher lord, who in turn owed services ultimately to the king himself.[1] The tenant could not give his land away or sell it without the permission of his lord, and if he refused to perform services, the lord could remove him from the land after a judgment by fellow tenants in the lord's court.[2]

In a series of reforms beginning in the middle of the twelfth century, this service-oriented relationship began to break down. King Henry II, who reigned from 1154 to 1189, sought to establish a sounder government in England by creating new legal procedures

The research for this article was generously funded by a grant from the Cleveland-Marshall Fund.

[1] For a discussion of the services and incidents to which a lord was entitled, see A. J. Casner and W. B. Leach, *Cases and Text on Property*, 3rd ed. (Boston: Little, Brown & Co., 1984), pp. 191–194.

[2] See S. F. C. Milsom, *Historical Foundations of the Common Law*, 2d ed. (Toronto: Butterworth's, 1981), p. 104; F. Pollock and F. W. Maitland, *The History of English Law*, 2nd ed. (Cambridge: University Press, 1898; reissued 1968), 1:354.

as an alternative to traditional procedures he found inadequate.[3] The effect was to diminish the authority of lordship[4] and ultimately to pave the way for a new economic relationship in society characterized by individual ownership. Chief among King Henry's accomplishments in this regard was the assize of novel disseisin.

The assize of novel disseisin played a major role in shaping the course of the common law.[5] As an action to recover land that had been usurped,[6] it provided landowners with security under the king's law by substituting trial by jury for trial by battle, by shortening the time period for obtaining recovery, and by providing easier access to the courts.[7] For all its importance,

[3] See W. L. Warren, *Henry II* (Berkeley and Los Angeles, University of California Press, 1973), pp. 360–361.

[4] Milsom, *Historical Foundations*, p. 124.

[5] In fact, Professor H. Berman in *Law and Revolution: The Formation of the Western Legal Tradition* (Cambridge, Mass.: Harvard University Press, 1983), p. 457, states: "Henry II created the English common law by legislation [such as the assize of novel disseisin] establishing judicial remedies in the royal courts."

[6] Disseisin, the term used in the common law, is a usurpation of the right of seisin. Seisin describes the feudal concept of ownership whereby a person held land under claim of a freehold estate. The term is derived from the French *saisir*, meaning to take hold of.

[7] D. Sutherland, *The Assize of Novel Disseisin* (Oxford: Clarendon, 1973), pp. 2–3. Enacted sometime between 1155 and 1166, the assize of novel disseisin remained an extraordinarily vital institution for over two hundred years. Ibid., p. 1. It was brought in the king's court. Twelve jurors would be picked to inspect the property and learn the facts of the case. These investigative jurors would then declare the facts to the court which would determine, on the basis of the jurors' declarations, whether the plaintiff had been disseised (that is, removed) unjustly and without judgment within a particular time period by the person alleged. Warren, *Henry II*, pp. 338–341. The assize of novel disseisin soon attracted many plaintiffs seeking recovery of their land to the king's court. It was summary in nature and more rational than the cumbersome and oft-times dangerous traditional action brought on a writ of right. This latter action was proprietary in nature. It was brought in the lord's court and required the establishment by the plaintiff of proof of ownership. If the evidence was not strong enough to constitute a proof, the defendant might be required to support his claim by trial by battle, a bloody device introduced in England by the Normans after the Conquest of 1066. See W. Holdsworth, *A History of English Law*, 7th ed. (London: Methuen, 1956), 1:299–312; Pollock and Maitland, *History*, 2:598–603, 604–610. Battle required the plaintiff and defendant, or their champions, to engage in single combat on the theory that God's intervention would give victory to the side of justice. See R. Bartlett, *Trial by Fire and Water: The Medieval Judicial Ordeal* (Oxford: Clarendon, 1986), pp. 103–104, 108–113, 115–116. It is no surprise that this form of justice soon gave way before the investigative jury of the assize of novel disseisin. Trial by battle was irrational. (See J. Makdisi, "Formal

a mystery has remained throughout the centuries as to its place of origin. Henry of Bracton in a much-quoted passage from the thirteenth century claimed that the assize had been "thought out and invented through many wakeful nights."[8] Yet where did King Henry and his advisors glean the idea for this assize? Even today it is asserted that "the assize was created in the reign of Henry II, but beyond that basic fact almost nothing about its origin is agreed on anymore."[9]

It is commonly believed that the origins of the assize may be traceable to the interdict *unde vi*,[10] a similar action in Roman law to recover possession of property.[11] There were features which the English assize and the Roman interdict shared in common. For example, both actions made it illegal to remove an owner from his property by force. Property governed by the two actions included land and fixtures but not movables, although movable property on land which was usurped could be recovered along with the income the land had produced during the period of usurpation. Also, the plaintiff who had been ejected must have been in actual possession.[12]

Rationality in Islamic Law and the Common Law," *Cleveland St. L. Rev.* 34 (1985-86): 98, for a discussion of the concept of rationality.) The assize, on the other hand, offered an effective means to protect tenants against unjust takings by their lords. See Sutherland, *Assize*, pp. 30–31, 90–97, citing Milsom with approval.

8 S. Thorne, trans., *Bracton on the Laws and Customs of England* (folio 164b) (Cambridge, Mass.: Belknap Press, 1977), 3:25. See Sutherland, *Assize*, p. 6; Pollock and Maitland, *History*, 1:146.

9 Sutherland, *Assize*, p. 5. Indeed, Lady Stenton, speaking more generally of the judicial development of this period, has stated, "It is probable that the early stages by which the momentous results of Henry II's reign were achieved will never be adequately recalled." D. Stenton, *English Justice between the Norman Conquest and the Great Charter, 1066–1215* (London: Allen & Unwin, 1964), p. 26.

10 T. Sandars, ed., *The Institutes of Justinian* (4.15.6) (Westport: Greenwood Press, 1922), p. 495; T. Mommsen and P. Kreuger, eds., A. Watson, trans., *The Digest of Justinian* (Philadelphia: University of Pennsylvania Press, 1985), 4:582–588.

11 See Sutherland, *Assize*, p. 22; Pollock and Maitland, *History*, 2:48, 52. A canonist action similar to the assize of novel disseisin was the *actio spolii*. Although Pollock and Maitland, *History*, 2:48, believe that the assize was suggested by the *actio spolii*, Sutherland, *Assize*, p. 21, n. 5, discounts the influence of this action on the formation of the assize because "it cannot have been much earlier than the assize and may have been later." See also S. Milsom, "Select Bibliography and Notes," in Pollock and Maitland, *History* 1:lxxxvii.

12 Sutherland, *Assize*, pp. 22–23. One feature not shared with the interdict was the assize's investigative jury, whose origins have been ascribed to the Frankish *inquisitio*,

Yet there was a major discrepancy between the two institutions which makes the comparison unsatisfactory. This discrepancy appeared in the type of person protected by each of these two actions. If an owner took land back from a non-owner, the non-owner could not recover the land in an action on the English assize if the owner could prove his ownership.[13] Of course, the assize was a summary action and proof of ownership was allowed only if it did not delay the proceedings;[14] yet such proof was allowed. In the same type of case under the Roman interdict *unde vi*, the non-owner won the suit. The owner was not allowed to offer any proof of ownership because ownership was not a defense. The interdict protected possession as an end in itself. Justinian's *Institutes* describes the situation as follows:

By [the interdict *unde vi*] he who has expelled him is forced to restore to him the possession, although the person to whom the interdict is given has himself taken by force, clandestinely, or as a concession, the possession from the person who has expelled him.[15]

---

the prerogative rights of the Frankish kings. Pollock and Maitland, *History*, 1:140–143; Holdsworth, *History*, 1:312–313; C. Haskins, *Norman Institutions* (Cambridge, Mass.: Harvard University Press, 1918), pp. 196–197.

[13] This point has been clarified only recently by Sutherland. Before Sutherland, Maitland interprets Bracton to hold that an owner was not permitted to eject a non-owner from possession after a lapse of about four days because such a disseisin would be "unjust" in the sense of "without process of law." Pollock and Maitland, *History*, 2:49–52; F. Maitland, "The Beatitude of Seisin," *Law Quarterly Rev.* 4 (1888): 38. That is, if an owner lost possession to a usurper and then retook possession more than four days later, the usurper would have an action to recover the land under the assize, according to Maitland. This conclusion has been largely refuted by Sutherland who, after months of searching the records of thirteenth-century courts for just such a case, could not find a single record where the four-day rule was applied. He in fact concluded from many of the assize cases that he read that the law was generally permissive of the owner's right to retake land on his own, provided that he acted without too much delay. Thus, if an owner was sued for retaking his own land from a usurper, ownership was a defense. Sutherland, *Assize*, pp. 77, 97–104, 118–121. See O. Holmes, *The Common Law*, ed. M. Howe (Boston: Little, Brown & Co., 1963), p. 166. *Contra*, Berman, *Law and Revolution*, p. 455.

[14] Sutherland, *Assize*, pp. 19–20. There were also restraints on the methods by which a disseisin might be effectuated. For example, weapons could not be used or displayed and a possessor could not be driven out by direct force. Ibid., p. 124.

[15] *The Institutes of Justinian* (4.15.6), p. 495. See B. Nicholas, *An Introduction to Roman Law* (Oxford: Clarendon, 1962), p. 109; *The Digest of Justinian*, 4:582–588. For a contrary view, see Berman, *Law and Revolution*, p. 454.

The scope of protection accorded possession under the Roman interdict was absolute: a possessor was protected even against repossession by the owner. The scope of protection accorded possession under the English assize was circumscribed: a possessor was not protected against repossession by the owner. The difference in function between the Roman and English actions is clear. The Roman interdict emphasized the maintenance of peace and quiet.[16] The English assize emphasized the protection of property rights.[17]

The assize protected property rights by providing a summary means for an owner to recover property which another had usurped. By establishing possession as a new category of proof of ownership, it differed from the proprietary action in England brought on a writ of right. This latter action, which predated the assize, was a claim of ownership. It is brought by one who had better right than mere prior possession to a piece of property. Prior possession was not sufficient to establish a claim of ownership under this proprietary action.[18] The assize, on the other hand, was a possessory action insofar as a mere prior possessor could prevail over a subsequent usurper.[19] That is, if A was thrown off his land

[16] Maitland describes this principle as follows: "It is a prohibition of self-help in the interest of public order. The possessor is protected, not on account of any merits of his, but because the peace must be kept; to allow men to make forcible entries on land or to seize goods without form of law, is to invite violence." *History*, 2:41.

[17] Maitland describes this principle as follows: "In order to give an adequate protection of ownership, it has been found necessary to protect possession. To prove ownership is difficult, to prove possession comparatively easy. Suppose a land-owner ejected from possession; to require of him to prove his ownership before he can be reinstated, is to require too much; thieves and land-grabbers will presume upon the difficulty that a rightful owner will have in making out a flawless title. It must be enough then that the ejected owner should prove that he was in possession and was ejected; the ejector must be precluded from pleading that the possession which he disturbed was not possession under good title. Possession then is an outwork of property." *History*, 2:42. He continues: "But though the object of the law in protecting possession is to protect the possession of those who have a right to possess, that object can only be obtained by protecting *every* possessor" (emphasis added). This is not a necessary part of this policy concern, and as we have noted, the assize did not operate when the usurper was able to prove true ownership, provided, of course, that such proof was possible within the summary confines of the assize.

[18] See Pollock and Maitland, *History*, 2:75–77.

[19] Ibid., pp. 47–51; W. Walsh, *A History of Anglo-American Law*, 2nd ed. (Indianapolis: Bobbs-Merrill, 1932), pp. 102–104.

by B, A would win an action under the assize to regain possession from B by showing merely that he had possessed the land before B. Under the proprietary action brought on a writ of right, A would have had to show a better right than mere prior possession in order to have prevailed against B.

What gave rise to this new concept of protecting mere prior possession under the assize? As we have seen, Roman law is not the answer.[20] The etymology of the term *assize* is itself uncertain. "Assize" was used in these early years to describe a decree by the king. The term was rarely used before the twelfth century or after the thirteenth. The earliest known assizes were those of Jerusalem in 1099 upon the conquest of the First Crusade.[21] Scotland had a couple of assizes during the course of the twelfth century.[22] Sicily had the Assizes of Ariano promulgated by Roger II in 1140.[23] By far the greatest number of assizes issued by any one king were those of Henry II in the late twelfth century.[24]

According to the *Oxford English Dictionary*, "assize" comes from the old French *assise*, meaning an act of sitting down or settlement. From this root it might refer to the legislative sitting of the king at which he made his decree. On the other hand, it is not inconceivable that the term *assize*, which means an administrative regulation, comes from the Arabic term *siyāsah*, which describes the administrative power of the sovereign to regulate and dispense justice in Islam.[25] *Assize* has appeared in several different forms,

[20] In addition to the Roman possessory action where ownership was not a defense, a person asserting title in the *vindicatio* (a Roman action to recover ownership) had to prove his absolute title (not merely prior possession). It is no wonder that this proof was characterized as the *probatio diabolica dominii*. R. Monier, *Manuel élémentaire de droit romain*, 6th ed. (Paris: Domat Montchrestien, 1947), 1:374; Nicholas, *Introduction*, pp. 153–157.

[21] See Beugnot, ed., *Assises de Jérusalem*, 2 vols. (Paris, Imprimérie Royale, 1841 and 1843; republished, Farnborough: Gregg Press, 1967).

[22] E. Jenks, "Comparative Chronological Table of Medieval Legal Sources," in *A General Survey of Events, Sources, Persons and Movements in Continental Legal History* (New York: A. M. Kelley, 1968), pp. 736–737.

[23] See Berman, *Law and Revolution*, pp. 419–421. Professor Berman calls these Assizes "the first modern code of royal law in the history of the West."

[24] See Pollock and Maitland, *History*, 1:136–138.

[25] See J. Schacht, *An Introduction to Islamic Law* (Oxford: Clarendon, 1964), p. 54, for a short discussion of *siyāsah*. William Stubbs in *The Constitutional History of England* (abridged by J. Cornford, Chicago: University of Chicago Press, 1979),

including the form "assys."[26] *Siyāsah* is composed of three consonants *s-y-s*[27] (vowels are not usually written in Arabic) and when the definite article *al* (pronounced *as* before the *s*) is attached to these letters the word spells "assys."

There may or may not be an etymological relationship between the two terms *siyāsah* and *assize*, but the possibility encourages an examination of Islamic law to determine what influence it may have offered in the formation of the English assize. In fact, in the twelfth century there was an Islamic action for recovery of land called *istiḥqāq*. As in the English assize and the Roman interdict, the Islamic *istiḥqāq* restored the owner who was removed from his property.[28] It was an action for recovery of land upon usurpation (*ghasb*). Contrary to the Roman action and consistent with the English, however, it was not intended to restore the non-owner who was removed by the owner from property. The non-owning possessor of property had no action against the proven owner of the property after the owner took his property back. As Joseph Schacht has stated, "the concept of protection of possession is absent from Islamic law,"[29] at least in the Roman sense of the term.

Yet the *istiḥqāq* was a possessory action in an important sense of that term. Possession offered a presumption of ownership. There was a presumption that the possessor of property who had his property taken was the owner and thus entitled to the return of his property. If the dispossessor could prove that he had a better right to the property (in other words, that he was the owner as

---

p. 137–138 n. 1, states that "there is no reason to look for an Arabic derivation [of the form *assisia*], as is done in the editions of Du Cange." (I did not find the reference in Du Cange.)

[26] See *The Oxford English Dictionary* (Oxford: Oxford University Press, 1933), 1:511.

[27] Actually the root of *siyāsah* is composed of three radicals *s-w-s* but the *w* changes to a *y* in this form of the Arabic word.

[28] See Khalīl ibn Isḥāq al-Jundī, *Abrégé de la loi musulmane selon le rite de l'Imām Mālek*, trans. G.-H. Bousquet (Algiers: La Maison des Livres; Paris: A. Maisonneuve, 1961), 3:100–107.

[29] Schacht, *Introduction*, p. 139. See also J. El-Hakim, *Le Dommage de source délictuelle en droit musulman*, 2nd ed. (Paris: Librairie Générale de Droit et de Jurisprudence, 1971), p. 170 n. 5. Cf. C. Chehata, *Etudes de droit musulman: 2, La notion de responsabilité contractuelle; Le concept de propriété* (Paris: Presses Universitaires de France, 1973), p. 150.

far as the possessor was concerned), the action for recovery by the dispossessed person failed. The presumption of ownership which initially operated in his favor was rebutted. Otherwise, the prior possessor was considered the owner.[30] It is this presumption of ownership based on possession that we see in the English assize.

Beyond the presumption of ownership there was another characteristic of possession under the English assize which existed in the Islamic *istiḥqāq*. As between two strangers in title to a piece of property, prior possession was the better ownership even if absolute title could be shown in a third person. Thus, if B usurped land from A, and C usurped this same land from B, B had an action for recovery of the land from C under the English assize even though A was the proven owner.[31] The same was true under the Islamic *istiḥqāq*. Sarakhsī, an eleventh-century Ḥanafī jurist, tells us that when a bailee held land which was then usurped by a stranger, the bailee could recover from the usurper even though he proved not to be the owner, because otherwise a usurper would have been encouraged to take property, knowing that the bailee would have no recourse against him.[32] One could argue in this case that the bailee stood as an agent of the owner in recovering the property. However, it is also indicated by a later Ḥanafī author that a simple possessor was protected as well. A person who usurped a slave from an owner and in turn had the slave usurped from him could bring an action for recovery against the second usurper.[33]

[30] See Schacht, *Introduction*, p. 139; L. Milliot, *Introduction à l'étude du droit musulman* (Paris: Recueil Sirey, 1953), pp. 624, 626–627; M. Morand, *Avant-Projet de code présenté à la Commission de Codification du Droit Musulman Algérien* (Algiers: A. Jourdan, 1916), p. 377.

[31] See Pollock and Maitland, *History*, 2:46. The *jus tertii* defense also was not available in an action on a writ of right and continues to fail today. See ibid., pp. 76–77; C. Donahue, T. Kauper, and P. Martin, *Cases and Materials on Property: An Introduction to the Concept and the Institution*, 2nd ed. (St. Paul: West Publishing Co., 1983), pp. 56–57.

[32] Sarakhsī (d. 1090), *al-Mabsūṭ* (Beirut: Dār al-Ma'rifah, 1978), 11:124–125, discussed in Chehata, *Etudes*, pp. 150–152.

[33] See 'Ālamgīr (Sultan from 1659 to 1707), *al-Fatāwī al-hindīyah*, 3rd ed. (Cairo, 1892; reprinted Beirut), 5:147 (which actually gives the case where the slave escapes from the second usurper and the first usurper is permitted to recover the value of the slave even though the true owner does not hold the first usurper liable). See also El-Hakim, *Dommage*, p. 170 n. 5 (citing Art. 910 of the *Majallah*). Maitland describes

These similarities between the Islamic and English actions for recovery of land are significant. They suggest a cross-cultural influence that opens an inquiry into whether there was in fact opportunity for King Henry II, creator of the assize of novel disseisin, to have known about the Islamic *istiḥqāq*. King Henry, a strong, broad-shouldered, energetic man who not only excelled at the hunt but mastered the art of eloquent argument, enjoyed contacts far and wide throughout the Western world. His participation in the Second Crusade and the later offer of the throne of Jerusalem, which he declined, are well documented. In particular he had close connections with the Normans to the south in Sicily.

The Normans were renowned for their administration both in England and in Sicily. Of course, before the Normans conquered Sicily it was ruled for over two hundred years from the ninth to the latter half of the eleventh century by the Muslims, enlightened rulers who had made it "the centre of an Arab civilisation as splendid as that of Cordova itself."[34] The advent of the Normans did not destroy this culture; with a genius for imitation, they integrated it with their own.[35] The Muslims continued to practice their religion freely and to be governed by their own judges and laws.[36] They, in turn, provided a large number of infantry troops as mercenaries.[37]

The Norman conquest of the Muslims which led to a blending of the two cultures was the work of Roger I, who died in 1101. His son Roger II grew up imbued with the Muslim culture and assumed the government of Sicily from 1112 to 1154. Continuing in the steps of his father, he maintained an intimate relationship with his Muslim subjects, delighting in the company of Muslim poets

---

the principle of protection in a case such as this as follows: "He who possesses has by the mere fact of his possession more right in the thing than the non-possessor has; he of all men has most right in the thing until someone has asserted and proved a greater right. When a thing belongs to no one and is capable of appropriation, the mere act of taking possession of it gives right against all the world; when a thing belongs to A, the mere fact that B takes possession of it still gives B a right which is good against all who have no better." *History*, 2:43.

[34] E. Curtis, *Roger of Sicily and the Normans in Lower Italy, 1016–1154* (New York and London: G. P. Putnam's Sons, 1912), p. 62.

[35] Berman, *Law and Revolution*, p. 414.

[36] Curtis, *Roger of Sicily*, pp. 67–68.

[37] Ibid., pp. 94–95.

and scholars.[38] Roger II, who promulgated the Assizes of Ariano in 1140,[39] was adept at incorporating many Islamic elements into the government of Sicily.[40] A closer look at the contacts and cross-influences which England and Sicily shared suggests that Henry II may have learned about the Islamic *istiḥqāq* through the Sicilian legal culture.

To mention just a few ties between the two states, the English judicial system seems to have furnished the model for the justiciarship in Sicily,[41] and the feudal registers of Sicily (which in at least one view were of Arabic origin[42]) appear to have influenced the military policy of Henry II.[43] There is also evidence of a relation between the English and Sicilian chanceries.[44] Furthermore, there were many visitors from north to south and vice versa.

> The northern Normans showed pride in the achievements of their Italian kinsmen, and it is characteristic that the splendour of Rouen and the glory of King Roger form the joint theme of a Latin poem of c. 1150. No list can be attempted of the Norman and English students at Salerno or of the pilgrims and crusaders who went or returned by way of Bari or Messina, nor can we hope to recover many traces of the commercial intercourse which must have existed.[45]

Many officials made both states their homes. Peter of Blois was an intimate friend of both King William II of Sicily,[46] whom he tutored, and King Henry II. The relations between these two

[38] Ibid., pp. 309–319. A close friend of the King was the famous Arab geographer Idrīsī, who wrote *The Book of Roger*, describing among many other things the world to be round. This book was published in 1154, the year of the King's death.

[39] See note 23 above.

[40] See Curtis, *Roger of Sicily*, pp. 333–375, and esp. 418–425; C. Haskins, *The Normans in European History* (Boston and New York: Houghton Mifflin, 1915), pp. 223–235.

[41] C. Haskins, "England and Sicily in the Twelfth Century," *The English Historical Review* 104 (1911): 643, 650–651, 664.

[42] Ibid., pp. 656 n.195, 665.

[43] Ibid., pp. 655, 661–664.

[44] Ibid., 103:446–447.

[45] Ibid., p. 435 (footnotes omitted).

[46] King William ruled Sicily from 1166 to 1189. William Stubbs in "The Chronicle of Roger of Hoveden," in *Historical Introductions to the Rolls Series*, ed. A. Hassall (New York: Haskell House, 1968), pp. 194–195, states that "William the Good was connected by blood very closely with the Beaumonts of Leicester and Warwick, a family which supplied Henry II with several ministers in his early years.... As his

kings were cemented further by the marriage of William to Henry's youngest daughter Joanna in 1177. Most striking of all, however, was the "ever-ready source of information" which King Henry had in his special advisor, Master Thomas Brown.[47]

Thomas Brown was born in England about 1120. He first appeared in Sicily about 1137 and was likely the protégé of the chancellor Robert of Selby, who also came from England. In 1149 he appeared as Kaid Brūn in the *dīwān*, the fiscal department of the Sicilian government, which took its origin from Muslim antecedents. *Dīwān* is the Arabic term for an Islamic administrative office or for account books of the Islamic treasury.

The *dīwān* kept records of boundaries, bought and sold land, and under the king's direction issued official certificates of boundaries and privileges. Its voluminous registers were called *dafātir*, another Arabic term. The officers of the bureau were mostly Muslim. In fact, Thomas Brown appeared with the secretary 'Uthmān in the *dīwān*, where he attached his *'alāmah* (distinguishing mark) to a transcript from the records of the bureau. The officers of the *dīwān* recovered the king's property, enforced the payments due him, and held court to determine boundaries and decide disputes. It was in this bureau that Master Thomas appeared as an important and trusted officer of the royal administration.

By 1158 it appears that Thomas Brown was in England on the personal invitation of Henry II and he remained there until his death in 1180.[48] He enjoyed a position of considerable importance, enjoying a high degree of personal and official confidence from the king. He had a seat at the exchequer and kept a third roll as a check on the rolls of the treasurer and chancellor. As Professor Charles Homer Haskins has noted, a "restless experimenter like

health failed he made a will, by which he left to Henry not only all the provisions collected for the expedition [Crusade], but a vast treasure besides, going moreover so far as to offer the succession to his crown to him or one of his sons [which proposal Henry declined]" (footnotes omitted).

[47] Haskins, "England and Sicily," 103:438. The information which follows on Thomas Brown and the *dīwān* is given in vol. 103, pp. 438–443, and vol. 104, pp. 652–653.

[48] Thomas Brown may have been forced to flee Sicily for his life when King William I (1154–1166) came to power. Richard, Fitz Nigel, *Dialogus de Scaccario: The Course of the Exchequer*, trans. C. Johnson (Oxford: Oxford University Press, 1983), p. 35. See Haskins, "England and Sicily," 103:441.

Henry II was not the man to despise a useful bit of administrative mechanism because it was foreign."[49] There could not have been a better opportunity for King Henry II to learn of the Islamic *istiḥqāq* than through this personal confidant who had been an important official in the Islamic Sicilian bureau which recovered land for the king of Sicily. Within eight short years after Thomas Brown appeared in England, the assize of novel disseisin was decreed.[50]

This evidence of the contact which King Henry II had with Islamic administration in Sicily strongly suggests an Islamic influence. The remarkable similarity in nature between the English and Islamic actions for recovery of land, when contrasted with the marked difference in Roman law, suggests one avenue where that influence may have materialized. In the absence of direct evidence of such influence more cannot be said at this juncture, but perhaps, as we begin to lift our eyes from the glories of Roman law to the glories that lay beyond, we may come to realize the tremendous impact which Islam and its legal system must have exercised on the West.

[49] Haskins, "England and Sicily," 103:434.

[50] It is estimated that the assize was enacted sometime between 1155 and 1166. See note 7 above.

III

ISLAMIC LAW IN MODERN TIMES

8

A Reassertion of the Sharī'ah: The Jurisprudence of the Gulf States

WILLIAM BALLANTYNE

THERE can be no doubt whatever, in my view, that there is in the majority of the Arab jurisdictions the feeling that in adopting wholesale legislation based upon Western, mainly French, civil codes, they went too far too fast: the feeling that they should have adhered to the Sharī'ah as a base—possibly devising some kind of new *Majallah* (Ottoman codification of Sharī'ah civil law). Now, to anticipate and to try to put the crux of this issue immediately in the spotlight: the difficulty (perhaps impossibility) lies in the fact that the Gulf states, since the dramatic onset of oil wealth, have become economically tied to the West. The Western economic system of banking and interest is anathema to the Sharī'ah, and while that is perhaps the main difficulty, it is not by any means the only one. There are, as we all know, many incidents of complicated modern commercial contracts which would simply be illegal at the Sharī'ah. Those who talk of a new *ijtihād* (interpretation) tend to overlook the fact that, even admitting that the door of *ijtihād* may be reopened (now, I think, admitted by the majority), there are few indeed who would venture to contend that express provisions (*nuṣūṣ*) of the Qur'ān and Sunnah can be tampered with. Of such is *ribā* (interest). It may be that the way forward is by a new and restrictive definition of *ribā*, *gharar* (hazard or risk), and other such aspects of the Sharīʿah, but that will take great unity and political courage at the present time. In my opinion, anything short of a new *Majallah* redefining Sharīʿah concepts in the light of contemporary conditions—a new *Majallah* passed by the Arab states as a uniform law—must continue to beg the question and leave in the Arab jurisdictions that uncertainty which will increasingly bedevil the Western lawyer. What a dream—a true *lex arabica*! There are at the moment few signs that it can be achieved or that such a code could be devised without resorting to what many Muslims would regard as heresy.

In order to assess current trends, we must consider briefly the position occupied by the Sharīʿah as a source of legislation in Kuwait, Bahrain, Qatar, the United Arab Emirates, and Saudi Arabia. They are all Islamic states, and it is almost trite to point out to this audience that where there are written constitutions—in all save Saudi Arabia and Oman—the Sharīʿah is prescribed as a, or the, main source of legislation. Saudi Arabia has no written constitution in the current sense, but the ancient Organic Instructions of the Hijazi Kingdom of 1926, amended or supplemented by the Statute of the Council of Deputies of 1932 and the Constitution of the Council of Ministers of 1953, make it clear that the law of the Kingdom is the Sharīʿah, and it may be confidently submitted that no regulation of the Kingdom which could be shown to be contrary to the Sharīʿah would be applied by the courts. In Oman, the position is perhaps least defined of all the states; there is no written constitution, and it must be stressed, therefore, that despite the apparently liberal trends to which I shall refer, the Sharīʿah could be applied to any matter in Oman at any time.

Apart from Saudi Arabia and Oman, we find varying shades. In my long practice, I have found that, in other than matters of personal affairs (*aḥwāl shakhṣīyah*), the Sharīʿah has had minimal relevance, particularly in commercial matters. However, whatever may have been the position in practice over recent years, the trend towards a reassertion is quite apparent, and it is thus illuminating to consider the extent to which the Sharīʿah *could* be applied under the existing constitutions and the variety of legislation promulgated under them.

Now, one hears too often from one's Arab colleagues the dictum, "No, we have civil courts in our country; the Sharīʻah is not relevant." That is, of course, a dangerous non sequitur; the crucial matter is not the label put upon the courts, but the law which those courts are directed to apply. While it may be true to say that a Sharīʻah *qāḍī* will apply the Sharīʻah exclusively, it is certainly not true, indeed it is entirely misleading, to say that a civil or commercial court will *not* apply the Sharīʻah. In considering the Gulf states, we may indeed indicate two extremes—in Saudi Arabia, it may be submitted that no court or judicial committee may do other than apply the Sharīʻah; whereas in Kuwait, at the other end of the scale, it would be rare indeed to find the Sharīʻah mentioned in a commercial court; the same may be said of Bahrain or, to a lesser extent, Qatar. We find, however, as we have said, varying shades.

Given, then, that the Sharīʻah may be taken in these states to be at least a principal source of legislation according to the constitution, what is the extent to which it is applied by law and in practice, with especial reference to commercial matters? To a large extent, this issue, embarrassing to regimes which have perforce adopted in the last two decades Western codes and, even more importantly, become absorbed into the Western economic system, has been swept under the rug. I do not believe that it will continue to be so.

As we have seen, in Saudi Arabia the Sharīʻah reigns paramount, and such regulations as have been promulgated must in my opinion be subjected to the test of validity at the Sharīʻah. Let us take the other states from Kuwait round the Gulf to Oman.

Kuwait

Article 1 of the Kuwaiti Civil Code of 1980[1] provides for an apparent hierarchy of sources to which a judge shall make reference: (1) express legislative provisions, which apply to matters to which they relate both expressly and by implication, (2) custom, and (3) the *fiqh*.

[1] Promulgated by Law 67 of 1980; published in *Al-Kuwait al-yaum* No. 1335 (1981).

Although contract is not expressly referred to in this context, Article 196 of the code covers this by the hallowed precept that "the contract is the law of the parties" (*al-'aqd sharī'at al-muta'āqidayn*).

While the Kuwaiti Civil Code shows a great deal of Sharī'ah influence in its make-up, by Article 3 of the law issuing that code special laws are expressed to take precedence over general laws such as the Civil Code. One such special law, the Kuwaiti Commercial Code, was published contemporaneously with the Civil Code, and legislates specifically in the modern commercial context.[2] In particular, while loans according to the Civil Code must be without interest, the Commercial Code, as a special law, allows interest on commercial loans, and indeed contains detailed provisions as to its regulation. Thus, in general, it would be rare indeed to find the Sharī'ah adduced as an authority in a purely commercial transaction in Kuwait, where express legislative provisions exist. However, where there is no such provision, and where the judge is directed to custom, the position is different. The learned commentary to the code points out that customs must not offend public policy or morals (*al-niẓām al-'āmm wa-ḥusn al-'ādāt*), and it goes on to state: "Customs (*'ādāt*) which contradict the social, political, economic or moral principles upon which the community rests can never be elevated to the rank of custom (*'urf*) even if of long duration; in a country such as Kuwait, whose religion is, by the constitution, Islam, it is not possible that anything which contravenes one of the bases or established precepts of Islam should constitute custom."

Bahrain

In Bahrain, the matter of sources was, until the promulgation of the new Commercial Code in March 1987[3] regulated by the Judicature Law of 1971.[4] The structure prescribed by that law,

[2] Promulgated by Law 68 of 1980; published in *Al-Kuwait al-yaum* No. 1338 (1981). Article 96 of the Commercial Code confirms the precedence of that code's provisions in the matter of commercial obligations and commercial contracts, where there is any variance with those of the Civil Code.

[3] Promulgated by Decree Law 7 of 1987; published in the *Supplement to Official Gazette* No. 1739.

[4] Law 13 of 1971, *Official Gazette* No. 929.

which must, from its wording, be taken to be hierarchical, is: (1) provisions of law, (2) the principles of the Sharīʿah, (3) custom, and (4) natural law or the principles of equity and good conscience.

This formula is interesting as clearly envisaging that secular legislation is to be preferred to the Sharīʿah, even, presumably, if it does not accord with the Sharīʿah. It also envisages that the Sharīʿah may be deficient in supplying a solution to a problem, in which case custom applies. Would such custom be applicable if itself contrary to the Sharīʿah? Finally, would the tenets of natural justice or the principles of equity and good conscience be applicable in defiance of the Sharīʿah?

As far as commercial matters are concerned—and it must be remembered that Bahrain is par excellence, and has been for thousands of years, an entrepôt state with great commercial interests, and latterly a developed banking community—the new Commercial Code of 1987 takes the matter a step further. As far as I am aware, this code has not been generally published in English. I have translated the relevant Article 2:

1. There shall apply to commercial matters that which the two contracting parties have agreed to unless such agreement conflicts with mandatory legislative provisions (*nuṣūṣ tashrīʿīyah āmirah*).
2. In the absence of express agreement, the principles of commercial custom shall apply unless there be in that respect provision in this law or in any other law relating to commercial matters. Special or local custom shall be preferred over general custom.
3. If there be no commercial custom, the laws relating to civil matters shall apply, failing which the judge shall deduce the bases of his judgment from the principles of the law of nature and the principles of justice.

It may now be said in the light of these provisions that, as with Kuwait, in Bahrain in a commercial matter where there is express legislative provision, such provision would be applied even if contrary to the Sharīʿah.

Taking *ribā* once again as the yardstick in our current context, we find that the new Bahraini code has, like Kuwait's in 1980, finally grasped this nettle and legislated sanctioning banking interest. Article 76 defines a commercial loan, and goes to the length of providing for a presumption that interest be charged in the absence of a contrary intention expressed by the contracting parties. The article further provides for an upper limit of interest to be set by the Central Bank. Article 275 of the code, which deals with bank deposit, again expressly allows the stipulation of interest thereon, and refers back in this respect to the general provisions of Article 76.

One may recall in passing that Bahrain still has a contract law and a law of torts based on the common law.[5] It is to be presumed that the state will eventually issue a comprehensive civil code in replacement of these two survivals, but in the meantime it will be interesting to study the conflicts which must inevitably develop between the old code and the new commercial code, based as it is upon European commercial concepts.

Qatar

The Civil and Commercial Code of Qatar of 1971[6] provides for the sources of law to be in essence as follows: (1) the contract between the parties provided it accords with the law, (2) express legislative provision, (3) custom, and (4) the Sharī'ah.

We may recall that, unlike the constitutions of Kuwait, Bahrain, and the U.A.E., which provide for the Sharī'ah as *a* principal source of legislation, the Qatari constitution provides that it shall be *the* principal source thereof. The question therefore arises as to whether the hierarchy of sources prescribed under the civil and commercial code must be read subject to the proviso that they are not contrary to the Sharī'ah. My own view is that, despite the more stringent wording of the constitution, this should not be the test, but the matter is clearly controversial and confirms doubts about the ever-looming presence of the Sharī'ah which exists in greater or less degree in the other jurisdictions. We shall note in a moment recent important and illuminating judgments delivered by the Supreme Constitutional Court of Egypt construing the effect

[5] The Bahrain Contract Law first appeared as Queen's Regulation No. 1 of 1961 in Supplement No. 32 to the *Persian Gulf Gazette*. It was reissued by the Ruler of Bahrain in 1969 (see *Official Gazette* No. 852). The Law of Civil Wrongs first appeared in 1970 (see *Official Gazette* No. 870).

[6] Law 16 of 1971, *Official Gazette* No. 7 (1971).

upon past existing legislation of the changes in the constitution made in 1980, whereby the Sharīʻah was promoted from being *a* principal source of legislation to *the* principal source.

The United Arab Emirates

The sources of law to be applied by the courts in the U.A.E. are to be found basically in Union Law No. 10 of 1973 setting up the Union Supreme Court[7] where it is provided (Article 75):

> The Supreme Court shall apply the provisions of the Islamic Sharīʻah, Union laws and other laws in force in the member Emirates of the Union conforming to the Islamic Sharīʻah. Likewise it shall apply those rules of custom and those principles of natural and comparative law which do not conflict with the principles of the Sharīʻah.

Here the paramountcy of the Sharīʻah is evident. Again, Union Law No. 6 of 1978[8] setting up the Union Courts of First Instance and Appeal prescribes the following sources (Article 8):

> The Union courts shall apply the provisions of the Islamic Sharīʻah, Union laws, and other laws in force, just as they shall apply those rules of custom and general legal principles which do not conflict with the provisions of the Sharīʻah.

The matter is taken further by the new Code of Civil Transactions for the United Arab Emirates,[9] which came into force in March 1986, and which provides (Article 1) that legislative provisions shall apply to all matters contained therein either expressly or by implication; that there shall be no place for construction or interpretation where a provision is clear; and that if the judge does not find any provision in the law, then he must adjudicate in accordance with the Islamic Sharīʻah. In so doing, the judge is directed to the Mālikī and Ḥanbalī schools; if he finds no answer there, then he adverts to the Shāfiʻī or Ḥanafī schools as the matter may require. If the judge still does not find the guidance he requires, then he gives judgment in accordance with custom, which custom, however, must not be contrary to public policy or

7 *Official Gazette* No. 12/1973

8 *Official Gazette* No. 58/1978.

9 Promulgated by Law 5 of 1985; published in *Official Gazette* No. 158.

morals, and if it is a custom peculiar to a particular emirate, then his judgment applies to such emirate. Article 2 of the code provides definitely that in the comprehension and interpretation of a provision, reference shall be made to the principles of the Islamic *fiqh*; while Article 3, in defining public policy, lays it down that nothing shall be contrary to the mandatory provisions and the basic principles of the Sharī'ah. The new code contains for the first time conflict of law provisions but, although Article 19 respects the principle of *autonomie de la volonté*, Article 27 provides that "it shall not be lawful to apply principles of law designated by the foregoing provisions if such principles are contrary to the Islamic Sharī'ah or public policy or morals of the U.A.E."

It may be deduced, therefore, that in the U.A.E. principles of law contrary to the Sharī'ah should not, whether in a civil or commercial transaction, be adverted to by the courts. Be that as it may, in a recent case in Abu Dhabi, the judge, in finding interest on a loan to be legal despite arguments produced before him based upon the new code, made a differentiation between a civil loan and a commercial loan. This was a commercial loan, he said, and thus the provisions of the civil code did not apply to it! I would submit that, in view of the weight of legislation existing in the U.A.E. to which I have referred, it is difficult to conceive how the judge could possibly have come to that conclusion. There is, as yet, no commercial code in the U.A.E.

Oman

Article 44 of the Law of Procedure for Hearing Cases and Applications for Arbitration before the Authority for Settlement of Commercial Disputes[10] prescribes:

> Decrees and laws in effect in the Sultanate; contracts between the litigants provided that such do not conflict with the laws, public order or morals; established and observed customs in the field of commercial activity; and that which will achieve justice between the adversaries and lead to stability in commercial transactions.

It may be noted also that certain provisions of the Omani Banking Law would appear to confer on contracting parties the

[10] Promulgated by Sultani Decree 32/84; published in *Official Gazette* No. 286.

right to choose both jurisdiction and law in their contract, although it seems doubtful whether those provisions go beyond matters of banking as therein defined. However, we may recall the basic constitutional position in Oman to which I have already referred and note that there is nothing to preclude the application of the Sharīʿah by the Committee; indeed, as a matter of jurisprudence, it may be anticipated that if points of Sharīʿah were made before the Committee, it would be obliged to take them.

In 1980, in the latter days of the Sadat regime, Article 2 of the Constitution of Egypt was amended to provide that the Sharīʿah should be *the* principal source of law. On 4th May 1985, the Constitutional Court of Egypt issued a judgment in this respect which was of great importance, not only for Egypt but for the other Arab jurisdictions whose codes owe so much to Egypt and where deference is paid to Egyptian jurisprudence. The case was brought before the Constitutional Court by no less a person than the Rector of al-Azhar, against the President, the Prime Minister, the President of the Legislative Committee of Parliament, and finally against the heirs of one Fuad Goudah, the latter being the person concerned with the substance.[11] In essence, the court held that the change in Article 2 of the Constitution did not affect existing legislation—notably Article 226 of the Civil Code of 1948, which the Rector claimed to be against the Constitution in its amended form in that it provides for interest in case of delayed payment. In another more recent judgment announced by the same Constitutional Court on 4th April 1987 the court ruled on a case brought by the public prosecutor, who was not satisfied with the sentence of fine or imprisonment prescribed for drinking wine and being intoxicated in a public place.[12] The prosecutor endeavored to invoke Sharīʿah punishment, but the court ruled, as before, that the new Article 2 of the Constitution applied only to subsequent legislation.

At the first conference of the International Banking Association to be held in an Arab country, that held in Cairo in February 1987, I had the honor to co-chair the section on "The

[11] Case No. 20, judicial year 1.

[12] Case No. 141, judicial year 4.

Sharīʿah and its Relevance to Modern Transnational Transactions." The burning interest in this subject at the present time and the appreciation of the current reassertion of the Sharīʿah generally were apparent. In particular, the first of the constitutional cases to which I have just referred came in for much criticism from Egyptian lawyers. The Sharīʿah as a main source of legislation was recognized, as was the problem of whether the Sharīʿah can be made compatible with modern transnational commercial transactions. Inevitably, these themes were developed by consideration of new *ijtihād*, and the papers read reflected the differences of opinion in this respect. A fascinating paper was read on behalf of the Rector of al-Azhar, in which he referred in particular to the Hague conferences and the resolutions that: (1) the Sharīʿah be considered as one of the sources of the general principles of law, (2) the Sharīʿah is living and capable of development, and (3) the Sharīʿah is unique and not taken from any other source. The paper outlined in particular how apposite was the Sharīʿah to commercial transactions, and dealt with this in detail. However, at the end of the paper came the punch line: the Rector's analysis was to illustrate the competence of the Sharīʿah to deal with commercial transactions, but it was now essential to return to the principle of Islam in the laws of Egypt, and much drafting had already been completed to that end. The Rector referred expressly to the amendment of the Constitution of Egypt to which I have referred.

The other papers, while stressing the need for a new *ijtihād*, did not explain—indeed, how could they?—how such a process could overcome immutable provisions which seem to conflict directly with occidental legal theories.

To sum up. At the present time it can only be said that uncertainty remains, not only in the Gulf states, but overall. I have ventured to express the view that only uniform legislation can solve the issues involved so as to remove all doubts; I have also referred to the unfortunate unlikelihood of this happening. We all know of the drafting committees operating within the Islamic conferences, but so far little has emerged. I must repeat that I for one fail to see how, even if it be desirable, such uniform legislation could, while remaining true to the basic precepts (*nuṣūṣ*) of the Sharī'ah, be consonant with Western legal systems or compatible with Western commerce and commercial law.

Invidious as it may be to quote too much from oneself, may I nonetheless do so from a book which I wrote in 1980.

> It is often said that the Qur'an (and hence the Shari'a) provides all the principles necessary for the regulation of relationships even in the world of commerce. As with Christianity or other major religions, that would be true in the context of the ideal society, wherein every member accepted and obeyed its dictates under spiritual sanction; in the modern commercial world, this would envisage also such obedience in general internationally by members of other cultures, including States. This is unfortunately at the moment unthinkable, and in the context of society as it exists, the lesser merits of man-made law must obtain. It is in the latter context that the Shari'ah must be viewed and, in its very nature, necessarily found inappropriate. It may be said that it is the material world that is at fault in this, and that either Islam or Christianity, restored to their essential validity amongst us, would do a better and more adequate job. Be that as it may, the inherent immutability of the Shari'a militates against its suitability in the system of international commerce which man has created. Acceptance of this truth is reflected in the publication by most of the States of the Muslim world of Commercial and other Codes in replacement of the Shari'a, which is now in many cases limited to matters of personal status.[13]

If I am correct in this overall view, then the Arabs are inevitably ever faced with the alternatives of adhering to Western-type codes (*vide* Kuwait, Bahrain) or adhering or reverting to Sharī'ah principles, perhaps with new *Majallah*s which merely codify the appropriate Sharī'ah principles (as an example we may recall the new *Majallah* issued in Saudi Arabia based on Ḥanbalī principles). No doubt the whole question will continue to be begged for as long as possible; but the pressures are there and are increasing; the swing back to the Sharī'ah is apparent in current legislation. It is the duty of the practising lawyer always to point out the possibility of its application.

[13] William Ballantyne, *Legal Development in Arabia* (London: Graham & Trotman, 1980), pp. 109–110.

9

The Development of Decennial Liability in Egypt

IAN EDGE

THE SUBJECT of this paper is an important species of liability for property damage, known as decennial liability, how it came to enter Egyptian law and the development of the legal rules concerning it up to the present day.[1]

Decennial liability is a vital aspect of property law not only in Egypt but in many other countries of the Middle East. No construction project would be entered into without a consideration of the application of this special liability—whether it applies to the project in question and, if so, how it is to be provided for and whether there are (as there often are) mandatory legal provisions requiring insurance against it.

Basically, decennial liability is a special legal liability imposed upon a contractor or constructor of buildings or construction

[1] There is already a considerable literature on aspects of decennial liability in the Middle East. See Michael Davies, *Business Law in Egypt* (Amsterdam: Kluwer, 1984), pp. 213–221; Attia, "Decennial Liability under Egyptian Law," *ALQ* 1.5 (November 1986): 504–524; articles in *Middle East Economic Review* (*MEER*) in issues June, July, and October 1979; June 1980; February 1981; August, October 1982; April 1983; and June 1984. As Professor Farhat Ziadeh is the author of the best monograph on property law in the Middle East, this slight paper is offered as a tribute to his immense scholarship and illumination in this field and I am honored to present it to him on the eve of his retirement.

projects under which the contractor, constructor, or construction engineers and architects are liable for the damage caused by any defect which is discovered in the construction after completion. The liability is not open ended. It is limited to a period of time during which it is assumed that any defects of construction will appear. In Egypt this period is ten years, hence the name by which the liability is known. It is an important protection for the owner on whose behalf the building or other project is constructed as it helps to ensure safe construction and it provides definite and clear rules on liability for subsequent defect.

ORIGINS

The concept of decennial liability was originally a French one. In French law it is known as "la garantie décennale" and was (and still is) found in Articles 1792 and 2270 of the Napoleonic Civil Code of 1804.[2] The introduction of this special liability was defended on a number of grounds:

(1) It is a general principle of contract that once a contract is completed by performance no contractual liability remains thereafter; but in the case of construction contracts, defects in construction may not be immediately apparent, only becoming noticeable at a much later date;
(2) Unsafe buildings are a public danger and not conducive to the public good; and
(3) Owners have little or no technical knowledge of a building and to impose liability in this way prevents the shifting of responsibility to people without technical knowledge.

In the late nineteenth century, when Egypt was looking to bring its civil law up to date, it adopted almost wholesale the civil law of France. Thus, the Napoleonic provisions of decennial liability came into Egyptian law almost unchanged. Initially, they were made part of the civil code of the mixed courts—the courts created in 1876 by the European capitulatory powers in Egypt

[2] Now see loi numéro 78-12 of 4 January 1978 and loi numéro 85-677 of 5 July 1985, which have replaced the older provisions and considerably added to them: *Code Civil* (Paris: Dalloz, 1986–87).

to deal with cases involving a foreign or a non-Egyptian party.[3] Later, in 1883, these same provisions (translated into Arabic) were put into the civil code of the national courts so that they applied also to cases involving Egyptians only.[4]

THE OLD PROVISIONS

The provisions were terse and short. Contractors and architects[5] were liable[6] for the total collapse of buildings owing to defects (including defects in the ground itself) for a period of ten years, although the architect was only to be liable if he actively supervised construction or the defect lay in his plans.[7] The two articles were in a section of the codes entitled "Hire of Persons or Industry," and there was no indication that the articles were limited in application to any form of hire contact. This was a mirror image of the provisions in the French civil code. However, the jurisprudence of France developed the notion that decennial liability only applied to a certain type of contract—basically a construction contract known as a "contrat d'entreprise"—and case law delimited its definitions and scope. This limitation did not occur in Egypt at the time of the mixed and national codes. However, the mixed and native courts did have many occasions to consider the scope of these articles and as a result a body of Egyptian case law developed which added to the provisions and extended them.[8] These modifications and interpretations were later used by Egyptian reformers to substantially amend the decennial liability provisions in the new Egyptian civil code of 1949.

In 1937 the Montreux Convention gave the mixed courts their final twelve-year lease of life—they were to be abolished in 1949 and their jurisdiction given to a newly unified set of national courts. During the 1940s, therefore, a committee was set up under

[3] Mixed Court Civil Code (MCC) 1876, Articles 500 and 501.

[4] National Court Civil Code (NCC) 1883, Articles 409 and 410.

[5] In French, "les entrepreneurs," in Arabic, "al-muqāwil"; French, "les architectes," Arabic, "al-muhandis al-mi'mārī."

[6] In the MCC "responsables"; in the NCC "mas'ūlān."

[7] It seems that the Arabic NCC was as close a translation of the French original as possible.

[8] See Grandmoulin, *Droit Civil Egyptien: les contrats* (Rennes: Librairie Thanoux, 1919[?]), pp. 220–225 and the cases there cited.

the chairmanship of 'Abd al-Razzāq al-Sanhūrī (Egypt's greatest modern jurist) to draft a new civil code for Egypt. His first draft (over 1500 articles long) was submitted to committees of both houses of Parliament and debated vigorously, resulting in a slimmed-down version of only 1150 articles.[9]

THE NEW DRAFT CIVIL CODE

In the first draft of the new Egyptian civil code six articles (articles 895–900) dealt with decennial liability. After deliberation in committee and redrafting, they were reduced to the four articles which appear as articles 651–654 in the new civil code promulgated in 1949.[10]

The aims of the 1949 civil code, as far as decennial liability was concerned, were: (1) to provide in the law for developments which the mixed and native courts had made, (2) to widen the basis of liability by adding to the law, and (3) to make clearer the boundaries of the liability.

I will look at each of those aims in turn and, by comparing the old and new codes, consider the important changes made by the 1949 law on decennial liability.

As to the first aim, the courts had already provided for some important lacunæ in the old codes. For example, the Mixed Court Civil Code talked of "destruction of the works"[11] but the mixed courts had soundly rejected any limitation of this to total destruction and included partial destruction.[12] This was explicitly added in the new code as part of Article 651(1).

[9] An extremely important source for this study is the *Majmū'at al-a'māl al-taḥḍīrīyah* (The collection of preparatory material) (hereinafter *Majmū'at*) of the committee which gives the civil code, with texts of the various drafts and comments of Parliament. It is in seven volumes.

[10] Law 131 of 1948, Egypt Government Printing Office. The most recent edition is of 1986 and incorporates some important amendments on evidence though unconnected with this study. A translation into English by the law firm of Perrot, Fanner and Sims Marshall is available.

[11] It must be said that the MCC in its French text provided for liability for "la destruction des travaux de construction"; but this was translated more vaguely in the Arabic text of the NCC as responsibility for "khilāl al-binā'" (faults of construction).

[12] See mixed court cases in *Bulletin de législation et de jurisprudences égyptiens* (hereinafter *BLJ*) 20 (1907–08): 110–116; 13 (1900–01): 221–222.

Again the courts had interpreted the word "construction"[13] widely so as to include any fixed structure (such as constructing a quay side, bridges, roads or dams)[14] and this too was explicitly provided for in the new code in Article 651(1).

As to the second aim, the liability was expanded from liability for mere collapse to include also inherent defect affecting the stability of the building (in Article 651[2]), and this was supported by reference to two minor and unreasoned mixed court decisions[15] and articles in the contemporary Portuguese and Brazilian civil codes.[16] An attempt in the first draft to distinguish between defects of minor importance which did not entail responsibility and defects of greater importance which did was not carried into the new code as the distinction was felt to be too difficult to draw, although Article 651(1) does say that the defect must be one which threatens the safety and strength or stability of the building.

As to the third aim, it was unclear whether under the old codes the liability could be excluded or limited by contract and further whether any fault on the part of the contractor needed to be proved. There were inconsistent decisions on both these matters and they were both important questions that were discussed at length by the drafting committee. In the end a special provision was added only in the former case, as I shall explain.

Under the old codes, there was no indication as to the types of liability (contractual or delictual) and whether the liability could be limited or excluded by a contractual provision. The majority view of the mixed courts seems to have been that the liability was contractual and therefore it could be limited by a contractual clause.[17] Article 899 of the first draft of the new civil code provided that the liability could be excluded or limited as long as the work of construction was a minor one but not if it

13 The Arabic of the NCC referring to "al-binā'" is perhaps even more restricted to the sense of buildings.

14 See *BLJ* 20 (1907–08): 110 (quay). It seems that the mixed courts did not admit structures without foundations as "constructions": see Grandmoulin, *Droit*, p. 222 and *BLJ* 13 (1901): 221, which rejected asphalting a road as a "construction." For a contrary (through unreasoned) view see *BLJ* 22 (1909-10): 271 accepting an ice rink as "a construction" within the decennial liability provisions.

15 *BLJ* 38 (29 April 1926): 379 and *BLJ* 29 (28 November 1916): 76.

16 See *Majmū'at*, 5:22.

17 Grandmoulin, *Droit*, p. 222.

was a major one ("al-muqāwalāt al-saghīrah," not "al-kabīrah"). The parliamentary scrutinizing committees, however, said that it was too difficult to draw such a distinction and that as the liability was a matter of public policy, no exclusion should be permitted at all.[18] This became Article 653 of the new code, and no exclusion or limitation is now possible at all.[19] Although the legislator appeared to accept that the liability was contractual (it is still not actually specified), it is a contract of a very special (and public) nature. This was recognized in the reorganization of the code itself. The provisions of the new code come under the heading of "contracts of work" (*'aqd al-muqāwalāt*),[20] which obviously has its roots in the French jurisprudential limitation of decennial liability to "contrats d'entreprises." That this is an important part of the make up of decennial liability is buttressed by the case law of the Egyptian Court of Cassation since 1949. In two cases (in 1975[21] and 1976[22]) the Cassation Court confirmed that decennial liability only applied to construction contracts (*'aqd al-muqāwalāt*) and not to contracts of services (*'aqd al-'amal*) or contracts of sale (*'aqd al-bay'*).

Secondly, under the old codes there were no provisions on whether the contractor must show some fault. The courts again produced inconsistent decisions but seemed to lean towards the view that liability was strict. In one case, an asphalted road subsided because of the collapse of an underground water sewer whose presence no one had known of. The Mixed Court of Appeal held that the contractor was not liable.[23] In another case a house collapsed after an exceptionally heavy and freak rainstorm washed away some of its supports. In this case, however, the contractor was held liable.[24] Sanhūrī in book 7 of *Al-Wasīṭ* quoted the drafting committee as saying that the courts developed two principles: (1) failure in the structure itself was not sufficient without

[18] *Majmū'at*, 5:28–30.

[19] See Sanhūrī, *A-Wasīṭ*, last ed., vol. 7, book 1, pp. 139–142.

[20] Heading of chapter 3 of book 2 of the code. For definition see Article 646. Compare this with the contract of services defined in Article 674.

[21] *Majmū'at aḥkām al-naqḍ* 26 (21 May 1975): 1048–1051.

[22] *Majmū'at aḥkām al-naqḍ* 27 (16 March 1976): 665–670.

[23] *BLJ* 13 (28 March 1901), p. 221; *Al-Wasīṭ*, vol. 7, book 1, p. 136.

[24] *BLJ* 15 (24 June 1903), p. 558; *Al-Wasīṭ*, vol. 7, book 1, p. 136.

some proven fault; but (2) if a building collapsed for no good reason, then the contractor would be *prima facie* liable, it being presumed that his materials or workmanship were defective.[25] Hence, in the case of a collapsed building the burden of proof was on the contractor to show that the collapse was not owing to his fault.

Sanhūrī comments on this that, "we should not make the rebuttal of this presumption easy through recourse to the opinion of experts since it is to be feared that the experts might show bias in favor of the members of their profession and the position intended by the legislator would be defeated" (p. 135). Accordingly, he continues, the draft code should restrict the cases in which *force majeure* can operate to discharge this liability.

For this reason, the first draft contained a limited provision which said that liability could be excluded by proof of *force majeure* and gave one example related to a default in the stability of the land.[26] After discussion this was altered to the following clause: "Breach of the provision is for the contractor unless he shows that the fault causing damage was caused through an extraneous cause."[27] This too was disliked by lawyers in the Senate (*majlis al-shuyūkh*) and eventually was deleted altogether. It was finally decided that the general provisions of *force majeure* in the civil code (now Article 165) covered the situation adequately and if applied would negate the causal connection necessary for liability.

SUMMARY OF CHANGES IN THE 1949 CIVIL CODE

The following main changes are, therefore, to be seen between the old and new codes: (1) the new provisions apply to "other fixed structures"; Sanhūrī refers to houses, villas, communal buildings, schools, hospitals, clinics, theaters, cinemas, factories, shops, mosques, and also bridges, dams, reservoirs, aqueducts, and things constructed underground[28] (but other writers

[25] See discussion in *Al-Wasīṭ*, vol. 7, book 1, pp. 235–238 on provisions of *Majmū'at*, 5:25–28 (footnote).

[26] Originally Article 898 of the draft code; see *Majmū'at*, 5:26–27.

[27] *Al-Wasīṭ*, vol. 7, book 1, p. 136; *Majmū'at*, 5:27 (footnote).

[28] *Al-Wasīṭ*, vol. 7, book 1, pp. 107–108.

dispute the application of this phrase to underground structures[29]); (2) the new civil code extended liability to defects that endanger property and people; and (3) in the new provisions it is clear that the ten-year period of liability runs from the date of delivery of the construction and not from the date of the failure in the structure or the date of recognition of the defect,[30] and other prescription periods do not apply to it;[31] and (4) in the new provisions there is a prohibition on exclusion or limiting clauses—this is a public policy provision—and recent cases add further that acceptance of a building does not negate any such prohibition;[32] and (5) in the new provisions the owner has a three-year period in which to make a claim once he knows of facts which give rise to it.

The conditions for a successful claim of decennial liability against a contractor are therefore as follows: (1) the existence of a *muqāwalāt* contract, defined in Article 646 as a contract where one of the parties contracts to do a piece of work or to perform a service on condition of remuneration; and (2) the claimant must prove that the defect occurred within the parameters of the articles 651–654; and (3) the contractor is then *prima facie* liable unless he can negate the presumed causal connections by showing that the defect occurred or the building collapsed by reason of something outside his control. It is not enough to show that the contractor was not negligent or that the defect or collapse were owing to an unknown cause.

MODERN ASPECTS OF DECENNIAL LIABILITY

Decennial liability is not merely an Egyptian phenomenon, for it is now found in the civil law of most Middle Eastern countries, often having been taken from Egypt originally. Iraq in 1950 adopted Egypt's civil code and along with it decennial liability, although limiting it to five years instead of ten. Syria adopted

[29] See Mohamed Labib Chanab, *Commentary on the Rules of the Aqd Muqawalat* (Cairo, 1962), pp. 125–127.

[30] Unlike the 1978 French law: see *Code Civil* (Paris: Dalloz, 1986–87).

[31] See Grandmoulin, *Droit*, p. 224 for the uncertain position in the mixed court period. Also Attia, "Decennial Liability," p. 509. Provisions on prescription are found in articles 382–388 of the new civil code.

[32] *Majmū'at aḥkām al-naqḍ* 16 (10 March 1965), pp. 736–747; 18 (13 April 1967), pp. 835–839.

decennial liability by decree in 1969 and Algeria adopted it by decree in 1975. In each case the provisions are indistinguishable from Egyptian law. Saudi Arabia in its 1977 tender regulations provided that a contractor in a public sector works contract was under such liability and must insure against it. Kuwait in articles 692–697 of its new 1980 civil code provides for decennial liability in the same way as Egypt (it was not in the earlier Kuwaiti commercial code, even though that was taken from Egypt), but even before the 1980 code decennial liability was considered by lawyers as part of Kuwaiti law by custom, and as such it was provided for in Kuwaiti standard form contracts for public sector works.

Decennial liability is therefore a fact of life in any contract of construction in the Middle East and is a considerable burden upon the contractor, the engineer, and the architect. In all cases, these persons generally insure against such liability and this has become the most important socio-legal feature of the whole idea of decennial liability. In any such Middle East construction contract, provision will need to be made for insurance against general liability for negligence against third parties and for this special liability. These insurance premiums then inevitably form part of the eventual contract price. In many countries, because of the public nature of decennial liability, insurance is mandatory and the state lays down the boundaries of the insurance, occasionally even stipulating that insurance will be the monopoly of a state insurance agency.

By Law 106 of 1976[33] Egypt followed suit. No license to build was to be issued to an owner or landlord without the production of a valid insurance policy covering certain basic liabilities. Article 8 of the 1976 law provided that the insurance must cover: (1) responsibility of engineers (not apparently limited to architects) and contractors for liability to third parties (including the landlord) during the execution of the works (presumably under the general negligence provisions in Articles 163 and 177 of the civil code, though this is nowhere stated); (2) liability under Article 651 (i.e., presumably decennial liability) for ten years after completion; and (3) liability to third parties (presumably again under articles 163 and 177) for the same ten year period.

[33] *Al-Jarīdah al-rasmīyah* (Official gazette) 37 (9 September 1976), pp. 811–817.

The language of Article 8 was by no means clear, but it seems likely that the above is the correct interpretation of its Arabic provisions. Thus, insurance was mandatory to cover both decennial liability and third party liability for at least ten years.

However, by amendments in Law 30 of 1983, Article 8 has been radically altered in an odd fashion. After 1983, insurance is mandatory to cover:

Civil responsibility of engineers and contractors for damages suffered by third parties, by reason of partial or total destruction of buildings or structures, with respect to:

(i) the responsibility of engineers and contractors during the period of execution, except towards their workers, and
(ii) the responsibility of the landlord (*mālik*) during the period of guarantee provided for in Article 651 of the civil code.

Although (ii) refers to Article 651, it seems to do so only for the purpose of determining the time for which the responsibility it refers to is to last (i.e., ten years), because by referring to the responsibility of the *landlord* it cannot possibly refer to decennial liability. In fact, it sits very oddly with the initial phrase, which refers to "civil responsibility of engineers and contractors," in that a landlord is generally neither. It seems then that, if any sense is to be made of the article at all, it provides that mandatory insurance covers the responsibility of engineers and contractors for damage to third parties during the execution of the works and further for the responsibility of the landlord to third parties for a period of ten years. It no longer requires mandatory insurance against decennial liability.

It may be that the change came about as a result of the systematic attempt by foreign state contractors to undermine the basis of Law 106 of 1976, by providing so many exceptions to its application that Law 30 of 1983 merely mirrored the prevailing legal position.

After the enactment of Law 106 of 1976, foreign contractors were required by law to provide for mandatory insurance for decennial liability up to 1 percent of the contract price. In the biggest contracts, the resulting hike in price could run to millions or tens of millions of dollars. U.K. and U.S. contractors were particularly affected by it and through them USAID or ODA (the U.S. and U.K. state development agencies), which often provided the funding for large construction projects. It was their high-handed actions against the new insurance provisions which most likely sparked a reconsideration of Law 106.

In one project, the Greater Cairo Sewage Project, U.K. and U.S. contractors were building a new sewage system for Cairo at a cost in excess of 1000 million dollars. The decennial liability premium on this project would be approximately 1 percent of the total price and therefore would have been approximately 10 million dollars. USAID/ODA, who were helping to fund the project, queried such a payment and so bullied their governments and Egypt that a tripartite treaty was signed by the United Kingdom, the United States, and Egypt on 19 October 1979[34] exempting the project contractors from the provisions of decennial liability and also the provisions on insurance in Article 8 of Law 106. The agreement provided expressly that the contractors were only to be bound by the terms of their contract. Essentially, if the project was to be protected against decennial liability, the Egyptian government would have to pay the premium itself—it was not part of the USAID/ODA loan package. Soon after this, all USAID projects in Egypt were similarly exempted by terms of a presidential decree, and in 1981 a similar treaty was entered into between Egypt and Australia over a Suez cold storage project.

These actions caused consternation among Egyptian lawyers: it was reminiscent of one law for Egyptians and another for foreigners—shades of the mixed courts!—and it is quite likely that it was one of the reasons behind the strange retraction in Law 30 of 1983.

THE FUTURE

Sanhūrī in defending his civil code said he had used all previous Egyptian jurisprudence and not left untouched any provision of the Sharīʿah. It is notable, however, in the commentary to the civil code that Islamic law is never once quoted to support

[34] Ibid., 8 May 1980; presidential decree no. 465 of 1979. For an English translation of this treaty, see *MEER*, Jan. 1980.

Articles 651–654. It refers to French, Spanish, Portuguese, Italian, Tunisian, Polish, and Japanese codes of law in support of it but nothing of Islamic origin.

In the 1980s, in Egypt, there was a call for Islamicization of its laws. Ṣūfī Abū Ṭālib, speaker of the Majlis al-Sha'b (the national assembly), was asked to chair a drafting committee to draft new Islamic legislation. Six codes of law were drafted by this committee: a commercial, civil transactions, and criminal code, each with its separate procedural code. Each code is provided with a substantial commentary which seeks to refer to Islamic law to support its provisions. Some codes, such as the draft criminal code, substantially alter the present law and provide for many new Islamic offenses and penalties; others, however, are little more than a reiteration of the present codes.

The new draft code of civil transactions is very little changed from the present civil code. Decennial liability is to be found in its draft Articles 650–653, and these are essentially the same provisions, with some cosmetic changes in language. In the commentary to the articles on decennial liability, the committee refers to a number of sources from which they drew in preparing the codes: (1) articles of the *Majallah* (the Ottoman civil code) of 1876, (2) articles in the so-called Ḥanbalī *Majallah*—a modern compilation of Ḥanbalī *fiqh* produced and published in Saudi Arabia, and (3) some general works of *fiqh*.

The main thrust of these provisions is that the modern contract known as the *'Aqd al-muqāwalah* is said to be comparable with one of the types of the Islamic contract of *ijārah* (hire) in which the hiree is in the position of an *ajīr mushtarak* (an independent contractor), a hired person who provides his own materials and is paid for a particular job, rather than in the position of an *ajīr khāṣṣ* (a servant) who is provided with materials and is supervised in what he is told to do. In this way the contract is a valid one according to Islamic law.

It is said further, however, that according to Islamic law the *ajīr mushtarak* is subject to civil liability (*ḍamān*) for things done in the course of completing his contract, and the commentary then equates this with decennial liability and hence accepts this form of liability, seemingly supporting its use from Islamic sources.

Unfortunately, these slight references to Islamic legal ideas are not sufficiently dealt with nor are they correct to describe this purported liability.

First, the concept of *ḍamān* is better considered as a form of tortious liability than as an extended form of contractual responsibility (which is what decennial liability is), even though the word *mutaḍāmin* comes from the same root. Even if it could be used to support this liability, it is clear that in classical Islamic law, before *ḍamān* could operate, one has to show positively some illicit act (*ta'addī*) or negligence (*tafrīṭ*) by the *ajīr mushtarak*,[35] whereas decennial liability is a form of strict liability (as we have seen above).

Second, the contract of *ijārah* is generally used for the hire or rent of animals or inanimate movable objects, and there is little reference in the books of *fiqh* to its use by classical Islamic lawyers in a contract of construction.

What could have been used to support decennial liability is not the contract of *ijārah* but rather the contract of *salam* (a contract of sale with future delivery) and particularly the contract of *istiṣnā'* (the sale of a thing to be manufactured and delivered in the future). Such a contract breaches fundamental principles of Islamic contract law—those of immediate delivery and certainty—but it was accepted by most jurists as an exception based on custom and it was justified by reference to *maṣlaḥah* (public interest) or, as Mālik put it, "because the people have need of it." However, even though the Islamic contract of *istiṣnā'* is closer to the modern contract of construction, it is still controversial whether the manufacturer in such a contract was subject to a form of strict liability for mismanufacture or misconstruction. In fact, it is controversial whether Islamic law accepted the idea of strict liability at all, and hence it is wrong and nonsensical to attempt to fit what is obviously a legal concept of French origin into an Islamic framework that is manipulated for that purpose.

[35] See, for example, Ibn Qudāmah, *Al-Mughnī*, 6:125, concerning *ḍamān* of a shepherd: "There is no *ḍamān* by the shepherd where he does not commit an unlawful act.... he is not liable unless there is an unlawful act or negligence (*ta'addī aw tafrīṭ*)." See also Article 607 of the Ottoman *Majallah*, and Articles 706–713 of the Ḥanbalī *Majallah*.

Nor are such arguments purely academic.

In a recent international arbitration between a large English oil company and a national oil company, a problem arose in the interpretation of decennial liability provisions and their existence in Islamic law.[36] The English oil company had agreed to build a gas plant in one of the Gulf states for a price of two billion dollars. The gas plant was built literally on a sand foundation and there was subsidence. As a result, a large gasometer cracked and blew up, causing a large amount of damage, and the rest of the gas plant was declared unsafe. The Gulf oil company claimed damages, or alternatively a return of the contract price, of two billion dollars. The Gulf state involved had taken its civil law from Egypt but had for some reason excluded from it the provisions of decennial liability in Articles 650–654. It was the argument of the Gulf oil company that the decennial liability provisions of the Egyptian code were part of Arab custom—they were so important and frequently occurring in the Arab Middle East that they had become part of Arab or Middle Eastern customary law and should be considered part of the law of that state, notwithstanding their absence from the civil law. Reference was made to previous decisions of courts of that state that had applied Egyptian case law to questions of this sort of liability. To bolster this argument, it was also said that decennial liability was recognized by Islamic law anyway as part of the law of *ḍamān* and hence should be applicable as part of Islamic law.

In the final result, the arbitral tribunal compromised on a solution which neither side wanted or enjoyed without really deciding on the above points, but it may be seen that the arguments are by no means academic.

CONCLUSION

Recent elections in Egypt have shown that the Muslim Brotherhood has now gained an effective voice in the Egyptian national assembly, and it remains to be seen whether as a result there will be any important changes to Egyptian law—and particularly

[36] Unfortunately this matter is still *sub judice* and the names cannot be revealed. The arbitral award was also ordered by the parties to remain unpublished.

whether there will be implementation of the six (so called) Islamic codes. The Muslim Brotherhood had as their voting slogan during the campaign "al-Islām huwa al-ḥall" (Islam is the solution), but it remains to be seen whether Islam can come up with viable alternatives to Western concepts of law (particularly commercial law) that are firmly entrenched in Egypt and indeed most of the other states of the Middle East. If there are not any viable alternatives, then any attempt to support the present law by spurious (and often wrong-headed) references to Islamic law (which may please bankers and entrepreneurs) should be treated by Islamic scholars as a dilution of classical Islamic law and vigorously challenged.

10

The Sharīʿah: A Methodology or a Body of Substantive Rules?

ANN ELIZABETH MAYER

INTRODUCTION

IN AN ARTICLE published in 1960 on the problems of modern Islamic legislation, Joseph Schacht discussed codifications of Islamic law. He made the following observation about codifications: "But traditional Islamic law, being a doctrine and a method rather than a code . . . is by its nature incompatible with being codified, and every codification must subtly distort it."[1]

Schacht was talking about what was then a relatively uncommon phenomenon. Since 1960, which is at least a decade before the impact of the Islamic resurgence made itself felt in the legal sphere, official campaigns to Islamize legal systems by adopting codified versions of Islamic law have been undertaken in many countries of the Middle East, such as Pakistan, Libya, Iran, the U.A.E., the Sudan, and Egypt. That is, there are many states that are currently pursuing Islamization in a form that Schacht would have argued means a distortion of traditional Islamic law—or, as

[1] Joseph Schacht, "Problems of Modern Islamic Legislation," *Studia Islamica* 12 (1960): 108.

others might prefer to put it, in a form that marks a new point of departure for the development of Islamic law.

There appears to be considerable support among Muslims for the general idea of codification of the Sharīʿah. If one accepts the argument that codification distorts traditional Islamic law, the existence of this support suggests that the Muslims who advocate codification are either prepared to abandon principles of traditional law that might conflict with codification or are unaware that codification is incompatible with traditional doctrines to which they adhere. Muslims have shown themselves reluctant to abandon the traditional theory of sources of Islamic law even as legal developments proceed in a manner that suggests the traditional theory is inadequate to account for the ways that Islamic law is currently evolving.

This paper will propose that the theoretical problems of adjusting traditional Sharīʿah doctrine and method to meet the demands of a codified legal system have yet to be fully appreciated and overcome and that these problems center on the traditional theory of sources of Islamic law. These problems are ones that arise when a theory of sources of law lags behind the developmental needs of a legal system, so that actual legal developments become hard to reconcile with the theory. It should be stressed that tensions between adherence to an outmoded theory of sources and actual legislative practice are not unique to the Islamic environment but are found in other legal systems as well.[2] That is, the existence of these tensions in no way implies that there are any peculiar defects or deficiencies in the Islamic legal heritage. Instead, the existence of such tensions should be seen as part of the normal history of growth of a legal culture and as indicative of a transitional stage in the historical development of a legal tradition.

This article will briefly discuss some of the issues that have been raised by the current Islamization campaigns and will attempt a tentative assessment of the significance of the codification movement in relation to traditional ideas regarding the nature of the Sharīʿah and the sources of Islamic law.

[2] Comparative historical problems of sources of law are treated in Alan Watson, *Sources of Law, Legal Change, and Ambiguity* (Philadelphia: University of Pennsylvania, 1984).

CODIFICATION AND THE SHARĪ'AH PRIOR TO ISLAMIZATION

Before considering the implications of modern codification of the Sharī'ah, it is instructive to review how the traditional Sharī'ah became a jurists' law, where one turned to qualified jurists to find out what the law was.

Although the Sharī'ah historically developed into a jurists' law, it might just as well have developed into a codified law. The tradition of codification was well established in the ancient world as well as in ancient Middle Eastern culture, and the choice could have been made at the outset of Islamic legal history to devise Islamic codes that would have been promulgated by the ruler. That is, it would have been perfectly possible for the Sharī'ah to have been introduced in a codified formulation.

One has the historical example of a high government official, Ibn al-Muqaffa' (d. ca. 759), who in the eighth century perceived the merits of codification and proposed that the Caliph should codify the Sharī'ah so that there would be one, uniform, official version of Islamic law.[3] This would have given the ruler centralized control over law-making and would also have precluded both the proliferation of diverging juristic interpretations of Sharī'ah requirements that followed the death of the Prophet in 632 and the development of the distinctive doctrines of the classical schools of Islamic law. Had Ibn al-Muqaffa''s proposal been implemented, Muslims would now be habituated to two assumptions underlying modern national codified systems—that it is for the state to select what rules to put in law codes and thereby to determine what the law is, and that one, unitary legal standard should prevail throughout a state's territory. Of

[3] Joseph Schacht, *The Origins of Muhammadan Jurisprudence* (Oxford: Clarendon Press, 1953), p. 95; Patricia Crone and Martin Hinds, *God's Caliph: Religious Authority in the First Centuries of Islam* (Cambridge: Cambridge University Press, 1986), pp. 85–87. There was even a report that the Caliph al-Manṣūr proposed to make Mālik's *Al-Muwaṭṭa'* the sole source of Islamic law for his subjects but was dissuaded from so doing by Mālik himself. Ibid., p. 86. Crone and Hinds offer a concept of "Caliphal law" that they believe existed from the death of the Prophet into the early 'Abbāsid period. Ibid., 43–57. It appears to be quite different from the codification idea of Ibn al-Muqaffa' and the Islamic codes and statutes that are currently being enacted. Its sources are said to be the Qur'ān, the Sunnah, and *ra'y*. Ibid., p. 54.

course, this early proposal for codifying the Sharī'ah was rejected.

Until the nineteenth century, there seem to have been no serious attempts to codify the Sharī'ah. One has the example of Ottoman *qānūns*, but these did not constitute realizations of Ibn al-Muqaffa''s ideal of codification. They covered very limited subject matter and did not challenge the theoretical supremacy of juristic interpretations of Sharī'ah requirements, not being treated as definitive statements of Sharī'ah law. Instead, the *qānūns* were conceptually marginal elements in the Sharī'ah system, supplementing the Sharī'ah in areas where it was relatively weak.

In the nineteenth and twentieth centuries Middle Eastern societies had to come to terms with the need to adopt codified versions of law, in spite of, rather than because of, their own legal traditions. The modern movement toward codification resulted from a secular impetus, designed to facilitate progress toward modernization, which was deemed by political leaders to require the abandonment of archaic elements in Middle Eastern legal systems.[4] In the process, the Sharī'ah law in its form as a jurists' law was discarded, except in Saudi Arabia, where there was greater resistance than elsewhere to codification.

The adoption of national law codes in the Middle East signifies the acceptance of the idea that it is rules formulated and enacted by the government that determine what the laws should be on the national territory.

The general shift to codified forms of law is not peculiar to Muslim countries, but is part of the adjustment that modern national legal systems have had to make to the need for greater efficiency and uniformity in law. The systematization and clarification of rules that codification permits have been universally adjudged to be the best ways to meet this need, while jurists' laws have generally been assessed as inadequate and thus have been

[4] Useful short surveys of legal reform and codification can be found in J. N. D. Anderson, *Law Reform in the Muslim World* (London: Athlone, 1976), pp. 34–85 and Herbert Liebesny, *The Law of the Near and Middle East: Readings, Cases, and Materials* (Albany: SUNY Press, 1975), pp. 46–125.

abandoned.[5] Of course, codification has lagged in the common law world, and the relatively few Middle Eastern countries influenced by the common law have not codified as extensively as civil law systems, but at least they have had to accommodate the idea that major areas of law need to be covered by statutory enactments. In other words, the universal contemporary pressures favoring the adoption of statutory or codified law seem overwhelming.

As Middle Eastern governments assumed the prerogative of legislation, they enacted codes that were largely of secular derivation, most of which were borrowed from French or French-inspired models. That is, until recently codification has generally been associated in the Middle East with the practice of borrowing law from the West and abandoning any pretense of following Islamic law in the areas covered by the new codes. However, even in the period when borrowing European codes was the major method of law reform, there were occasional instances of Middle Eastern governmental attempts to preserve substantive Sharīʿah rules by enacting them in codified form while discarding the old unwieldy juristic treatises. The most famous single attempt to reformulate the Sharīʿah in codified form was in the Ottoman *Majallah* of 1877, which set forth a streamlined, rationalized version of the law of obligations taken from rules in Ḥanafī treatises. The Ottoman Family Rights Law of 1917 was another such monument, although it did not limit its selection of rules to those in Ḥanafī sources. In the 1950s and 1960s there were also a number of noteworthy attempts to codify aspects of personal status law, but these took place against a background of previously applicable traditional Sharīʿah law, and the impetus behind these changes lay in a desire to implement liberal reformist policies, not in a drive for Islamization of the existing law.

Despite the exceptions that have just been noted, it is fair to say that in the Middle East the process of codification of law was predominantly associated with secularization, while Islamic law remained associated with the traditional, uncodified system

[5] A valuable study of how national codifications emerged out of a tradition of jurists' law in the West can be found in Alan Watson, *The Making of the Civil Law* (Cambridge: Harvard, 1981).

of jurists' law. The fact that today Islamization has become associated with codification initiatives therefore constitutes a major change.

CODIFICATION IN THE ERA OF ISLAMIZATION

With the Islamic resurgence in the Middle East, the tendency has grown to interpret the importation of Western law as a manifestation of Western cultural imperialism. The idea that Western legal imports should be eliminated and Islamic law should be revived as the law of the land has become very popular.

In the early 1970s in Libya Mu'ammar al-Qadhdhāfī inaugurated the first official attempt to Islamize a legal system by enacting Sharī'ah rules in the form of statutes replacing rules that had been taken from Western models. Other Islamization programs were subsequently undertaken elsewhere. In some countries, individual statutes were enacted, while in others, attempts were made to codify whole areas of law via newly formulated schemes of Islamic rules.

The consistent choice of codification and statutes to implement Islamization of legal systems is noteworthy, because on the basis of historical example it would not seem to be the case that governmental intervention via legislation would be necessary to make Islamic law applicable. After all, Islamic law was applied for over a millennium without there having been recourse to legislative measures by governments to bring it into force. Thus, a different and perfectly viable option would be to revert to the traditional system of jurists' law that preceded the borrowings of Western codified law. This would mean that the government would merely announce that there would be no more reliance on Western-inspired law and that Islamic jurists would again be in charge of interpreting the requirements of the Sharī'ah.

Following the latter option, however, would entail that governments relinquish the power that they gained over legal systems when European-style codified law was originally adopted. To cede their legislative prerogatives would constitute a setback for the governments involved, which, as their conduct indicates, want unitary national legal systems in which the political authorities retain the power to determine what will be treated as law. Naturally, governments interested in pursuing Islamization prefer to reinstate Islamic rules via a process of government-controlled legislative measures. Thus, governments have every reason to want to promote the idea that Islamization should be effectuated by governmental enactments—an idea that in any case happens to be supported by many private Muslims, as well.

THEORIES OF THE SOURCES OF ISLAMIC LAW VERSUS THE HIERARCHY OF SOURCES OF LAW IN MODERN LEGAL SYSTEMS

To appreciate the readjustments that are called for by the current movement to codify the Sharīʿah, it is important to recall the traditional Islamic theory of sources of law, or *uṣūl al-fiqh*. In brief summary, the theory establishes what are the material sources of the Sharīʿah (basically the Qur'ān and Sunnah), the techniques of reasoning that may be used to elaborate and interpret the former (such as *qiyās* or *ijtihād*), and the principle of ratification by juristic consensus (*ijmāʿ*).

In order to interpret and apply Sharīʿah law to a legal problem, it was traditionally thought essential that the interpreter should possess a mastery of the relevant texts and methodology, a mastery that until recently was largely the province of Islam's jurists. There was great diversity in the conclusions that jurists reached regarding what were the correct Islamic solutions to legal problems, but the widely differing substantive rules that were set forth in the juristic treatises of the classical Sunnī schools were treated as enjoying an equal claim to Islamic orthodoxy. What guaranteed the orthodoxy of legal rules in this system was not uniformity of results, a goal that the traditional system did not aim to achieve, but the common use of recognized methods of scholarship and interpretation of the sources. A demonstrable reliance on the criteria of *uṣūl al-fiqh* was what established the Islamic pedigrees of substantive rules of law.[6]

[6] The literature on *uṣūl al-fiqh* is vast. A summary treatment can be found in Joseph Schacht, *An Introduction to Islamic Law* (Oxford: Oxford University Press, 1964), pp. 58–68. An excellent recent article on the origins of *uṣūl al-fiqh* is George Makdisi, "The Juridical Theology of Shāfiʿī—Origins and Significance of *Uṣūl al-Fiqh*," *Studia Islamica* 59 (1984): 5–47. In this study, George Makdisi shows

One may contrast the traditional scheme of *uṣūl al-fiqh* and another scheme for ranking legal sources that is useful for comparative purposes. This ranking is critical when one needs to know where legal rules are set forth and to what sources one should turn for clarification of the legal rules.

In a modern legal setting, one can classify sources as primary sources, which one consults to find the actual texts of laws, and secondary sources, where one finds clarifications of the rules that are set forth in the primary sources. These should be distinguished from remote sources of law, such as customary norms and the religio-cultural heritage from which the law ultimately derives. Understanding the historical background and origins of legal rules, as found in the remote sources, enhances the understanding of primary and secondary sources, but one does not refer to the remote sources to find what the legal system actually treats as the definitive statements of legal rules.

This hierarchical ranking of legal sources may seem oversimplified, and one could object that it does not adequately reflect the historical complexity in the relationships among different types of legal sources. Still, it can be used as a starting point for analyzing where one should turn to find the law.

This ranking is instructive when applied to the traditional Sharīʿah system. By applying this scheme, admittedly with a bit of strain and oversimplification, we arrive at a classification that will be helpful in identifying how the current codification trend entails conflicts with the doctrine and method of the traditional Sharīʿah.

I believe that Muslims in the past made distinctions between what were to be treated as primary and secondary sources of Islamic law, while relegating others to the status of remote sources. However, the emphasis on the traditional ideas of *uṣūl al-fiqh* may have obscured the nature of these distinctions.

---

that the term *uṣūl al-fiqh* did not always have the meaning that eventually came to be associated with it. Although in traditional Islamic law it generally designated the methodology of Islamic law, there is evidence that at least into the tenth century its meaning was so unsettled that it could be used to designate not the science of interpreting the material sources but, rather, the principles of positive law or substantive legal rules. Ibid., pp. 8–9. I find the early ambiguity of this critical term intriguing, since it seems to anticipate the contemporary confusion about whether the Sharīʿah should be viewed as a methodology or a body of substantive legal rules.

In the premodern period, once the schools of Islamic law had sufficiently congealed and their distinctive rules had developed, the *fiqh* (jurisprudence) literature was generally treated as the primary source of law. That is, it was typically juristic elaborations of the meanings of the Qur'ān and Sunnah that were consulted to resolve legal questions, rather than the Qur'ān and Sunnah. Which jurist's views would be deemed authoritative on a legal problem would depend on a variety of factors, such as the school adherence of the parties involved, which law school was followed in the region, what legal treatise was most highly regarded in the relevant legal community, and the relative standing of local legal experts. To help clarify legal problems that were not resolved in a primary source, jurists could use sources such as legal handbooks, *fatwā* collections, commentaries, and supercommentaries, meaning that aspects of the *fiqh* literature might be utilized as secondary sources. In this scheme, the Qur'ān and Sunnah were effectively relegated to the status of remote sources of law, since what was set forth in their texts was superseded by school doctrine as developed by jurists.[7]

Despite the occasional strong objections that were voiced to the preeminence that *fiqh* assumed as the primary source of Islamic law, the historical record shows that Sharīʿah law in the premodern period was generally treated as a jurists' law, which meant that the actual legal rules were whatever the jurists said they were. Indeed, the prestige that Islam's jurists traditionally enjoyed was due to their status as the masters of legal interpretation and their monopoly of legal authority.

The traditional theory of sources of law survives today, albeit with greater attendant controversy than in the past. In the contemporary Muslim world, questions regarding the hierarchy of the Islamic sources have become more widely contested than they appear to have been in the premodern era.[8] The expansion of secular education, the increase in literacy, and the enormous

[7] Yves Linant de Bellefonds, *Traité de droit musulman comparé*, 3 vols. (The Hague: Mouton, 1956), 1:19–34. Although brief, this treatment of the problems of trying to determine how the comparative legal historian should classify and rank the sources of Islamic law is the best that I have encountered.

[8] Some sense of the current disputes regarding sources can be gleaned from the Pakistani cases cited below.

growth in communications have meant that voices of many different Muslims, not just eminent scholars, are now being heard on these questions. While in the past the authority of Islamic jurists was rarely challenged, many contemporary Muslims are inclined to dispute the notion that only highly trained religious scholars are qualified to interpret the Qur'ān and Sunnah. Among contemporary Muslims who question the authority of jurists as the sole interpreters of the Sharī'ah sources, there is a growing tendency to demote the juristic treatises embodying the *fiqh* to the rank of secondary sources and to deny that they have any binding legal force.

Today one also finds Muslims who entirely reject the authority of the *fiqh* and treat the Qur'ān and Sunnah as the primary sources of Islamic law. Other Muslims question the authenticity of the *ḥadīth* collections and are inclined to downgrade the importance of the Sunnah, treating the Qur'ān as the sole primary source of Sharī'ah law and the Sunnah, sometimes along with the *fiqh*, as a secondary source, at best.

In addition to mounting disarray on the question of how to rank the Qur'ān, the Sunnah, and the *fiqh* as legal sources, there is also a growing diversity in approaches to interpretation. Today, as Muslims without training in the classical religious sciences apply their own ideas of appropriate criteria to finding how the Sharī'ah deals with various legal problems, one finds that the traditional forms of legal reasoning are often abandoned and replaced by new and more free-wheeling methods of interpreting the sources.

In sum, the premodern consensus that supported the treatment of juristic interpretation as the primary source of Islamic law seems to have broken down.

Although contemporary Muslims are deeply divided on many aspects of the traditional theory of sources of law, I know of no serious argument that has been put forward for the proposition that, as a matter of Islamic jurisprudence and theology, Islamic law should be deemed to be whatever the government of a modern nation-state says that it is, or, in other words, that modern legislation should be treated as the primary source of Islamic law once the state transforms it into positive law via its enactments, or that the Qur'ān and Sunnah should thereby be demoted to the status of remote sources of law.[9]

I see this as the background of the problem to which Schacht alluded—the incompatibility of the traditional Sharī'ah and codification. Modern governments expect their codes and statutes, including their new Islamic codes and statutes, to be recognized and deferred to as the primary source—nay, the exclusive source—of law. But, how can Muslims be expected to accord the requisite deference to governmental codes of Sharī'ah rules when Islamic theories of sources of law still do not envisage the Sharī'ah as a body of substantive rules created by governmental fiat?

CHALLENGES TO ISLAMIZATION MEASURES AS PRIMARY SOURCES OF SHARĪ'AH LAW

As has already been noted, neither traditional ideas of *uṣūl al-fiqh* nor contemporary theories of the sources of Islamic law support the notion that a secular legislator is entitled to make binding determinations of what the principles of Islamic law are. Proponents of the Islamization of contemporary legal systems do not seem to have confronted this issue squarely or to have articulated a coherent theory explaining why Muslims should accept that legislative initiatives by modern governments that are pursuing Islamization policies are to be treated as authoritative statements of Islamic law. The result of this failure is that we today have the coexistence of newly-enacted "Islamic" legislation in various countries that is clearly intended to be used as the primary source of Sharī'ah law along with theories of *uṣūl al-fiqh*, whether traditional or contemporary, according to which the former has no claim to be treated as the primary source of Islamic law.

The neglect of this critical issue in the literature on Islamization should not be taken to mean that Muslims are in practice

[9] An argument offered by one supporter of governmental Islamic legislation is that it should be obeyed because of the general duty owed by citizens to obey those in power and what the latter proclaim as law and also because of the need for general, uniform law. Ayatullah Ahmad Jannati, "Legislation in an Islamic State," *Al-Tawhid* 2 (1985): 66. This argument does not begin to explain why as a matter of Islamic jurisprudential theory Muslims should accept governmental enactments as the primary and exclusive sources of Islamic law or abandon their ideas of *uṣūl al-fiqh*.

untroubled by the conflicts between theories of sources of law and legislative praxis that are created when modern states attempt to exercise a monopoly over the making of Sharī'ah rules. We have some examples in both Pakistan and Iran, where the two most extensive Islamization campaigns have been undertaken, that indicate the kinds of objections Muslims are making to the proposition that governmental legislation constitutes authoritative statements of Islamic legal rules that are binding upon Muslims as a matter of Islamic jurisprudence or theology.

In Pakistan an important challenge in the form of a court case brought in 1980 by one Kai Kaus, an ex-judge, was made to the premises of the Islamization campaign that has been pursued since shortly after President Zia ul Haq seized power in 1977.[10] The petitioner, who was seeking relief in the form of a number of declaratory judgments and injunctions based on the Qur'ān and Sunnah, professed adherence to the goal of Islamization but insisted that there was no need for human legislation to impose the Sharī'ah in Pakistan, since all legal rules were contained in the Qur'ān and Sunnah. Sharī'ah rules, he argued, came into force due to their divine character and were already binding on the Muslims of Pakistan.[11] He prayed the court to recognize the validity of his claim that Pakistani Muslims were absolutely free persons except for their obligation to abide by the rules in the Qur'ān and Sunnah and that they were entitled to resist any order that clearly seemed not to be the will of Allah.[12] By implication, he was indicating his refusal to recognize the binding character of the "Islamic" legislation that was being enacted by the Pakistani government and his rejection of the idea the latter could ever constitute the primary source of Sharī'ah law for Pakistan's Muslims. For Kai Kaus, only the Qur'ān and Sunnah enjoyed the status of primary sources of Sharī'ah law.

Obviously, no modern state could allow its citizens the freedom demanded by Kai Kaus to decide for themselves what their legal rights and obligations were, based on their own, independent interpretations of religious texts. Not surprisingly, the court

[10] *B. Z. Kai Kaus* v. *President of Pakistan*, 1980 PLD SC 160.

[11] Ibid., p. 163.

[12] Ibid., p. 164.

rejected Kai Kaus's petition—without, however, offering a satisfactory response to the theoretical objections that he had raised to the legitimacy of the government's Islamization program. The court acknowledged that codifications of Sharī'ah law could be objected to on Islamic grounds that included the stereotyping of law that codification entails, the abandonment of the principle that God alone is the Legislator, and the inadaptability of Islamic law to codification.[13] While the court seemed unable to find Islamic authority supporting the notion that the state could make Islamic law in the same way it made other laws, it justified dismissing the petition by reference to sources and authority from the legal tradition of the Subcontinent, which has been a hybrid of British and local cultures since the British consolidated their rule over India. The court asserted:

> It cannot be denied, as the above precedents show, that enforcement of laws—(and we may say so even under Islamic [*sic*])—is the function of the State, which firstly makes known the relevant law to the people by publishing or publicizing it so they may regulate their lives, dealings and conduct accordingly.[14]

According to the norms of the transplanted British legal system, it was, of course, correct and appropriate for the state to make the law known. Why that should be the case in an Islamic system was not really dealt with.

The political system in Pakistan, where military officers have ruled the country since overthrowing the Bhutto government in 1977, is very different from that in Iran, where after the revolution of 1978–79 Islamic clerics came to play a dominant role in the government. In Iran one might expect that more deference would be shown to the traditional prerogatives of jurists because of the powerful position Islamic jurists hold in the post-revolutionary regime. It is therefore surprising that in Iran the Islamization campaign has not involved a return to jurists' law as the primary source of Sharī'ah rules. Instead, in the wake of the Islamic Revolution, Iranian law has continued to be made, just as it was under the

[13] Ibid., p. 179.
[14] Ibid., p. 174.

Pahlavis, in the form of statutes and codes enacted by the Iranian Majlis, or parliament. To effectuate the Islamization of the legal system that was one of the express goals of the Islamic Revolution a variety of "Islamic" laws have been passed by the Iranian Majlis.

This result seems a strange one, given the power that Ayatollah Khomeini has over the regime, in which he enjoys considerable authority both as a charismatic political leader and the officially recognized preeminent jurist. Khomeini has stated that God is the sole Legislator in Islam and that there is no room for human legislative activity in Islamic government. Before coming to power in Iran, he asserted in his famous program for an Islamic government:

> The entire system of government and administration, together with the necessary laws, lies ready for you.... if laws are needed, Islam has established them all. There is no need for you, after establishing a government, to sit down and draw up laws, or, like rulers who worship foreigners and are infatuated with the West, run after others to borrow their laws. Everything is ready and waiting. All that remains is to draw up ministerial programs.[15]

That is, for Khomeini, Islamic law is already complete and enforceable without any need for governmental enactments. The sole role of government, according to his view, is an executive and administrative one—basically, that of seeing to it that the laws of Islam are implemented and observed.

Khomeini is not the only Iranian jurist to adhere to the traditional Islamic notion that human legislative activity is unnecessary in a system based on the Sharīʿah. For example, when in the aftermath of the Islamic Revolution the Majlis was considering enacting a new bill on retaliation and blood money, a bill designed to enact traditional Sharīʿah rules on these subjects into law, another prominent cleric, Ayatollah Tehrani, spoke out to denounce the project, condemning as obscene the assumption that rules set forth in the Qur'ān itself would require ratification by a human legislature.[16]

[15] [Ayatollah Ruhollah] Khomeini, *Islam and Revolution* (Berkeley: Mizan, 1981), p. 137.

[16] Shahrough Akhavi, "Ideology and Praxis of Shiʿism in the Iranian Revolution," *Comparative Studies in Society and History* 25 (1983): 216.

It is a matter of no small lego-historical significance that Khomeini's public position in opposition to the establishment of the legislature was ignored despite his prestige and the influence that he was able to exercise on other aspects of the governmental scheme adopted after the Islamic Revolution. The role of the Majlis is formally provided for in Chapter 4 of the 1979 Constitution of the Islamic Republic. Article 71 empowers the legislature to enact laws on all issues within constitutional limits. Article 72 qualifies this by saying that legislation may not contradict the principles and commandments of the official religion (Twelver Shī'ism).

It should be noted that, so far, there seems to have been no willingness on the part of the regime to concede that the government's undertaking acts of legislation—including Islamic legislation—as provided for in the constitutional scheme might in itself violate the commandments of Shī'ī Islam. Khomeini's acquiescence in the adoption of the Iranian Constitution seems a compromise of his earlier convictions, since, like many other Islamic conservatives and traditionalists, he had argued that the Qur'ān and Sunnah should be the constitution of an Islamic government, not a man-made document.[17] While one might have expected the Islamic Republic to honor the views of the figure who is officially treated as the most distinguished authority on Shī'ī Islam, it seems that modern legal culture had become so influential in the time since Iran imported French-style law in the 1920s that Khomeini's widely publicized prerevolutionary objections to Western-inspired legislative models and constitutions were overridden.

Leaving aside the dubious legitimacy of the constitution itself in relation to Islamic legal theory, in the scheme established by the Constitution of the Islamic Republic of Iran, it is unquestionably legislation that is enacted by the Majlis that assumes the role of the primary source of law. For example, in Article 167 of the Iranian Constitution judges are ordered to try to base their decisions in the first instance on Iran's codified laws, or *qavānīn-i mudavvanah*, and, if they cannot do so, to use reputable Islamic sources, or *manābi'-i mu'tabar-i islāmī*—which, presumably, include the *fiqh* literature—and *fatwās*. As this indicates,

[17] Khomeini, *Islam and Revolution*, p. 55.

the traditional primary (and perhaps secondary) sources of the Sharīʿah are to be referred to only *in the absence* of a dispositive code provision. True, "reputable Islamic sources" may be used as primary sources where the Majlis has not enacted an applicable rule. However, as they are referred to only where there is a legislative gap, in those instances where they might still occasionally be used as primary sources, they would clearly be, at the most, primary sources of the second rank.

As these examples from Pakistan and Iran illustrate, there are Muslims who are aware of the incongruity of raising man-made laws to the stature of primary sources of law in legal systems purportedly designed to reinstate Islamic law. However, the idea that it is governmental enactments that determine what enjoys the status of "law" has become so well entrenched in modern legal systems that the arguments of those who insist that Islamization programs should preserve the traditional Sharīʿah methodology have fallen on deaf ears.

THE CONFUSING RESULTS OF NEW ISLAMIC LEGISLATION: THE EXAMPLE OF *ZINĀ* LAWS

Interesting examples of national Islamic legislation can be seen in the different rules that have been enacted into law regarding *zinā*, or fornication and adultery, in Libya, Pakistan, the Sudan, and Iran. *Zinā* is one of the most serious crimes in the Sharīʿah and has a relatively large number of references in both the Qur'ān and the Sunnah. That is, it is a subject on which the texts in the material sources are quite extensive and regarding which the rules are set forth with greater specificity than they are on many other topics. Nevertheless, the *zinā* legislation in these countries varies on a number of points, leading to a situation where a single legal standard is applicable within the territorial limits of a state but where the *zinā* rules change depending on the country in which the offense is committed. This involves a notion of territoriality of law—something that was not contemplated in the traditional Sharīʿah.

On the question of the penalty for *zinā*, one finds a number of potentially applicable provisions in the material sources. For example, the Qur'ān in 24:2 provides for a penalty of one hundred lashes, and there are accounts in the Sunnah of offenders being stoned to death. One way, but not the only way, to reconcile the provisions regarding *zinā* penalties has been to say that the Qur'ānic penalty is for the offender who has never been married, while the stoning penalty is for the *muḥṣan* offender, one who has been married at the time of the offense. In the traditional *fiqh*, there were disputes about what constituted the proper *zinā* penalty that were never conclusively resolved.

Naturally, national legislation on the *zinā* penalty cannot reflect the ambiguities in the sources or the differences in their traditional interpretations but must in each instance select one, and only one, interpretation as the official standard for what the *zinā* penalty should be. Not surprisingly, given the lack of consensus about how *zinā* should be punished, the resulting national legislation has turned out to be very diverse.

In 1973 Libya enacted a *zinā* law providing a penalty of one hundred lashes for the offense,[18] while in 1979 Pakistan enacted a law saying that the penalty for *zinā* was one hundred lashes for a person who was not *muḥṣan* and stoning to death for a person who was *muḥṣan*.[19] The *zinā* provisions in the 1983 Sudanese Code of Criminal Procedure were similar to those in the Pakistani law, except that the penalty for the *muḥṣan* offender was hanging and for the male virgin flogging and also imprisonment and banishment for a period of one year.[20] Iran in 1982 adopted a *zinā* law that divided offenders into five categories with differing penalties, including stoning to death for the *muḥṣan*, a hundred lashes for the non-*muḥṣan*, a hundred lashes followed by stoning for elderly *muḥṣan* offenders, flogging and shaving of the head and a year's banishment for the married person who had not yet consummated the marriage, and execution where the offenses involve a number of special circumstances.[21]

[18] For a discussion of this law see Ann Mayer, "Libyan Legislation in Defense of Arabo-Islamic Sexual Mores," *American Journal of Comparative Law* 27 (1979): 297–298.

[19] Enforcement of Hudood Ordinance VII of 1979, Sections 5 (2)(a) and 6 (3)(a).

[20] Sudanese Code of Criminal Procedure of 1983, Article 318.

[21] The Iranian *zinā* rules were published as part of a law on *ḥudūd* and *qiṣāṣ* that was printed in the official gazette, number 10972 dated 1361/8/4. The relevant articles are 99–103.

In traditional Islamic law it was the use of recognized juristic methods of interpretation that guaranteed the orthodoxy of results, so that diversity in the results could be tolerated, but in the case of these new national *zinā* laws, the diversity in results is due solely to the choices made by the respective legislators. But, what in these circumstances guarantees the orthodoxy of the results in terms of Islamic theory? Why should a Muslim who is convinced that the sources mandate a certain penalty accept a different standard just because it has been enacted into law by the state as the Sharīʿah rule that is to be nationally applicable? It seems that there is no theoretical justification for expecting such acquiescence.

In Pakistan, where the opportunity for public challenge to the *zinā* law was greater than it was in the other countries, a legal challenge was brought to the stoning penalty provided for under the new *zinā* law by employing a procedure set forth in Article 203D of the Constitution Amendment Order of 1979, a Pakistani law that permits private citizens to bring suits challenging laws that are "repugnant to the Injunctions of Islam as laid down in the Holy Quran and the Sunnah."[22] The discussion of the validity of the stoning penalty revealed the inability of the government to provide a theoretical justification for its assumptions that Pakistani Muslims should recognize Pakistani legislation as a primary source of Islamic law. It also revealed Muslims' continued adherence to traditional ideas about the Sharīʿah sources and that the official Islamization measures could not necessarily expect to be recognized as primary sources of Islamic law. Indeed, the plaintiffs in the *zinā* case seemed to think that the *zinā* legislation could be treated as no more than an attempted paraphrase of the *zinā* rules as set forth in the true sources of Islamic law, so that it was subject to correction if it did not accurately state the applicable Islamic principles.

In their arguments, the plaintiffs appealed to both the Qur'ān and Sunnah and to juristic interpretations, which, to their minds, had obviously retained their traditional authority as primary and/or secondary sources of Islamic law. Based on their analyses and interpretations of passages in the Qur'ān and Sunnah, the

[22] *Hazoor Bakhsh* v. *Federation of Pakistan*, 1981 PLD FSC 145.

plaintiffs asserted that the Pakistani *zinā* legislation was flawed, because the correct standard was set forth in the Qur'ān (24:2). The plaintiffs argued that the Pakistani legislation improperly gave precedence to the stoning provisions found in the Sunnah, which, in their assessment, were of dubious authenticity and dealt with cases in which there were special or unusual circumstances. The plaintiffs were able to persuade the court that the stoning penalty was repugnant to the injunctions of Islam, and the court ruled that the law should be invalidated. Thus, the Pakistani stoning penalty for *zinā* was eliminated by the court ruling, leaving only the penalty of one hundred lashes provided for in the Qur'ān (24:2).

This ruling was one that had definite political implications in the Pakistani setting. At the risk of oversimplification, one could say that the Qur'ānic penalty, which is relatively mild, is one that is today supported by more liberal Pakistani Muslims, while the rule in the Sunnah that allows offenders to be stoned to death is favored by Islamic traditionalists and conservatives and Islamic jurists. Just as Islamic liberals had found the original *zinā* law unacceptable, so Islamic conservatives and traditionalists objected strongly to its invalidation and its replacement by the hundred lashes standard. The support of the conservative group was politically important to the Pakistani government. Reliance on this group had, presumably, been a factor in the adoption of the stoning penalty in the first place. The government therefore called for a rehearing of the case, changing beforehand the composition of the court by adding conservative clerics. The court in the second ruling in the case upheld the validity of the law as originally drafted, agreeing, as could have been predicted, with the government that stoning was the correct Sharī'ah penalty for the *muḥṣan* offender.[23]

Like the parties who criticized the law, the court in ruling that the original stoning penalty was correct made extensive references to the Qur'ān and Sunnah, but it interpreted the material sources differently, concluding that the Qur'ānic penalty applied only to the non-*muḥṣan*. It is significant that neither the Pakistani Government, as a party in the case, nor the courts were

[23] *Federation of Pakistan* v. *Hazoor Bakhsh*, 1983 PLD FSC 255.

prepared to assert that the Pakistani *zinā* law had to be treated as binding simply because the government had enacted it. Instead, both the courts and the governmental defendants acted as though the traditional theory of Sharīʿah sources were still intact and in place. Even though the law that permitted the challenge to Pakistani laws on the grounds that they violated Islamic injunctions had clearly been enacted to allow challenges to Pakistan's secular laws that were to be overhauled in the course of Islamization, the court did not rule that it was inappropriate to use the law to challenge the legitimacy of new "Islamic" laws that the government had been enacting as part of its Islamization campaign. That is, for all concerned the primary and secondary sources of the Sharīʿah were effectively the Qur'ān, Sunnah, or *fiqh*, or some combination thereof, and it was to these, not to Pakistani law, that they turned to ascertain whether the *zinā* penalty was valid or not under Islamic criteria.

But once the government had intervened so as to predetermine the outcome of the reconsideration of the case, it was clear that henceforth all Pakistanis, regardless of their readings of the relevant Islamic sources, would be expected to defer to the Pakistani *zinā* law as the definitive statement of the applicable Sharīʿah principles. That is, the law on the stoning penalty, having been submitted to the scrutiny provided for under the Pakistani Islamization program and having been officially decreed to embody the correct interpretation of the Islamic sources, was henceforth elevated to the status of the primary source on the penalty for *zinā* in Pakistan. But, leaving aside the issue of how this position could be reconciled with the traditional theory of sources, since this supposedly definitive law had already been changed twice by court rulings, whatever initial prestige it might have had had become considerably tarnished. Muslims who had not been disposed to accept the Islamic rationale for the stoning penalty in the original law could hardly be expected to defer to the court's second ruling, which reversed its own position. Despite the power of precedent in the Pakistani legal system, it would be hard to accept this decision as constituting a legitimate judicial ruling when it was so patently the product of extra-judicial forces—here, politically motivated interference and pressures by Pakistan's military rulers.

Sudanese Muslims became outspoken in their criticisms of Nimeiri's Islamization measures after his overthrow in 1985, including many features of his *zinā* law. The repressive policies of the Iranian and Libyan regimes make it dangerous for critics of the Islamic legislation there to speak out publicly, but there is no reason to believe that Muslims in these countries are any less inclined than those in Pakistan and the Sudan to evaluate governmental Islamization measures by reference to the traditional sources of Islamic law. One might add that, to the extent that Muslims become aware of the variety of penalties that have been chosen by the legislators in these countries, the fact that there are so many inconsistent national standards for how to penalize *zinā* will tend to exacerbate doubts about the credibility of all of these standards as definitive statements of the applicable Sharīʿah rules.

Therefore, one can say that, although the authority of codified versions of Islamic law requires that the government be accorded the exclusive prerogative to decide what will constitute Islamic law on its territory, Islamization has been proceeding at a time when Muslims are still clinging to a theory of sources of Islamic law that is incompatible with any governmental pretensions to monopolize legal authority.

THE FATE OF THE ISLAMIC THEORY OF SOURCES IN THE ERA OF ISLAMIZATION

Despite the instances of criticism of Islamization measures like the ones just described, Muslims do not seem to be disposed to abandon Islamization projects on the grounds that they cannot be reconciled with the traditional theory of sources of Islamic law. The priorities of today's Muslims seem to be changing, so that they are inclined to attach importance to seeing Sharīʿah rules enacted into law by governments—even though at the same time the awareness must be growing that this is placing enormous strains on the traditional Sharīʿah theory of sources, which Muslims are far from having renounced.

Governments pursuing Islamization are showing no inclination to cede either to jurists or to their citizens the prerogative of determining the rules of Islamic law by which they will deem themselves bound. Instead, all regimes seem eager to control what will be the official interpretations of Islamic requirements by elevating their own codes and statutes to the status of the primary source of Islamic law. Thus, as the pressures continue for Islamization of law, the practice of codification and systematization of Islamic law by governments will most likely also continue.

Since codification of Islamic law seems destined to proceed, eventually the conflicts between the traditional theory of sources and the practice of Islamization via government legislation will have to be resolved. They seem likely to be resolved by a process of detaching the substantive rules of the Sharī'ah from the traditional theory of sources, and the development of new ideas of sources that can accommodate the legitimacy of legislation by modern states. This process is sure to be a delicate and painful one, given Muslims' strong attachment to the traditional theory of sources and its centrality to the understanding of Islamic law as it has been known for over a millennium. When and if completed, the process may well have the effect of transforming the Sharī'ah from a legal tradition in which methodology is central to one in which certain principles in the substantive rules enacted into law by governments become its distinguishing feature.

11

Executive and Legislative Amendments to Islamic Family Law in India and Pakistan

DAVID PEARL

IT IS NOW more than a quarter of a century since Ayub Khan, then President of Pakistan, introduced into Pakistan law the Muslim Family Laws Ordinance 1961. This ordinance has played a very significant role in the domestic and political life of that country and, indirectly, in the political battles which have accompanied legislative and judicial pronouncements on Muslim family law in neighbouring India. The purpose of this paper is to review the impact of this ordinance on the family laws of the Muslim communities of South Asia, by placing the ordinance into the framework of the ideological commitment to an Islamic state, which is apparent to a degree in Pakistan from the beginning of its independence, although its manifestation is more central since the accession to power of President Zia in 1977. In India, the constitutional framework on which all discussion must be based is the important Article 44 of the Directive Principles of the Constitution with its clear philosophy of a uniform civil code.

Many attempts have been made to repeal the 1961 ordinance; all of them up to the present time have proved unsuccessful. The

This paper was written before the introduction of the Sharī'ah Bill into Pakistan by President Zia on 15 June 1988. It has been possible to make only minor references to this bill.

ordinance is seen by some to be modernist in substance and based, in its inspiration, on the falsehood of legislative intervention. Yet, notwithstanding major and significant Islamicization programs designed to introduce Islamic laws on crime, on evidence, and relating to the elimination of *ribā* (interest), the ordinance still prevails as the governing provision for the Muslims of Pakistan.

It is necessary at the outset to consider the broad currents of political life in Pakistan, first from partition to 1977 and then from 1977 to the present time. Only in this context can the specific family law material be seen in its context.

FROM PARTITION TO 1977

It has been suggested that one reason why Pakistan did not move quickly toward the introduction of Islamic laws was that regional differences and divisions tended to dominate the scene.[1] This was true of Bengal and the same phenomenon, although perhaps to a lesser extent, was apparent also in Baluchistan. The religious groupings themselves were hopelessly divided by sectarian differences. One illustration of the problem is the attempt faced by Pakistan from the start, to define and delimit the borders of Islamic adherence. The issue has appeared in its starkest form in the treatment of the Aḥmadīyah community with its unorthodox interpretation of the doctrine of the "seal of the prophets." After disturbances against that community, an inquiry was constituted to consider the reasons for the disturbances and the implications for the community at large.[2] The members of the inquiry were unable to draw a satisfactory definition of the term "Muslim." Neither did they believe that any two *ulamā'* would necessarily agree as to the definition of a Muslim. Given such divisiveness, it is little wonder that in its early period Pakistan to a very large extent ignored the implication of the meaning of the peculiar feature

[1] See R. Russell, "Strands of Muslim Identity in South Asia," *South Asia Review* 6 (1972): 21.

[2] The Munir Report. See E. I. J. Rosenthal, *Islam in the Modern National State* (Cambridge: Cambridge University Press), pp. 23–25. See also C. J. Adams, "The Ideology of Maulana Maududi" in *South Asian Politics and Religion*, ed. E. D. Smith (1960), p. 371.

of Islam as the legal basis, as opposed to the political and religious basis, for its existence as a separate entity.

If the ultra-religious groups had difficulty at that time in impressing on the body politic of Pakistan the need to introduce a program of full Islamicization, it must be stated also that communism had never been a serious contender for political power. Three reasons can be given for this. First, there has always been the spirit of competition amongst the peoples of northern India, making communism an unlikely flower; secondly, the doctrine of free trade was by now firmly planted; thirdly, Islamic ideology contains much which cannot exist side by side with communism. The disturbances which led to the resignation of Ayub Khan in 1969 were not designed to introduce a communist society, nor did this happen. The hero of the hour, of course, was Z. A. Bhutto, who had been detained by Ayub under the Defence of Pakistan Rules. Bhutto wrote these sentences in an affidavit placed before the High Court in Lahore on February 5th 1969:

> I want to hold high the banner of the Quaid [Muhammad Ali Jinnah, first president of Pakistan] and Iqbal [the famous Indian philosopher] to show to the world that this Islamic State of 120,000,000 gallant people can rise to the pinnacles of glory and translate into reality the ideal of free and equal men with which Islam lit the torch of civilization.... Pakistan is [a] formidable fortress of the millat of Islam, serving oppressed mankind everywhere.

These were not the words of a communist. Iqbal saw the Islamic ideal as a "spiritual democracy," dynamic in nature and conscious of social needs. Jinnah's Muslim state was based on the concept of the separate development of the Muslims on the subcontinent. Bhutto's "Islamic socialism" was no more than a continuation of these traditions.

The creation of Bangladesh strengthened the hand of those who wished Pakistan to go in a direction far beyond Bhutto's vision and create an Islamic state governed by the Sharī'ah. It was accurately stated by one observer that the "cry of Islam betrayed" is something that no politician in Pakistan can afford to dismiss lightly.[3] It was indeed for reasons such as these that the 1973

[3] Michael Hornsby writing in the *Times*, 15 July 1973.

Pakistan constitution prescribed a time limit of seven years for the Council of Islamic Ideology to submit a report recommending steps to give effect to appropriate injunctions of Islam and making suggestions on how to bring all existing laws into conformity with those laws. The council was given four functions. By Article 230, the council was empowered to make recommendations to legislative bodies as to the ways and means of enabling and encouraging the Muslims of Pakistan to order their lives in accordance with the principles and concepts of Islam as enunciated in the "Holy Quran and Sunnah." Secondly, the council advises government on any question which is referred to it bearing on whether a proposed law is or is not repugnant to the injunctions of Islam. Thirdly, it has the duty to make recommendations on the measures for bringing existing laws into conformity with the injunctions of Islam and the stages by which such measures should be brought into effect. Finally, it is obliged to compile such injunctions as can be given legislative effect. It is in the context of this process of Islamicization that the family laws of the Muslims must be viewed.

FROM 1977 TO THE PRESENT DAY

When Zia came to power in 1977, he moved quickly in the direction of Islamicization. A Federal Shariat Court was created by Article 203(C) of the constitution. The powers, jurisdiction and functions are set out in Article 203(D):

(1) The Court may, on the petition of a citizen of Pakistan or the Federal Government or a Provincial Government, examine and decide the question whether or not any law or provision of law is repugnant to the injunctions of Islam as laid down in the Holy Quran and the Sunnah of the Holy Prophet, hereinafter referred to as the Injunctions of Islam.

(2) If the Court decides that any law or provision of the law is repugnant to the Injunctions of Islam, it shall set out in its decision
  (i) the reason for its holding that opinion; and
  (ii) the extent to which such a law or provision is so repugnant; and specify the day on which the decision shall take effect.

(3) If any law or provision of law is held by the Court to be repugnant to the Injunctions of Islam

(i) the President in the case of a law with respect to a matter in the Federal Legislative List or the Concurrent Legislative List, or the Governor in the case of a law with respect to a matter not enumerated in either of those Lists, shall take steps to amend the law so as to bring such law or provision into conformity with the Injunctions of Islam; and

(ii) such law or provision shall, to the extent to which it is held to be repugnant, cease to have effect on the day on which the decision of the Court takes effect.

A very important point to mention about Article 203(C) is that the word "law" for the purposes of the article includes any custom or usage having the force of law, but it does *not* include the constitution itself, Muslim personal law, or any law relating to the procedure of any court or tribunal. This last proviso has not prevented the introduction in 1984 by the Qanun-e-Shahadat Order of the Islamic rules of evidence.

The constitutional mechanisms, however, are to an extent limited. This can be illustrated by a consideration of *B. Z. Kai Kaus* v. *President of Pakistan.*[4] In this case, the Supreme Court had to consider the relationship between the judiciary on the one hand and the executive and the legislature on the other in the context of the process of Islamicization. The petitioner, a retired judge of the Supreme Court of Pakistan, sought a declaration and an injunction from the court. He argued as follows:

[The Muslims of Pakistan] being bound only by the divine law, i.e. the Sharia, the Sharia is the only law in this State, the status of the so-called remaining laws including the Constitution being only that of orders whose validity depends on their acceptance as Allah's will by the judicial ulama or the judiciary, and that any order or so-called law including the Constitution which is in conflict with any part of the Holy Qur'an and Sunnah ... including the directions relating to justice and righteousness is null and void.

The Supreme Court refused to grant the relief sought. The court placed the process of Islamicization firmly in the hands of government. In its view no court had jurisdiction to interfere

[4] 1980 PLD SC 160.

with that process except to the limited extent laid down by the constitution itself:

> The point which we want to emphasise is that the job ... is of a legislative and political character to be performed by the State by enacting the necessary laws for Islamicisation of the existing laws or even to promulgate new laws on that pattern but within the hemisphere of the Holy Qur'an and Sunnah.

President Zia has not been slow to introduce such changes. Four important ordinances on criminal law were introduced as long ago as 1979; those relating to *zinā* (illicit sexual relations), *qadhf* (false allegations of unchastity), drinking, and theft. The banking infrastructure has been progressively placed on an interest-free basis for both Pakistan and foreign banks.[5] As we have already stated, Islamic laws of evidence have been introduced.[6] But Muslim personal law as contained in the Family Laws Ordinance has escaped reform. Sharī'ah bills have up until the present time met with little governmental support. We shall have cause to comment on why the move towards Islamicization has avoided any significant change of Ayub Khan's ordinance. For the moment, we must sketch out, in brief, the major aspects of the Ḥanafī family law, the reforms introduced in 1961, and the judicial interpretations of these reforms.

ḤANAFĪ FAMILY LAW

The classical Ḥanafī law as applied on the sub-continent can be outlined in brief as follows.[7] The husband has the right to marry four wives, so long as he feels able to treat them equally. In this regard, equality is traditionally defined in the context of external criteria; namely, food, clothing, support, and so on. The husband has the capability of divorcing his wives unilaterally and extra-judicially (*ṭalāq*). There are different forms or modes of *ṭalāq*, but historically the most often used in Pakistan amongst the Ḥanafī

[5] See T. Ingram, "Islamic Banking: A Foreign Bank's View" in *Islamic Banking and Finance*, ed. Butterworths editorial staff (London: Butterworths, 1986).

[6] Qanun-e-Shahadat Order (10 of 1984).

[7] See also D. Pearl, *A Textbook on Muslim Personal Law*, 2nd ed. (London: Croom Helm, 1987).

is the three-fold pronouncement which first, renders the divorce irrevocable from the moment of the pronouncement, and second, makes the parties incapable of remarrying each other unless and until the wife has been married to another man and this marriage has been consummated and she is divorced from him. The wife has no corresponding right although she can initiate a separation process from her husband known as the *khul'*. However, the husband must give his consent, and, in addition, the wife usually provides compensation. Since 1939, the wife can obtain a divorce from a court on grounds based in large part on the culpability of the husband. In Ḥanafī law, the marriage is a contract effected by an offer by one side followed by an acceptance on the other side. There have to be witnesses: two male Muslim witnesses or one male and two females. No other formalities are technically necessary. A girl, once she attains the age of puberty, has the capacity to contract herself in marriage. Before puberty, her guardian (usually the father or the paternal grandfather) has the right to contract the marriage for her on her behalf. A girl married in such circumstances can terminate the marriage as soon as she attains the age of puberty. This right is now regulated, to an extent, by the Dissolution of Muslim Marriages Act 1939. Consummation with her consent will terminate her right to exercise the option of puberty and avoid the marriage.

Inheritance is, of course, a major area in its own right. Suffice it to say that the Ḥanafī law, although not to the same extent as the Shī'ī law, provides little in the way of support for the orphaned grandchild out of the estate of his grandfather if he is in competition with a closer survivor, for instance, a brother or a son of the deceased.

THE 1961 MUSLIM FAMILY LAWS ORDINANCE

In common with many other Muslim countries, Pakistan in the 1960s experienced a wave of governmental intervention in family law. Earlier, in the 1950s, a commission had been appointed to consider reform in this area. The commission had recommended far-reaching reforms based to a very large extent on social need. But it was not until Ayub Khan assumed power that many of these recommendations were introduced into law by the Muslim Family Laws Ordinance 1961. This ordinance has its base on the two political concepts of local responsibility and the principle of arbitration. Local officials are given a major role in adjudicating domestic disputes in their neighborhood within the spirit in effect of the preservation of the peace in that district.

By section 5(1) of the ordinance, marriages solemnized under Muslim law are to be registered in accordance with certain procedures laid down by the ordinance. Lack of registration does not render the marriage void, although in certain circumstances it may well be difficult to prove its existence. By section 6, a married man is permitted to marry a second wife only when the approval has been given to him by an arbitration council comprising a representative of his first wife and his own representative together with a neutral chairman, who is the chairman of the local administrative unit known as the union council. If the arbitration council is satisfied that the proposed second marriage is necessary and just in accordance with the rules laid down, then a second marriage is permitted. Otherwise, it will be refused. Rule 14 of the rules states that in making a judgement on what is "just and necessary" and without prejudice to its general powers, the arbitration council should have regard to the following circumstances: sterility, physical infirmity, physical unfitness for the conjugal relationship, wilful avoidance of a decree for the restitution of conjugal rights, and insanity on the part of the existing wife. Although a second marriage solemnized without approval remains a valid marriage, the husband is liable to criminal penalties[8] and the first wife has the *locus standi*, if she so wishes, to petition the court for a divorce under an amendment to the Dissolution of Muslim Marriages Act 1939. The second marriage, however, cannot be registered, and the lack of registration may make it difficult to prove the existence of a valid marriage.

Arguably by far the most contentious provision is that dealing with the right of *ṭalāq*. The ordinance by section 7 establishes the position that a *ṭalāq* can always be revoked regardless of its mode of pronouncement. Subsequent to the pronouncement, the husband must inform the chairman of the appropriate union

[8] Section 6(5)(b) MFLO 1961.

council.[9] The purpose of the notification is to "freeze" the effect of the *ṭalāq* for a period of ninety days. During this time the chairman of the union council summons an arbitration council made up of himself and two representatives, one each from either side, to attempt a reconciliation. After the expiry of the ninety-day period, the *ṭalāq* becomes operative unless a reconciliation has been successful or the husband has in any event revoked the *ṭalāq*. No further procedure is required and no order from a court or the arbitration council is necessary. One of the interesting aspects of these provisions concerns the marital status of the parties when the husband does not inform the appropriate chairman that he has pronounced the *ṭalāq*. It has been argued by some that the introduction of notice is contrary to the Qur'ān and Sunnah. The Pakistan courts have consistently taken a different view, and the position is established that notification to the chairman is mandatory.[10]

The constitutionality of section 7 has been considered by the Federal Shariat Court in *Noor Khan* v. *Haq Nawaz*.[11] This was a case brought under the provisions of the Offence of Zina Ordinance 1979. On 18 November 1979, Noor Khan filed a report in a police station alleging that some ten years before that date, the wife of his uncle Fatah Khan had gone on to her fields to cut grass when a certain Haq Nawaz forcibly took her away. It was stated by Noor Khan that the woman, Naziran Bibi, had given birth to three children and that Haq Nawaz was the father. The complainant further stated that Haq Nawaz had not returned the woman to Fatah Khan and that he had continued to commit *zinā* (illicit sexual relations). Fatah Khan himself told the police that he had married Naziran Bibi some thirty years before and that she had borne him children, five of whom were still alive. He stated that he

[9] Section 7(1) MFLO 1961. The appropriate chairman is laid down by the West Pakistan Rules, Rule 3.

[10] *Syed Ali Nawaz Gardezi* v. *Lt. Col. Muhammad Yusuf*, 1963 PLD SC 51; *The State* v. *Tauqir Fatima*, 1964 PLD (WP) Kar 306; *Fahmida Bibi* v. *Mukhtar Ahmad*, 1972 PLD Lah 694; *Abdul Mannan* v. *Sufaran Nessa*, 1970 SCMR 845; *Ghulam Fatima* v. *Abdul Quyyum*, 1981 PLD SC 460. See, however, *Chuhar* v. *Ghulam Fatima*, 1984 PLD Lah 235, and recently the surprising case from Karachi, *Qamar Raza* v. *Tahira Begum*, 1988 PLD Kar 169, which is reported too late for consideration in this paper.

[11] 1982 PLD FSC 265.

had not divorced Naziran Bibi. The accused was acquitted by the Additional Sessions judge. This judge formed the view that Fatah Khan had divorced Naziran Bibi. It was clear that notification to the chairman had not taken place, yet nevertheless the judge held that the provisions of section 7 of the ordinance were inapplicable as the section was contrary to the injunctions of Islam "to the extent of giving notice of *ṭalāq* to the chairman by the husband and in respect of the notice becoming effective within ninety days." The judge relied on Article 227, which obliges the Pakistan law maker to bring all laws into conformity with Islam as laid down by the Qur'ān and Sunnah. On appeal, the Federal Shariat Court repelled this proposition:

> Article 227 of the Constitution is controlled by Article 230 and unless Parliament enacts laws in accordance with the recommendations of the Islamic Council the provisions of Article 227 do not have the effect of rendering existing laws unislamic automatically.... this view that s.7 of the Muslim Family Laws ordinance is unislamic is evidently unjustified.

Unfortunately, this aspect of the judgment of the court is *obiter*. The court decided that none of the parties was aware of the requirements of notice under section 7. The court stated:

> It would be making a technicality of the provisions of notice under section 7 of the Muslim Family Laws Ordinance too cumbersome on the parties who have been living together as husband and wife without any challenge for 10/12 years.

Another attempt to attack the validity of section 7 on the ground that it is contrary to Qur'ān and Sunnah failed in *Aziz Khan* v. *Muhammad Zarif*.[12] Aftab Hussain J. said:

> It is not within our jurisdiction to declare s.7 of the Muslim Family Laws Ordinance as repugnant to the Holy Qur'an in view of the embargo placed on our jurisdiction in this respect by article 203(B) of the Constitution.

[12] 1982 PLD FSC 156.

The other provision of the ordinance which has been discussed in the courts in the context of its constitutionality is section 4. This provision states:

> In the event of the death of any son or daughter of the propositus before the opening of succession, the children of such son or daughter, if any, living at the time the succession opens, shall *per stirpes* receive a share equivalent to the share which such son or daughter, as the case may be, would have received if alive.

The provision has met considerable criticism in any event. For instance, Noel Coulson argued that although the section was intended to operate within the framework of the traditional law, its effect is actually so far reaching that he wonders whether all its implications were fully appreciated.[13] Likewise, Sir Norman Anderson considered that the section makes chaos of the Islamic law of succession.[14] For example, if a man were to die leaving an orphaned son's daughter and a full brother, in the classical Ḥanafī law the son's daughter would inherit one half of the estate and the brother would receive the other one half as the agnatic heir. In Pakistan, however, the son, if alive, would have excluded the brother; thus the son's daughter takes the entire estate to the exclusion of the brother.

The religious elements in Pakistan are equally disturbed by the provision.[15] Their main concern is that children of daughters are introduced into the line of inheritance as primary heirs. Thus distant kindred are converted into sharers in contravention of the principles of Ḥanafī succession law.[16]

An attempt was made to attack the basis of section 4 as contrary to the principles of Islam as laid down in the Qur'ān and Sunnah. This failed, however: the Supreme Court in *Federation*

[13] See, for example, in *Succession in the Muslim Family* (Cambridge: Cambridge University Press, 1981), pp. 143 ff.

[14] *Law Reform in the Muslim World* (London: Athlone Press, 1979), p. 155.

[15] See, for example, A. B. M. Sultanul Alam Choudhury, "Problems of Representation in the Muslim Law of Inheritance," *Islamic Studies* 3 (1964): 375.

[16] Choudhury states: "If for the sake of finding a short-cut to these problems, we amend and abrogate the divorce law for our convenience, then the sacrosanctity of and reverence for divine law will be gone forever." Ibid.

of Pakistan v. *Farishta*[17] holding that the ordinance was a special statutory ordinance intended to be applied only to Muslim citizens of Pakistan and therefore the court was without jurisdiction to review its provisions constitutionally. As Keith Hodkinson has said: "*Farishta* reduces the potential role of the judiciary in Islamicisation by excluding from its scrutiny almost all the controversial legislation in matters of family and succession law."[18]

We have seen, therefore, that the courts' position is that the Muslim Family Laws Ordinance 1961 is protected from any attack on its constitutionality. Until such time as the lawmaker actually reforms the law, the courts will continue to apply the legislation as binding. We must now turn our attention to consider those cases in recent years which have developed the basic provisions of the ordinance.

THE ORDINANCE IN PRACTICE

Divorce

Pakistan courts have considered the implications of the divorce provisions of the ordinance on many occasions.[19] One of the first cases was the Supreme Court decision in *Syed Ali Nawaz Gardezi* v. *Lt. Col. Muhammad Yusuf*.[20] The ordinance was reviewed in the context of a matrimonial dispute which resulted in a husband suing in a civil action another man accused of enticing his wife away. The alleged enticer defended the action by suggesting that the husband had in fact divorced his wife. The court was obliged to consider the purpose of the 1961 ordinance. The Supreme Court stated:

> The object of section 7 is to prevent hasty dissolution of marriages by talaq, pronounced by the husband unilaterally, without an attempt being made to prevent disruption of the matrimonial status. If the husband himself thinks better of the pronouncement of talaq and abstains from giving a notice to the chairman, he should perhaps, be deemed, in view of section 7, to have revoked the pronouncement and that would be to the advantage of the wife.

[17] 1981 PLD SC 120.

[18] *Cambridge Law Journal* 40 (1981): 248.

[19] For further discussion see Pearl, *Textbook*, pp. 123–130.

[20] See above, note 10.

The Supreme Court is insistent in this case that notice delivered to the chairman is mandatory. If the husband abstains from giving notice, then the court takes the view that the husband must be presumed to have revoked the *ṭalāq*. This opinion has been followed on many occasions in the Pakistan courts. For example, in *The State* v. *Tauqir Fatima*,[21] the court said, "as no notice had been given [to the chairman] the talaq could not have become effective."

There have been two recent authorities which have adopted a different position. The first case which requires some discussion is *Chuhar* v. *Ghulam Fatima*.[22] This case concerned the question of legitimacy of a child. A previous pronouncement of divorce bringing to an end the mother's first marriage was clearly of relevance, but only as a preliminary point. The court said that "as the main object of section 7 . . . is to prevent hasty dissolution of marriage by talaq," the object would not be defeated in this case by the clear evidence that no notice had been given. The case is certainly understandable on its own facts, for the *ṭalāq* was pronounced some fifteen to eighteen years beforehand. The law leans in favor of legitimacy, and an overreliance on the technicality of section 7 would have had an adverse effect. Nonetheless, the case certainly runs counter to the earlier authority.

The second case which adopts a similar approach is the criminal case, *Noor Khan* v. *Haq Nawaz*, which has already been discussed.[23] The Federal Shariat Court thought that the provisions on notice in the ordinance are too cumbersome when there is evidence that the wife and the second husband have been living together without challenge for many years. Thus, for the purposes of legitimacy and the criminal prosecution of *zinā*, undue emphasis on the mandatory obligation to inform the chairman might produce a harsh result. In these circumstances the court is willing to waive the strict application of the ordinance. In other cases, however, where the issue is simply the effectiveness of the divorce between the two principals, there would seem to be a uniform approach that notification to the chairman is mandatory. This

[21] See above, note 10.

[22] See above, note 10.

[23] See above, page 207 and note 11.

pragmatic interpretation of the words of the ordinance fits into the Islamic notions of interpretation, as well as providing a sensible distinction between the effectiveness of a *ṭalāq* at the time of the pronouncement or shortly thereafter, and the legitimacy of any child born out of a subsequent *nikāḥ* (marriage).

The ordinance states that the husband shall supply a copy of the notification to the chairman to the wife. Is this mandatory? In a Lahore case, *Inamal Islam* v. *Hussain Bano*,[24] the court gave mandatory force to the need to inform the wife: "The supply of a copy of notice to the wife is a necessary part of the requirement of service of notice on the chairman."

In contrast, a Karachi court, *Parveen Chaudhry* v. *VIth. Senior Civil Judge, Karachi*,[25] has expressed itself in a slightly different way:

> The only impediment to immediate effectiveness of the divorce is information to the Chairman and the forming of the Arbitration Council. To such extent it is very clear to us that the mere fact of absence of communication of the divorce before moving the Chairman under subsection (i) of section 7 of the ordinance does not invalidate the divorce.

Did the court mean that it is not mandatory to inform the wife of the divorce (which is indeed the position in classical law and has not been changed by the ordinance) or alternatively that it is not mandatory to inform the wife of the notice to the chairman? It is submitted that the former view is the more appropriate interpretation.

A final matter deals with the formation of the arbitration council by the chairman. The thrust of Pakistan decisions in this area is that the formation of the arbitration council is a matter for the chairman alone. Failure to summon the council, either because of negligence on the part of the chairman or for some other reason, does not in any way invalidate the effectiveness of the *ṭalāq*; that is ninety days after notification being delivered to the chairman.[26]

[24] 1976 PLD Lah 1466.

[25] 1976 PLD Kar 416.

[26] *Sobhan* v. *Ghani*, 1973 Dacca Law Reports 227; *Fahmida Bibi* v. *Mukhtar Ahmad*, 1972 PLD Lah 694; *Maqbool Jan* v. *Arshad Hassan*, 1975 PLD Lah 147;

Judicial and legislative developments have also produced important developments in the law relating to *khul'*, traditionally the consensual extrajudicial separation initiated by the wife. Here, however, it has been the court which has led the way. After some hesitation, the Supreme Court in *Khurshid Bibi* v. *Muhammad Amin*[27] decided that *khul'* could be effected without the consent of the husband, so long as the wife can show to the satisfaction of the court that married life has in effect irretrievably broken down. The involvement of the arbitral procedures is ensured by section 8 of the Muslim Family Laws Ordinance.[28]

The question of culpability has occupied the Pakistan courts. In *Siddiq* v. *Sharfan*,[29] where the wife was wholly to blame for the breakup of the marriage, the court refused to grant the wife a *khul'* divorce, for to do so was seen to be contrary to the policy of Islam. However, in *Hakim Zadi* v. *Nawaz Ali*,[30] where admittedly the wife was not at fault, it was stated by the court that it would not be necessary to prove that each and every allegation was in fact true. More recently, in *Rashidan Bibi* v. *Bashir Ahmad*,[31] the judge stated:

> The principle of khul' is based on the fact that if a woman has decided not to live with her husband for any reason and this decision is firm, then the court, after satisfying its conscience that not to dissolve the marriage would mean forcing the woman to a hateful union with the man, it is not necessary on the part of the woman to produce evidence of facts and circumstances to show the extent of hatred to satisfy the conscience of the Judge, Family Court or the Appellate Court.

The legal decisions relating to divorce provide a valuable case study of how the courts, using as their text the reformist provisions of the 1961 ordinance, have gradually introduced a law of divorce which to an extent is more "even handed" than the traditional

---

Akhtar Hussain v. *Collector Lahore*, 1977 PLD Lah 1173; *M. Zikria Khan* v. *Aftab Ali Khan*, 1985 PLD Lah 319.

[27] 1967 PLD SC 97.

[28] *Princess Aiyesha Yasmien Abbasi* v. *Maqbool Hussain Qureshi*, 1979 PLD Lah 241.

[29] 1968 PLD Lah 411.

[30] 1972 PLD Kar 540.

[31] 1983 PLD Lah 549.

Ḥanafī law. Arbitration, which plays such a significant role in Islamic law, is introduced into the Ḥanafī law; the disapproved forms of *ṭalāq* are rendered ineffective in any event; nonetheless a man is not prohibited from divorcing his wife unilaterally and extrajudicially. Although such movements in the law can be criticized for being contrary to the strict interpretation of Ḥanafī jurisprudence, the thrust of the case law is broadly welcomed by most sections of Pakistan society.

Polygamy

It will be recalled that Section 6(1) of the 1961 ordinance states:

> No man, during the subsistence of an existing marriage, shall, except with the previous permission in writing of the Arbitration Council, contract another marriage, nor shall any such marriage contracted without such permission be registered under this ordinance.

The section on polygamy illustrates how the ordinance has steered a path midway through the outright abolition of polygamy, even when based on interpretations of Qur'ānic verses,[32] and simply leaving matters as they were and relying on the combined effect of education and the economic realities to reduce the impact of polygamy. The ordinance is in effect a guideline provision: polygamy is discouraged, Islamic arbitral techniques are introduced, evidential difficulties and criminal sanctions act as a deterrent, but at the end of the day the possibility of polygamy still exists. The criminal sanction may not deter many but it has been used even, as in *Fauzia Hussain* v. *Khadim Hussain*,[33] when the first marriage was solemnized in civil form in the United Kingdom.

Succession

The final example from Pakistan concerns the approach taken in relation to section 4, the section on inheritance. It is indeed in this area that most of the criticism of the ordinance has been directed, not only because the provision interferes with the Ḥanafī law of succession in a clear disregard of Ḥanafī jurisprudence,

[32] As in Tunisia in 1956.

[33] 1985 PLD Lah 166.

but also because it does not in any event solve the alleged social problems it was designed to alleviate. A recent case is *Kamal Khan* v. *Zainab*.[34] The case involved the distribution of the estate of Sufaid Khan (P) who died in 1972. In 1977, the entire estate was transferred to the surviving granddaughter (Z) of a predeceased son (R). The action challenging this distribution was brought by a nephew (K). K was the son of P's brother. The court held that Z could not receive more than one half of the estate of her father, and the remaining half must revert to K. The Judge said, "The legislature never intended to give greater benefit to the grandchildren of a predeceased parent than would have been his due, if the grandparent was alive."

He distributed the estate in the following manner:

> The starting point is that notionally the off-spring of the propositus is deemed to be alive for the purpose of succession at the time of the death of the propositus, and the succession of the grandchildren is to be calculated again notionally as if the parent of the grandchild died after the death of the original propositus.

Thus he determined that R would have inherited the entire estate of Sufaid Khan (P) as he was the only son, and, further, that Z would inherit only one half of the estate of R as R had no son, but only the one daughter. The remaining one half of R's estate (originally, of course, P's estate) therefore reverted to the collateral, namely, K.

Some would say that the decision undermines the whole basis of section 4. However, it is as clear a judicial reflection as one has on how the ordinance will inevitably be interpreted in such a way as to reflect the fundamentals of Ḥanafī distribution in cases involving Ḥanafīs. Thus, in *Iqbal Mai* v. *Falak Sher*,[35] although the Supreme Court refused to consider the issues on the particular facts of that case, the court raised, although it did not answer, the question whether it was the intention of the lawmaker to provide the opportunity for the orphaned grandchild simply to obtain the "Islamic share," and not to provide a system of strict

[34] 1983 PLD Lah 546.

[35] 1986 PLD SC 228.

representation. Judicial interpretation on Islamic principles would appear to be the way the law will develop in this area.

THE CONCLUSION to the examination of the case law on divorce, polygamy and succession suggests that the courts reflect public opinion in Pakistan to a very great extent. There is little resistance to the provision on polygamy, there is a consensus that *ṭalāq* should be controlled and that rights for women should be acknowledged in that area, and the system of representation introduced by section 4 was seen by most observers as a flagrant breach of Islamic mores. The judicial determinations we have discussed fit neatly into the consensus views.[36]

In contrast, in India, it was partly because of the very fact that the Supreme Court did not reflect the aspirations of the dominant view of the Muslim community that serious disturbances arose in 1986 with allegations of religious harassment by the majority community and by secular judges. It is to these questions that we now turn.

THE INDIAN DIMENSION

Identity for the Muslim community in India, regardless of whether they be Shīʿī or Sunnī, carries with it the acknowledgment that the personal law is an essential element. There is a powerful feeling that without the framework of the personal law within which to live their lives it would be only a matter of time before the Muslims would be swallowed up by the absorptive power of the Hindus. The directive in Article 44 of the constitution to secure for the citizens of India a uniform civil code is seen as a threat to the very identity of the Muslim community. For instance, one religious leader, Maulana Abul Lais of the Jamaat-e-Islami, is quoted as saying, "This provision for a uniform civil code is the root cause of all the evil and tirade against Muslims in our country."[37] Although

[36] It is too early to assess the impact of President Zia's ordinance of 15 June 1988 introducing the Shaʿrīah Bill as the governing force. However, it is probable that the approach already reflected in some cases, such as *Qamar Raza* v. *Tahira Begum* (1988 PLD Kar 168) to the effect that certain provisions of the Muslim Family Law Ordinance 1961 are contrary to the Qur'ān and Sunnah, and thus unconstitutional, will gain support.

[37] *India Today*, 31 January 1986, p. 50.

this view perhaps represents the extreme position, there are many Muslims in influential positions whose views are not so different.

The political dimension came to the fore in the judicial discussion of the right of a Muslim divorcee to maintenance from her ex-husband. In classical Ḥanafī law a divorced wife is entitled only to maintenance during her period of *'iddah* (three menstrual cycles).[38] In India, imperial legislation was amended in 1973 which, *inter alia*, enabled a woman who has been divorced from her husband to seek an award of maintenance payable until her remarriage (s.125). An additional provision, section 127(3)(b), was inserted into the code as a result of pressure from Muslim groups who wished to retain the Muslim personal law. The section reads:

> Where any order has been made under s.125 in favour of a woman who has been divorced by, or has obtained a divorce from her husband, the Magistrate shall, if he is satisfied that (b) the woman has been divorced by her husband and that she has received, whether before or after the date of the said order, the whole of the sum which, under any customary or personal law applicable to the parties, was payable on such divorce, cancel such order.

The exact meaning of this provision has been the subject of considerable judicial comment. It was first held that the payment of the deferred dower by the husband at the time of the divorce would satisfy section 127(3)(b); accordingly the court would have no jurisdiction to order maintenance under section 125.[39] However, in Kerela, it was held that a dower payment was outside the purview of the act.[40] A trilogy of Supreme Court decisions resolved the argument in favour of the Kerela authority. The decisions are *Bai Tahera* v. *Ali Husain*,[41] *Fuzlunbi* v. *K. Khader Vali*,[42] and finally *Mohd. Ahmed Khan* v. *Shah Bano Begum*.[43]

[38] Pearl, *Textbook*, p. 53.

[39] *Ruckhsana Parvin* v. *Sheikh Mohamed Hussein*, 1976 79 Bom LR 123.

[40] *Muhammed* v. *Sunabii*, 1976 KLT 71 1; *Kunhi Moyin* v. *Pathumma*, 1976 KLT 87.

[41] AIR 1979 SC 362.

[42] AIR 1980 SC 1730.

[43] AIR 1985 SC 945.

In the third case, the man's defence to the claim for maintenance was that he had divorced her by *ṭalāq*, that he had paid her 3,000 rupees by way of dower, and that he was under no further obligation in the matter. A special bench of five judges affirmed the ex-wife's rights. The Chief Justice states that if there is any conflict, section 125 overrides the personal law. However, he is equally clear that there is in fact no such conflict in any event. He states that Muslim law does not countenance cases where the wife is unable to maintain herself after a divorce. He states:

> Since the Muslim Personal Law, which limits the husband's liability to provide for the maintenance of the divorced wife to the period of 'idda, does not contemplate or countenance the situation envisaged by section 125, it would be wrong to hold that the Muslim husband, according to his personal law, is not under an obligation to provide maintenance, beyond the period of 'idda, to his divorced wife who is unable to maintain herself.... The true position is that, if the divorced wife is able to maintain herself, the husband's liability to provide maintenance for her ceases with the expiration of the period of 'idda. If she is unable to maintain herself, she is entitled to take recourse to section 125 of the Code.

There is little justification for describing the Muslim law obligation in this way. It is an unorthodox approach and the Qur'ānic authorities cited by the judge are given a novel interpretation by him. The decision produced an immediate reaction amongst the Muslim community, culminating in the enactment of the Muslim Women (Protection of Rights on Divorce) Act 1986. This act is headed "An Act to protect the rights of Muslim women who have been divorced by, or have obtained divorce from, their husbands..." Section 3 lays down the rights of *mahr* (dower) and maintenance during *'iddah*.

(1) Notwithstanding anything contained in any other law for the time being in force, a divorced woman shall be entitled to
  (a) a reasonable and fair provision and maintenance to be made and paid to her within the iddat period by her former husband;
  (b) where she herself maintains the children born to her before or after her divorce, a reasonable and fair provision and maintenance

to be made and paid by her former husband for a period of two years from the respective dates of birth of such children;

(c) an amount equal to the sum of mahr or dower agreed to be paid to her at the time of her marriage or at any time thereafter according to Muslim law; and

(d) all the properties given to her before or at the time of marriage or after her marriage by her relatives or friends or the husband or any relatives of the husband or his friends.

There are many difficulties in interpretation of this provision[44] but section 3(2) provides a Muslim woman who has been married under Muslim law and who has "been divorced by, or obtained a divorce from her husband in accordance with Muslim law," with a right of action to seek from the magistrate an order for payment against the husband during the *'iddah* period. The magistrate has jurisdiction to make an order, having satisfied himself that the husband has sufficient means, and has failed or neglected to make the relevant payment. Subsequent to the *'iddah* period, if a magistrate is satisfied that a divorced woman who has not remarried is not able to maintain herself, he may make an order directing "such of her relatives as would be entitled to inherit her property ... to pay such reasonable and fair maintenance to her" (s. 4[1]). If the woman has children, the first responsibility falls on the children, failing whom the responsibility falls on her parents. If there are no relatives, then the responsibility to provide support falls on the appropriate State Wakf Board (s. 4[2]). It is important to mention that the provisions of sections 125 to 128 are not excluded if at the time of the application under section 3(2) both the applicant and her former husband declare (either jointly or separately) that they would prefer to have the dispute settled under the general law.

The 1986 act (and the bill which preceded it) has been described by Tahir Mahmood as "a symbol (for the Muslims) of their legal and constitutional equality with the majority community." He states that the majority community in contrast "viewed it as a symbol of victory for a religious minority which had 'no

[44] See T. Mahmood, "The Muslim Women (Protection of Rights on Divorce) Act 1986—Perspectives and Prospects," *Islamic and Comparative Law Quarterly* 6 (1986): 159.

right to claim equality of rights and status' with them."[45] These remarks illustrate very well the particular problem of the application of Muslim personal law in India, a problem, of course, which does not exist in neighboring Pakistan.

The observer from outside the region is entitled to contrast the legislative intervention in Muslim family law in Pakistan with that of India. It is interesting to observe that reform of the methods of divorce popular amongst the Sunnī community has not been attempted there. There have been judicial initiatives to restrict the rights of the husband.[46] There is also the opinion of academics such as Tahir Mahmood, who believes that the classical law has been corrupted: "An extremely rational and humanistic law on divorce has indeed been awfully corrupted to the detriment of women by ignorant laymen, unscrupulous law-men and tradition bound god-men."[47] But, inevitably, attempts by legislation to reform this area of the personal law of the Muslim community are bound to arouse political opposition. In contrast to this position in India, in Pakistan successive governments have been able to protect the 1961 ordinance from amendment. This success probably has as much to do with political power as it has to do with acceptance by the community. But from the perspective of either country, it is apparent that further "modernization" has now run its course. Further developments in the last decade of this century are likely to take the form of solutions from a specifically Islamic perspective.

[45] Ibid.

[46] *Jiauddin Ahmed* v. *Anwara Begum* (1978), where the Judge stated: "Talaq must be for a reasonable cause and be preceded by attempts at reconciliation between husband and wife and by two arbiters. . . . if the attempts fail, talaq may be effected." See *Islamic and Comparative Law Quarterly* 2 (1982): 38, where the case is reproduced and cited as *Ziauddin Ahmed* v. *Anwar Begum*.

[47] See above, note 44.

Contributors

WILLIAM BALLANTYNE, M.A. (Cantab.), is a barrister and currently Visiting Professor in Arab Laws at the School of Oriental and African Studies of the University of London. He has been a practising lawyer in London and the Middle East for over forty years, and is the author of *Legal Development in Arabia*, *Commercial Law in the Arab Middle East: The Gulf States*, and *A Register of the Laws of the Arabian Gulf*. He is the General Editor of the *Arab Law Quarterly*.

IAN EDGE is Lecturer in Law at the School of Oriental and African Studies of the University of London and a barrister. His main area of research and writing is Egyptian law.

DAVID F. FORTE is Professor of Law at the Cleveland-Marshall College of Law of Cleveland State University. He has written books and numerous articles on various aspects of law in the United States and on Islamic law. He is former Chief Counsel to the United States Mission to the United Nations.

WAEL HALLAQ is Associate Professor of Islamic Law and Theology at the Institute of Islamic Studies of McGill University. He has written on Sunni legal theory, on logical aspects of Islamic law, and Islamic legal reasoning.

GEORGE MAKDISI is Professor of Arabic and Islamic Studies, and Director of the Center for Medieval Studies at the University of Pennsylvania. He is the author of *L'Islam hanbalisant* and

The Rise of Colleges: Institutions of Learning in Islam and the West.

JOHN MAKDISI is Professor of Law and Associate Dean at the Cleveland-Marshall College of Law of Cleveland State University. In addition to several books and articles on law in the United States, he has written on family law, contract, intestate succession, bibliography, teaching, legal reasoning, and formal rationality in Islamic law.

ANN E. MAYER is Associate Professor in the Department of Legal Studies at the Wharton School of the University of Pennsylvania. She is the editor of *Property, Social Structure, and Law in the Modern Middle East.*

DAVID S. PEARL is Dean of the School of Law at the University of East Anglia, Norwich, England. He is the author of *A Textbook on Muslim Personal Law* (2nd ed., 1987), and *Interpersonal Conflict of Laws in India, Pakistan and Bangladesh* (1981).

JEANETTE WAKIN is Senior Lecturer in Arabic and Islamic Studies at Columbia University. She is the author of *The Function of Documents in Islamic Law*, an edition of a work by al-Ṭaḥāwī with an introduction on the use of documents as evidence in Islamic law and on legal formularies.

BERNARD WEISS is Associate Professor of Arabic in the Department of Languages and the Middle East Center at the University of Utah. He has written numerous articles on classical Islamic theory of law and methodology of legal interpretation.

FARHAT J. ZIADEH is Professor Emeritus in the Department of Near Eastern Languages and Civilization at the University of Washington. He is the author of *Lawyers, the Rule of Law and Liberalism in Modern Egypt*, and *Law of Property in the Arab World: Real Rights in Egypt, Iraq, Jordan, Lebanon and Syria*, and has published an edition of *Kitāb adab al-qāḍī* by al-Khaṣṣāf.

Index